150
2/20

The Jewish Home Cookbook

Published by
The Worcester Jewish Healthcare Center
629 Salisbury Street
Worcester, MA 01609

The photographs reproduced in this book are provided with the permission of The
Jewish Healthcare Center and its Auxiliary, the Worcester Jewish Community Center,
the East Side Reunion Committee, the Worcester Historical Museum, and members of
the Worcester Jewish Community. We appreciate their generosity.

Cover photograph © 1995 Larry Stein
Book design and layout Font & Center Press

Library of Congress Catalog Card Number: 95-079136

ISBN 0-9647977-0-4

First Printing 1995
Printed in the United States of America

1 2 3 4 5 6 7 8 9 10

Acknowledgments

The Jewish Home Cookbook represents the efforts of many people. More than nine hundred recipes were submitted. One hundred and fifty of Worcester's (Massachusetts) best cooks kitchen tested and evaluated each recipe. In all, two hundred and fifty people have had an active role in the creation of this cookbook. But, as is true in all major community-wide projects, it is a core group of tireless workers whose monumental vision, skill, and determination have brought this book to publication. To them, The Home community says, "Thank You."

Shirley Kane, Chairperson
80th Anniversary/Cookbook Project

Table of Contents

Introduction

The Jewish Home Cookbook *is presented in celebration of 80 years of service.*

"The Jewish Home," founded in 1914 was the result of a community's conscience: its feeling of religious and moral obligation to care for the deprived and needy. The Jewish community of Worcester, Massachusetts originally founded "The Home" as an orphanage, for Jewish children. However, the needs of the elderly broadened the focus and its first residents were three children and one elderly couple who were cared for in a nine room house. By 1921, "The Home's" population had grown to 28 children and five elderly residents. In that same year, the Ladies Auxiliary was formed. Those women helped expand "The Home's" program for children from the simple provision of food, clothing, and shelter, to a variety of religious, educational, and recreational activities. Historically, there has been a long association with "The Home" and the publication of cookbooks. The Auxiliary created the first edition of **The Jewish Home Cookbook** to fund their numerous projects. That first cookbook is now a cherished family heirloom, having been printed in 1927 on the occasion of "The Home's" Bar Mitzvah year.

Serving the constantly growing community, "The Home's" facilities repeatedly proved inadequate. To underwrite construction costs for expanding the physical plant, the annual "Home Show" was born. First held in 1926, these star-studded galas became the premiere event of the Worcester social season. They continued until 1941 when World War II brought them to a halt. (To mark "The Home's" 50th anniversary the "Home Show" was gloriously revived in 1964.) In the late 40s an extensive infirmary wing was built at "The Home's" Pleasant Street site. At about the same time the children's section was closed as better and more effective ways were found to care for children.

The 60s brought important changes in healthcare. Geriatrics was becoming both highly professionalized and specialized. Government funds helped "The Home" improve its facilities for medical and nursing care, and expand its professionally trained staff.

Today, "The Home," known as The Jewish Healthcare Center, is a model facility, serving 140 residents and other community elderly who benefit from the newest concepts in geriatric medical care and an expanded mission of "The Home's" goals: to extend beyond the walls — out into the community to implement new concepts for the aged. Day care programs for those living outside "The Home" now exist, as well as, medical care and rehabilitative therapy programs for outpatients. There is an extensive "Meals on Wheels" program. "The Home" has become a major geriatric center for research, student training, and the development of demonstration projects. As in the past, and throughout the 80 years since its founding, "The Home" has been the symbol and manifestation of the Jewish community's conscience and compassion.

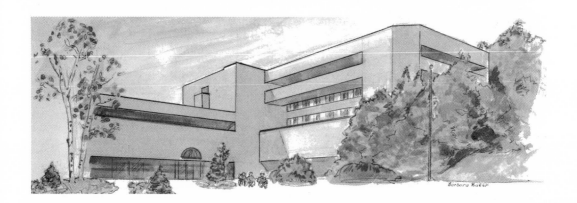

Preface

Our hope is that the new **Jewish Home Cookbook** will become a useful and comfortable culinary friend in your kitchen. Earlier editions have been prized possessions in our community, frequently given as gifts to newly married couples. Through the tireless efforts, dedication, and good taste of Nancy Benjamin and Lisa Honig, the recipes compiled within are true generational links between past and future. They were contributed by young and old, new cooks and experienced cooks. We have preserved many of the all time favorite recipes from our community's most legendary cooks. Their delicious specialties which have appeared in our earlier cookbooks are designated by the symbol ⌂.

As before, **The Jewish Home Cookbook** is a reflection of many ethnic and regional influences and following established tradition, all the recipes can be used by those adhering to the Laws of Kashruth.

Appetizers

Spicy Pecans

Nancy Benjamin

1 pound pecan halves
¹/₄ cup rum
¹/₂ cup sugar
1 tablespoon Worcestershire sauce
1 tablespoon corn oil

¹/₂ teaspoon cayenne pepper
¹/₂ teaspoon salt
¹/₂ teaspoon ground pepper
2 teaspoons cumin

- Preheat oven to 325°F.
- Put pecans in boiling water and cook 1 minute, then drain.
- Combine rum, sugar, Worcestershire, and oil, and stir. Add pecans and mix and let set 10 minutes.
- Spread in jellyroll pan and bake 35 minutes. Mix every 10 minutes or until liquid is absorbed.
- Mix the spices in a bowl, and add the nuts, and mix until well coated.
- Return to baking sheet and let them stand until cool and dry. Store in a tightly covered container.

Easy Dip with Black Bread

Lissa Kasakoff

1 cup cottage cheese
1 cup Miracle Whip salad dressing

8 ounces sour cream
1 package vegetable soup mix

- Mix ingredients.
- Refrigerate a few hours before serving.
- Serve with black bread. Serves 6–8.

Hummus

Sue Seder

1 16-ounce can chick peas, drained
1 large clove garlic, minced
¹/₄ cup lemon juice
2 tablespoons sesame tahini paste

¹/₄ cup water
salt to taste
¹/₂ tablespoon cumin (optional)

- Put all ingredients into food processor and blend until smooth.
- Add salt to taste and cumin, if desired.
- Serve with pita bread and/or vegetables.

Tzatziki

Simone Weinert

Serve with pita bread or plain (over potatoes).

2 cups yogurt
1 cucumber, peeled and seeded
1 clove garlic, crushed

juice of 1 lemon
fresh dill (lots of chopped dill)
salt and pepper, to taste

- Drain yogurt through cheesecloth overnight.
- Dice and salt the cucumber overnight, then drain it thoroughly.
- Mix remaining ingredients together and combine with yogurt and cucumber. Serves 6.

Artichoke Spread

Sandra (Robbins) Scheibel

I'm forever asked for this recipe! Takes 10 minutes to prepare, 15 minutes to bake.

2 6-ounce jars marinated artichokes,
    quartered
1/2 cup Parmesan cheese
1/2 cup mayonnaise

garlic powder
ground red pepper
water chestnuts, diced, optional
diced mushrooms, optional

- Drain marinade from artichokes and place them in a paper towel. Squeeze out excess fluids and chop artichokes more.
- Add 1/4 cup of cheese, the mayonnaise, and a sprinkle of garlic powder (about 4 shakes), or to taste. Add 2 quick dashes red pepper and mix.
- (Note: If water chestnuts and mushrooms are used, add a touch more mayonnaise.)
- Put in baking dish and sprinkle top with remaining cheese.
- Bake at 350°F 12–15 minutes, until hot and bubbly.
- Serve with deli rye or Triscuit crackers. Serves 4–6.

Artichoke and Fresh Spinach Dip

Elizabeth Tapper

A crowd pleaser. Guests rip apart and eat the "bowl" when the dip is gone.

2 8 1/2-ounce cans artichoke hearts,
    drained and minced
12 ounces fresh spinach with stems,
    cooked, squeezed dry, and minced
1 cup mayonnaise
1 large garlic clove, minced
1/4 cup parsley leaves, minced
2 tablespoons fresh lemon juice

2 large shallots, minced
2 tablespoons freshly snipped chives
2 teaspoons dried dillweed
1 teaspoon salt, or to taste
freshly ground pepper
dash of hot pepper sauce
*crudites
*small round dark rye bread

- Combine all ingredients (except crudites and rye bread) and mix well. Transfer to a bowl, cover, and chill overnight. Taste and adjust seasoning.
- Slice off a thin "top" piece of the dark rye. Using a curved knife (grapefruit knife works well) dig out the inside of the bread, making a "bowl." Fill the "bowl" with the dip and arrange crudites around the bowl on a platter. Makes 3 cups.

Caponata

Carol S. Glick

Great appetizer, freezes well.

4 cups peeled and cubed eggplants
1/3 cup green pepper, chopped
1 large onion, chopped
1 14-ounce can sliced
    mushrooms, drained
2 cloves garlic, crushed
1/4 cup olive oil

1 large can tomato paste
1/4 cup water
2 tablespoons red wine vinegar
1 1/2 teaspoons sugar
1/2 teaspoon oregano
1 teaspoon each salt and pepper
1/2 cup stuffed olives, sliced

- Sauté eggplant, pepper, onion, mushrooms, and garlic in oil, and cook approximately 10 minutes.
- Add tomato paste and remaining ingredients and mix thoroughly.
- Simmer covered until eggplant is tender, approximately 30 minutes.
- Cover and refrigerate overnight. Serves a lot.

Mushroom Almond Pâté

Sylvia Davidson

1 cup slivered almonds
4 tablespoons butter
3/4 pound fresh mushrooms, sliced
1 small onion, sliced
1 clove garlic, minced

3/4 teaspoon pinch salt
1/4 teaspoon ground thyme
1/8 teaspoon pepper
2 tablespoons oil

- Toast slivered almonds over medium-low heat in a wide frying pan about 5–7 minutes, stirring frequently until lightly browned. Turn out of pan to cool.
- Melt butter in pan. Add sliced mushrooms, onion, garlic, salt, thyme, and pepper. Cook over medium-high heat, stirring occasionally, until most of the liquid evaporates.
- Chop 2 tablespoons of almonds and set aside.
- Whirl remaining nuts in blender or processor until finely ground. Continue blending, gradually adding oil, until creamy and smooth. Add mushroom mixture and blend until smooth. Stir in chopped nuts.
- Serve at room temperature with crackers or raw vegetables.

Provolone Loaf

Melody Rose

Unique appetizer that draws raves — a requested recipe.

Garlic Mixture:
8 ounces cream cheese
1/4 cup butter or margarine
1 clove garlic, smashed
1/8 teaspoon pepper
1/4 cup pistachios (or almonds
    or walnuts)

1 pound Provolone cheese, sliced
1 container pesto sauce
1/2 cup chopped sun-dried tomatoes

- In a small bowl, blend the cream cheese, butter, garlic, pepper, and pistachios until smooth.
- Wet cheesecloth and line a loaf pan, loose ends hanging over the sides.
- Divide cheese slices in half and arrange so they overlap bottom and up sides of pan (approximately 2 1/2 inches). Divide remaining cheese in half.
- Layer cheese with 1/2 of pesto, 1/2 of remaining cheese, and 1/2 of tomatoes. Spread with garlic mixture and then layer remaining pesto, cheese, and tomatoes.
- Pull cloth over loaf, press until firm, chill and set. Unmold by flipping onto platter. Garnish with fresh basil and pistachio nuts. Serves 20.

Warmed Cranberry Brie

Anne McDonald Kelly

1/3 cup whole cranberry sauce
2 tablespoons brown sugar
1/4 teaspoon rum or orange extract

1/8 teaspoon nutmeg
1 8-ounce round Brie
2 tablespoons pecans

- Combine cranberry sauce, brown sugar, rum or orange extract, and nutmeg.
- Peel off top rind of Brie leaving 1/4-inch rind.
- Top with cranberry mixture and sprinkle pecans.
- Bake at 500°F, 4–5 minutes. Serve with crackers. Serves 2.

Special Brie Appetizer

Sandra (Robbins) Scheibel

Everyone seems to enjoy this one! Takes 5 minutes to prepare and 8 minutes to bake.

1 small round or 2 large wedges
    plain Brie
1 handful brown sugar, light or dark

1 6-ounce package of pecan halves
2 ounces brandy or cognac

- Place Brie in serve/bake dish, like a quiche dish.
- Pack brown sugar generously on top of cheese.
- Cut some pecan halves into smaller pieces. Place all on top of brown sugar with overflow on sides. Drizzle brandy on top.
- Place in 375°F oven for 8 minutes. Serve with crackers. Serves 6.

Baked Brie

Merna Siff

Everyone comments. Big hit at party. Easy to prepare. Yummy.

a piece or a round of Brie
Pepperidge Farm pastry dough,
    not shells

1 jar apricot preserves
slivered almonds, lightly toasted
crackers or French bread

- Cut Brie in half horizontally. Spread tops of both pieces with apricot preserves and slivered almonds, and then put cheese back together.
- Roll out dough (1 piece). Mold dough all around the Brie. Flatten and seal top (with wet fingertips). Invert covered cheese and place in a pyrex dish sprayed with Pam.
- Bake in a 350°F oven for 20–25 minutes. Serve with French or Syrian bread, or crackers. Hors d'oeuvres for 8–20.

Savory Cheesecake Appetizer

Sandra Honig

Elegant presentation — great for Passover.

1 cup creamy, small curd cottage cheese
3 eggs
3 8-ounce packages cream cheese,
    softened
1 1/3 cups sour cream
1/2 cup (2 ounces) grated Romano cheese

2 tablespoons potato starch
2 cloves garlic, minced
1 tablespoon dried basil
1 tablespoon oregano
1 teaspoon cracked black pepper

- Heat oven to 300°F.
- Place cottage cheese and eggs in blender, cover and blend on medium speed for 30 seconds or until smooth.
- Beat cream cheese in large bowl until smooth. Add cottage cheese mixture, sour cream, and remaining ingredients. Beat until smooth.
- Pour into greased 9-inch springform pan. Place on cookie sheet. Bake 60–70 minutes in lower third of oven until top just starts to turn brown.
- Turn oven off and leave pan in oven with door ajar for 30 minutes. Remove. Serves 16 or more.

Three Cheese Nacho Dip

Marlene Persky

Best hot Mexican dip.

1 cup sour cream
3 ounces cream cheese, at room
    temperature
1 16-ounce can refried beans
1/2 cup salsa (mild, medium, or hot)

2 teaspoons chili powder
1/2 teaspoon cumin
1 cup shredded Cheddar cheese (mellow)
1 cup shredded Monterey Jack cheese
1 7 1/2-ounce bag tortilla chips

- Combine sour cream, cream cheese, beans, salsa, chili powder, and cumin in food processor.
- In an 8 x 8-inch baking dish, or 9-inch pie plate, spread one-half of mixture. Top with one-half of cheeses. Repeat ending with cheeses.
- Bake in a 350°F oven for 20–30 minutes. Serve with chips. Serves 8.

Taco Pie

Marlene Persky

The best!

1 8-ounce package cream cheese,
    softened
1/2 cup sour cream
2 tablespoons mayonnaise
1 tablespoon lemon juice
1 avocado, mashed
3/4 teaspoon chili powder

1 teaspoon garlic salt
pepper, to taste
shredded lettuce
1/2–3/4 cup taco sauce
1 large chopped tomato
1 cup shredded Cheddar cheese
2 tablespoons chopped onion

- Combine first 8 ingredients in food processor. Process until smooth.
- Pour into serving dish or 9-inch pie plate. Top with lettuce, taco sauce, tomato, cheese, and chopped onion. Serve with taco chips. Serves 8.

Mexican Bean Pie

Sue Seder

2 10 1/2-ounce cans Jalapeño-
    flavored bean dip
1 cup sour cream
2/3 cup mayonnaise
1 package taco seasoning mix
2 4-ounce can green chiles, drained
4 medium-sized ripe avocados

2 tablespoons lime juice
1 teaspoon pinch salt
1/4 teaspoon garlic powder or salt
8 ounces sharp Cheddar cheese, shredded
    (mellow)
4 tomatoes, chopped
1 bunch green scallions, chopped

- In a 9 x 13-inch dish or 2-inch pie plate, spread bean dip on bottom.
- Combine sour cream, mayonnaise, taco mix, and chiles. Spread over bean dip.
- Mash avocados with lime juice, salt, and garlic, and spread over mayonnaise layer. Sprinkle with chopped cheese, tomatoes, and scallions.

⌂ Chopped Liver

Mrs. Nathan Jacobson

1 pound liver, chicken or calves
2 hard-boiled eggs
1 stalk celery, chopped and sautéed,
    optional

1 medium-sized onion, sautéed
2 tablespoons chicken fat

- Broil liver until done.
- Chop or grind all ingredients together.
- Mix and season with salt and pepper to taste.
- Serve on crackers, toast, or celery.

Vegetarian Chopped Liver

Hazel Holsborg

The best faux liver you've ever tasted.

2 large onions
¼ cup vegetable oil
6 hard-boiled eggs

1 large can peas, or frozen, thawed
6 ounces walnut meats
salt and pepper

- Dice onions and sauté in oil until golden brown. Put in processor and add 2 whole eggs, whites from 4 eggs, peas, walnuts, and salt and pepper to taste. Process until desired texture.
- Serve on bed of greens.

Mock Chopped Liver

Marjorie Bernstein

Appearance and taste is identical to liver.

1 cup lentils
chicken soup
1 large onion, chopped
olive oil

1 cup walnuts
6 egg whites, cooked
salt and pepper
garlic powder

- Cover lentils with chicken soup and cook ½ hour.
- Sauté onion in olive oil.
- Grind walnuts in food processor until fine.
- Add lentils (all broth will be dissolved), onions, and eggs to processor. Process until all ingredients are thoroughly mixed.
- Season to taste. Serves 8.

Vegetarian Kishka

Ethel Chaifetz

Great for hors d'oeuvres.

1 box Tam crackers
3 large carrots
2 stalks celery
1 large onion

¼ pound unsalted margarine
pepper, to taste
¼ teaspoon garlic powder, optional

- Crush crackers. Grate carrots, celery, and onion.
- Melt margarine. Mix all ingredients thoroughly together.
- Press into rolls and tightly cover each roll with aluminum foil, sealing sides.
- Bake in 350°F oven on a cookie sheet for approximately 1 hour. **Do not** slice while hot. Refrigerate several hours or overnight.
- To serve, slice to desired thickness and reheat in oven before serving. Can be frozen after initial baking.

Ellen's Herring Salad

Judy Rubin

2 jars schmaltz herring, drained
  (approximately 1 pound)
1 small jar sliced pickled beets
4 pickle spears, cut into small pieces
1 large apple, diced

2 hard-boiled eggs, diced
$^1/_4$ cup walnuts, chopped
1 pint sour cream
$^3/_4$ jar beet juice

- Mix all ingredients together and serve chilled.

Israeli Herring Salad

Anita "Aschie" Epstein

Great appetizer — can be made in advance.

1 2-pound jar pickled herring in wine
  sauce
2 large white Spanish onions, diced
2 large tart apples, peeled and diced

$^1/_4$ cup wine or cider vinegar
$^1/_3$ cup oil
$^1/_4$ cup sugar
1 6-ounce can tomato paste

- Drain herring, discard the onions, and cut herring into small pieces.
- Add remaining ingredients to herring and mix well.
- Place mixture in jar and refrigerate until ready to serve. Serve on party rye or crackers.

Ruth's Herring Salad

Ruth Short

Meat grinder is best to use. If not, use processor.

1 16-ounce jar herring in wine sauce
6 hard-boiled eggs
2 medium-sized tart apples, pared and
    cored

2 medium-sized onions
2 slices toasted white bread
salt and pepper, to taste
sugar, to taste

- Drain herring and set liquid aside.
- In a separate bowl, grind eggs and set aside.
- Into a large bowl, grind herring, apples, onions, and bread. Mix together, and add eggs.
- For a little vinegary taste, add some of the reserved liquid. Serve on crackers or toasted pita triangles. Serves a good-sized crowd.

Herring with Cranberry Sauce

Rae Budnitz

This is an hors d'oeuvre — hard to say how many it will serve.

1 16-ounce jar party herring in wine
    sauce
1 1-pound can whole berry cranberry
    sauce

1 cup sour cream
1 red onion, thinly sliced

- Drain herring and remove onions.
- Mix together cranberry sauce and sour cream. Add herring and onion.
- Let stand 24 hours. (For larger quantity, use 3 jars of herring, but only double the cranberry sauce and sour cream.)

Chopped Herring

Dorothy Smith

Do not use herring in sour cream sauce.

1 16-ounce jar herring in wine sauce
2–3 slices "challa" or white bread
2 hard-boiled eggs
1 carrot, grated
1 apple

1 large onion
½ green pepper, optional
1 tablespoon sugar
2 tablespoons vinegar
¼ teaspoon pepper

- Drain herring, reserving liquid.
- Soak "challa" or bread in liquid. Squeeze liquid out of bread.
- Chop each ingredient in food processor. Mix together.
- Taste. May need more vinegar or sugar.
- Stays well in refrigerator. Serves 10.

Make Your Own Lox

Lolita Baker

This is unusual and unique.

1 fresh fillet of salmon (not steak)
oil
1 tablespoon sugar

1 tablespoon liquid woodsmoke
   flavoring
2 tablespoons kosher salt

- Rub salmon fillet with oil.
- Make a paste of sugar, woodsmoke flavoring, and kosher salt. Rub fish with paste, using the flesh side only. Wrap fish well in Saran Wrap, and store in refrigerator for seven days, turning daily.
- Wash and dry fish. Freeze partially for 35 minutes, before slicing — it slices better when frozen.

Smoked Fish Log

Lilyan Spiegel

Delicious appetizer — serve with wheat crackers.

1 8-ounce package cream cheese, softened
1 tablespoon lemon juice
2 teaspoons grated onion
1 teaspoon horseradish

2 cups flaked smoked fish (1 pound mixed fish or 3/4 pound bluefish)
2 tablespoons chopped parsley
1/2 cup chopped walnuts

- Combine cheese, lemon juice, onion, and horseradish. Add to fish and mix thoroughly. Chill mixture for several hours.
- Combine nuts and parsley. Shape fish mixture into a log form and roll in nut mixture. (I use waxed paper or Saran Wrap to roll.) Serves 8–10.

Salmon Roll

Evelyn S. Heller

1 7½-ounce can red salmon
1 8-ounce package cream cheese
1 teaspoon lemon juice
1 ounce Cheddar cheese, grated
2 teaspoons white horseradish

1 scallion, cut very fine, optional
1/4 teaspoon salt
1/4 teaspoon liquid woodsmoke flavoring
1/2 cup chopped pecans
3 tablespoons finely chopped parsley

- Drain and flake salmon.
- Mix cream cheese with lemon juice, cheese, horseradish, scallion, salt and smoke flavoring. Add salmon and mix. Refrigerate for at least 1 hour.
- Shape into roll, and roll in nuts and parsley. Serves 8–10.

Nova Scotia Mousse

Jean Freed

1 envelope gelatin, dissolved in
    ¹/₄ cup water
¹/₂ cup light cream, heated
8 ounces cream cheese
1 cup sour cream
1 teaspoon Worcestershire sauce
¹/₄ teaspoon hot pepper sauce

1 clove garlic
1 teaspoon lemon juice
1 tablespoon parsley
1 tablespoon white horseradish
¹/₄ pound lox, chopped
¹/₄ cup black olives, chopped
4 ounces red caviar

- Add dissolved gelatin to cream and cool.
- Mash together until smooth cream cheese, sour cream, Worcestershire sauce, hot pepper sauce, and garlic. Stir in the gelatin mixture.
- Add lemon juice, parsley, horseradish, lox, and olives. Fold in caviar.
- Pour into greased 3 cup fish mold. Refrigerate until firm.

Salmon Mousse

Augusta H. Kressler

1 15-ounce can salmon, drained,
    reserve liquid
1 tablespoon unflavored gelatin
2 tablespoons white or red horseradish
1 tablespoon lemon juice
1 tablespoon chopped fresh dill weed

1 tablespoon chopped fresh parsley
1 teaspoon chopped garlic
1 cup regular or light sour cream
¹/₂ teaspoon salt or soy sauce
Worcestershire sauce, or hot sauce to
    taste

- Place salmon in a small bowl.
- Sprinkle gelatin over reserved liquid in another smaller bowl to soften. Melt the gelatin mixture in a double boiler over hot water.
- Place all ingredients, including bones, into a blender or food processor and blend until smooth.
- Pour mixture into an oiled, 4-cup attractive mold — use a fish mold if you've got one. Chill until firm.
- Unmold onto a plate and garnish with dill. Serve with thinly sliced cucumber or crackers or both. Serves 18–20.

Pearl of the Sea Mousse

Jean Freed

Egg Mixture:
6 hard-boiled eggs, finely chopped
1 cup mayonnaise
1 teaspoon salt and pepper

Gelatin Mixture:
1 envelope gelatin
2 tablespoons lemon juice
2 tablespoons water
1 teaspoon Worcestershire sauce
1 teaspoon anchovy paste
dash onion powder

1 4-ounce jar black caviar
small jar pimentos
black olives

Egg Mixture:
• Combine all ingredients in a small bowl.

Gelatin Mixture:
• Combine all ingredients and heat until smooth.
• Combine gelatin and egg mixture. Carefully fold in caviar.
• Decorate bottom of 1 1/2-quart ring mold with strips of pimento. Spoon this over the egg and caviar. Chill until firm.
• Fill center with black olives.

"Gifelteh" Fish Mold

Freda Weintraub

Best served as an hors d'oeuvre.

1 can Rokeach Sweet Vienna fish
  (8 pieces)
2 cups strained borscht

2 packages lemon jello
1/2 bottle **strong** horseradish
1/3 cup lemon juice

• Slice fish in half horizontally. Place in a jello mold.
• Heat borscht and dissolve Jello in it. Add horseradish and lemon juice.
• Pour 1/2 of **cooled** liquid over fish.
• Refrigerate till almost firm (15–20 minutes).
• Pour remaining liquid over fish and keep in refrigerator. May be prepared a day before serving. Serves 10–12.

Tortilla Roll-ups

Ann Sloane

Excellent hors d'oeuvre. Easy, colorful, tasty.

1 8-ounce package cream cheese, softened
3 tablespoons chopped green onion
3 ounces smoked salmon, chopped
2 tablespoons sour cream

1 tablespoon chopped fresh dill or 1 teaspoon dried dill
4 9–10-inch flour tortillas
1 1/2 cups fresh spinach leaves

- Combine cream cheese, onion, salmon, sour cream, and dill in medium-sized bowl.
- Spread a generous 1/4 cup filling on each tortilla. Place spinach leaves on top, leaving 1/2-inch border.
- Roll up tightly and wrap in plasatic wrap. Refrigerate at least 1 hour or up to 6 hours. To serve, cut into l-inch pieces.

Santa Fe Roll Ups

Karen Hodes Turk

Can be made ahead of time and frozen.

1 8-ounce package cream cheese, softened
1/3 cup chunky salsa
1/4 cup chopped green onions
1/2 teaspoon chili powder

1/2 teaspoon garlic powder
3 tablespoons fresh chopped cilantro, optional
salsa for dipping
1 package small flour tortillas

- Mix all ingredients except tortillas in blender or food processor.
- Spread 1 heaping tablespoon of mixture on tortilla with spatula. Roll tightly and refrigerate for 1 hour.
- Trim edges and cut into 1/2-inch slices. Serve on platter with extra salsa for dipping.
- Makes approximately 50–60 pieces. Serves 10–12 people.

Mock Blintzes

Harriet Lowe

These freeze very well and can be frozen for a few months if necessary.

³/₄ cup sugar
2 teaspoons cinnamon
1 large loaf white bread (20-ounce)

12 ounces cream cheese, softened
³/₄ cup butter or margarine (1¹/₂ sticks),
   melted

* Combine sugar and cinnamon and set aside.
* Remove crusts from white bread slices. Using a rolling pin, roll each slice flat. As you roll each one, spread with a thin coating of cream cheese. Roll each jellyroll-style the long way.
* Cut each roll in half. Roll each in melted butter, and then in mixture of sugar and cinnamon.
* Freeze at this point or bake at 350°F for about 15 minutes or until crispy. When placing in baking dish, try to be careful that blintzes do not touch each other.

Cheese Boregas

Irene Garber

1 tablespoon Parmesan cheese
1 package grated sharp white
   Cheddar cheese
1 package Feta cheese, crumbled
1 egg, beaten

2 tablespoons flour
2 packages Pepperidge Farm puff pastry
4 ounces sesame seeds
1 extra large egg, beaten, for glaze

* Combine Parmesan, Cheddar, and Feta cheeses. Add egg and flour.
* Unfold pastry. Cut each sheet into thirds and then each strip into thirds to make squares. Place 1 tablespoon of mixture into center of square.
* Fold to form triangle and press edges closed. Brush beaten egg over top of triangle then dip top in seeds. Refrigerate or freeze.
* Bake at 400°F until slightly brown.

Mushroom Gratinée Cups

Barbara W. Burwick

Hors d'oeuvres. Superb!

Cups:
white bread, cut into circles with a 2-inch round cookie cutter

Filling:
2 pounds mushrooms (don't wash, wipe with damp cloth)
1/4 pound butter
2 tablespoons shallots, finely chopped
juice of 1/2 lemon
1/4 cup Madeira or dry sherry
1 tablespoon flour
1 teaspoon salt
2 cups heavy cream
ground pepper, to taste
Parmesan cheese, freshly grated

* To prepare cups, press bread into small muffin tins. Push around sides to make a cup. Bake 350°F for 15 minutes.
* To prepare filling, cut off mushroom stems until even with caps. Chop mushroom caps coarsely.
* Melt butter, add finely chopped shallots, and stir. Add mushrooms and cook over high heat until moisture evaporates, approximately 10–15 minutes.
* Squeeze in lemon juice and stir. Add Madeira or dry sherry when more liquid evaporates. Sprinkle in flour and salt.
* Add heavy cream and ground pepper to taste. Bring to boil, then simmer. Cook until not too liquidy — until mushrooms are just covered with reduced cream (can be refrigerated at this point).
* Fill bread cups to top with mushroom mixture. Sprinkle lots of freshly grated Parmesan cheese over top.
* Bake 350°F for 15 minutes. Serve immediately as hors d'oeuvres.

Spinach Balls

Joy Goodwin

An excellent hors d'oeuvre.

2 10-ouunce packages frozen spinach
2 2 1/2 cups packaged herb stuffing
3/4 cup melted margarine or butter
1/2 cup Parmesan cheese, grated
2 small onions, minced

Spices:
salt
pepper
garlic powder
Mrs. Dash or thyme

* Cook and drain spinach well.
* Combine all ingredients and roll into balls made from 1 teaspoon of ingredients, about the size of a walnut.
* Bake 350°F for 20 minutes on a greased cookie sheet.
* Remove at once and drain on paper towels. Serve **hot**. Makes about 75 balls.
* May be frozen. Reheat at 400°F for 3–5 minutes.

Spinach–Cheese Croustades

Hannah Laipson

Delicious hors d'oeuvres/appetizers. Freezes very well before baking.

Croustades (Basic Recipe):
6 tablespoons butter, at room temperature
48 slices fresh thin-sliced bread

Filling:
1 onion, finely chopped
3 tablespoons oil or butter
1 10-ounce package frozen chopped spinach, thawed and well drained
1 teaspoon salt
1/4 pound Feta cheese, crumbled
1/2 cup cottage cheese
1 egg, beaten

Croustades:
* Coat inside of 2-inch muffin cups with butter.
* Cut circles (2 1/2– 3 inches) from slices of bread with cutter. Press each circle gently but firmly into muffin cup to fit snugly.
* Bake at 350°F for 10 minutes or until golden.
* When filled, heat 10 minutes at 350°F on baking sheet.

Filling:
* Sauté onion in oil until soft. Add spinach and salt. Cook until tender and remove from heat.
* Mix cheeses together and stir in egg. Stir into spinach–onion mixture and blend well.

Spanaki Kroketes

Lorraine Lonstein

Greek recipe for fried spinach balls.

2 10-ounce packages frozen chopped spinach
1 egg
1 cup dry bread crumbs
2 tablespoons grated Parmesan cheese
2 tablespoons grated Mozzarella cheese
2 tablespoons grated onion
2 tablespoons butter, melted
1/2 teaspoon dried oregano
1 egg
1 tablespoon water
seasoned bread crumbs
salt and pepper, to taste
oil for frying

* Cook spinach according to package directions. Drain thoroughly in a colander, pressing out excess water.
* Combine spinach with next seven ingredients and mix well. Let stand 10 minutes.
* Shape into balls, about 1 1/4 inches in diameter.
* Beat egg and water together.
* Roll spinach balls in bread crumbs. Dip in egg mixture and roll again in bread crumbs.
* Fry in deep fryer until golden. Drain on paper towel and serve. Makes 15 balls.

Variation: Cooked, well-drained yellow squash, zucchini, or eggplant can be chopped and prepared in the same manner.

Zucchini Squares

Jean Freed

1 cup Bisquick
1/2 cup chopped onion, sautéed in butter
    or olive oil
1/2 cup grated Parmesan cheese
2 tablespoons minced fresh parsley and
    mint leaves
1 pinch salt

1/2 teaspoon dried oregano
pepper, to taste
1 clove garlic, minced
1/2 cup vegetable oil
4 eggs, beaten
3 cups thinly sliced zucchini

- Mix the above ingredients.
- Bake in a 350°F oven for 25 minutes in greased 9 x 13 x 2-inch pan.

Cheese Squares

Bobbie Hirshberg

Wonderful. Great at parties.

1 bag of frozen onions, chopped,
    10–12 ounces
2 tablespoons butter
10 ounces Cracker Barrel cheese,
    extra sharp (divide in half and
    grate into separate bowls)

2 cups milk, at room temperature
2 eggs, at room temperature
3 cups Bisquick
1/2 stick butter, melted
2 tablespoons poppy seeds

- Sauté onion in 2 tablespoons butter until soft and transparent.
- Place in a bowl with grated cheese. Stir in milk, eggs, and Bisquick.
- Grease a 13 x 9-inch pan. Pour in mixture and sprinkle remaining cheese over top. Drizzle the 1/2 stick melted butter over top. Sprinkle poppy seeds over top.
- Bake at 400°F about 20 minutes until golden.
- Chill in refrigerator. Slice into 1-inch squares. Heat before serving in a 375°F oven about 5 minutes. Can be frozen! Serves 30.

Chinese Chicken Wings

Marilyn F. Karsh

Great appetizer as well as ethnic.

2–3 pounds chicken wings
salt and pepper
1/2 cup honey
4 tablespoons brown sugar

1/4 cup soy sauce
1 garlic clove, crushed
1/4 cup ketchup

- Clean and dry wings. Season with salt and pepper.
- Bake covered at 375°F for 3/4 hour. Pour off juice.

Sauce:
- Mix together honey, brown sugar, soy sauce, garlic clove, and ketchup and pour over wings.
- Bake uncovered at 400°F basting every 15 minutes for 45 minutes or until tender.
- Can be prepared day before and reheated.

Chicken Wings Appetizer

Linda Goldstein

2–3 pounds chicken wings (wingettes — separated at joint)
2/3 cup soy sauce

4 cloves garlic, minced or mashed
2/3 cup dark brown sugar
2 teaspoons dry mustard

- Combine ingredients.
- Marinate chicken wings 24 hours.
- Bake at 350°F for 1 hour. Serves 10–12.

Vidalia Onion Dip

Karen Hodes Turk

Easy hors d'oeuvre!

2 cups chopped Vidalia onions
2 cups mayonnaise
2 cups shredded Swiss cheese

1 teaspoon black pepper
paprika, to garnish if desired

- Mix together ingredients (except paprika). Arrange in 9-inch pie/quiche dish.
- Bake at 350°F for 20–30 minutes or until bubbling. Serve with crackers/crudites. Serves 6.

Baba Gannouj

Gerry Moss

Middle East Eggplant Dip. Best made early in the day.

1 eggplant, about 1 pound
2 teaspoons finely chopped garlic
2 tablespoons fresh lemon juice
¼ cup sesame paste (tahini)

1 tablespoon olive oil
3 tablespoons finely chopped parsley
salt and pepper, to taste

- Cook eggplant, preferably over a charcoal grill or gas grill, until it "wilts" and is softened throughout, approximately 25 minutes, turning 3–4 times. Remove from heat and let cool.
- Scrape pulp away from skin. There should be about 1 cup of pulp. Put in food processer, add garlic, and blend. Add remaining ingredients and blend to make a fine purée.
- Serve chilled or at room temperature with pita bread and fresh vegetables to dip. Serves 8–10.

Barbeque Bologna

Barbara Rubin

Excellent appetizer.

1 large onion, chopped
oil
1 jar chili sauce
¹/₂ cup water

¹/₄ box brown sugar
3 tablespoons vinegar
1 tablespoon lemon juice
2 pounds bologna, in 1 piece

- Sauté onion in small amount of oil. Add remaining ingredients (except bologna) to sautéed onion. Simmer for 20 minutes.
- Score whole bologna and place in baking dish. Add sauce making sure it covers the bologna. Bake in covered pan at 275°F for 2 hours, basting frequently.
- Cut in cubes — leave in sauce for serving. Serves large group.

Salami Hors d'oeuvre

Toby Richmond

Very simple and very well liked.

1 Kosher salami
1 jar Honeycup Mustard

- Cook salami which has been scored well at 250°F for 1 hour.
- Cover the salami very generously with the honeycup mustard being sure to get it into all the crevices. Cook 1 more hour.
- Cut and serve it as an hors d'oeuvre with a little accompanying Honeycup Mustard on the side. Serves 6.

Suzie's Sweet and Sour Meatballs

Harriet Robbins

Reheats beautifully! Freezes well.

Meatballs:
2 pounds ground beef or ground veal
1 egg
1 medium-sized onion, grated
salt, to taste

Sauce:
10 ounces grape jelly
12 ounces chili sauce
juice of one lemon

- Combine ground beef or veal, egg, onion, and salt.
- Using about 1 tablespoon of mixture, roll into balls.
- Combine in saucepan grape jelly, chili sauce, and lemon. Add meatballs to sauce.
- Simmer to brown 1^1/$_2$ hours. Serves 8–10.

Tangy Sweet and Sour Meatballs

Dorothy Heitin

Easy!

1^1/$_2$ pounds minced beef, uncooked
1 teaspoon salt
^{1}/$_4$ teaspoon pepper
1 clove garlic, minced

1 egg
2 tablespoons matzoh meal
1^1/$_2$ cups ketchup
2 cups ginger ale

- Combine first 6 ingredients and form into small balls.
- Combine ketchup and ginger ale in a large saucepan and bring to a boil. Drop meatballs into sauce. Cover and simmer for 2 hours (or less). Serves 4–6.

Aunt Ethel's Champagne Punch

Debbie Fins

Great for brunches.

2 2-liter bottles ginger ale, chilled
2 bottles champagne, chilled
1 pint sherbet (strawberry or raspberry)

1 large can of pineapple juice
fruit (strawberries, sliced oranges etc.)

- Freeze can of pineapple juice
- Gently mix ginger ale and champagne in large punch bowl. Add 1 pint sherbet.
- Place frozen pineapple juice in bowl and stir gently.
- Float sliced fruit.

Refreshing Fruit Punch

Harriet Robbins

1 12-ounce can frozen orange juice,
  defrosted
1 12-ounce can frozen lemonade,
  defrosted

1 large can pineapple juice
1 liter club soda
fresh lemon and lime slices
cherries

- Mix first 3 ingredients together. Add club soda before serving.
- In an ice cube tray, put cherries, lemon, and lime pieces, add water, and freeze.
- Add these cubes to fruit punch when serving.

Soups

Chicken Soup (Clear)

Shirley Kane

The traditional first course to most family gatherings.

2 chickens (3–4 pounds each), cut-up or
    1 chicken, plus extra wings, giblets,
    necks (no liver)
2 medium onions
8–10 carrots, cut into thirds

8 stalks celery, with tops cut into thirds
1/3 bunch fresh parsley
salt and pepper, to taste
2 parsnips, optional

- Place all ingredients (except parsley) in a 6–8-quart pot. Over medium-high heat, sear contents, stirring frequently.
- When lightly browned add water to cover and bring to a boil. Skim top and add parsley and seasoning.
- Reduce heat, covering tightly, and simmer 1 1/2 hours.
- When cool, remove chicken and carrots. Strain soup through sieve and refrigerate soup overnight.
- Remove fat from top.
- Soup can be served with noodles, rice, or matzoh balls. Deboned chicken and carrots can be added back in.
- Soup keeps in refrigerator for 5 days and freezes for 3 months. Keep frozen in containers. Soup stock is good base in many recipes. Serves 12–14.

Light and Fluffy Knaidlach

Frances Berger

They rise to the top.

1/3 cup shortening, melted and
    cooled (nyafat — onion flavored,
    if desired)
1/2 cup water

1 teaspoon salt
1 dash pepper
4 eggs, beaten
1 cup matzoh meal

- Melt shortening (measure before heating). Cook slightly, being sure it remains liquid.
- Add water, shortening, salt and pepper to beaten eggs, and mix well. Add matzoh meal and stir thoroughly. Refrigerate for 1 hour.
- Form into balls, (wet hands makes it easier).
- Drop into 1 1/2 quarts boiling water with 1 tablespoon salt. Cook for about 20 minutes. Transfer to soup to serve. Serves about 8.

Aunt Sadie's Knaidlach

Esther Freeman

2 eggs
¹/₄ teaspoon salt
¹/₃ cup matzoh meal, plus 1 tablespoon

Or:
6 eggs
1 teaspoon salt
1¹/₄ cups matzoh meal

- Beat eggs and salt very, very well in electric mixer.
- Add matzoh meal and mix on slow speed.
- Refrigerator at least 15 minutes.
- Bring water to boil (2–4 quarts).
- Wet hands and form mixture into ball. Drop into water. Cover and cook on low for 45 minutes. Do not peek.
- If too light and fluffy, add another tablespoon of matzoh meal.

🗂 Meat Kreplach

Mrs. Samuel Stayman

Meat Mixture:
3 pounds cooked meat, shoulder steak
    or chuck
1 large onion
salt and pepper, to taste
2 eggs

Dough Mixture:
3 cups flour
2 eggs, slightly beaten
³/₄–1 cup water

Meat Mixture:
- Chop meat and onions fine. Add seasoning and eggs, and mix together well.

Dough Mixture:
- Mix all ingredients together. Divide in 3 parts.
- Roll each part thin on well-floured board. Cut into small squares, put meat on each square, and press together into triangles.
- Drop in boiling water and cook each batch for 15 minutes. Drain and rinse in cold water.
- Freezes well, either raw or cooked. Fry crisp for hors d'oeurves or drop into soup.

Hearty Russian Chicken Soup

Jayne Singer

An original Russian recipe

4–5 pound roasting chicken, cut-up
1 tablespoon salt
4 carrots, sliced
2 parsnips, sliced
1 large turnip, diced
4 stalks celery with leaves chopped

1 medium-sized onion, diced and sautéed
    in butter or olive oil
2 teaspoons minced garlic cloves
1/2 teaspoon pepper
1/2 teaspoon celery seed
1 tablespoon dill

- Place cut-up chicken in large stock pot. Add water to cover and bring to boil. Skim surface.
- Add remaining ingredients and simmer for 1 hour.
- De-bone chicken. Return meat to pot and simmer for another hour. Serves 6–8.

Egg-Lemon Soup

Natalie Rosenkrantz

6 cups chicken broth
1/2 cup rice, medium- or long-grain white
3 large eggs

2–4 tablespoons lemon juice, to taste
season with salt and pepper

- In a 3- or 4-quart pan over medium-high heat, bring broth to a simmer. Add rice and simmer, covered, for 20 minutes or till tender. Turn down heat so broth stays hot but does not boil.
- In a medium-sized bowl, beat eggs with a wire whisk or fork until they are light. Beat in lemon juice.
- Slowly add 3/4 cup hot broth to egg mixture, stirring constantly. Gradually add egg mixture back to the remaining broth in pan, stirring constantly. Continue stirring and heating for 1–2 minutes longer, or until soup thickens slightly. Do not boil or the eggs will curdle. Makes about 6 servings.

Vegetarian "Borshch"

Eva Honig

1 tablespoon olive oil
1 large onion, chopped
2 large beets, chopped
1 large carrot, diced
1 small can tomato paste
1 stalk celery, diced
1 large parsnip, diced
1 medium-sized purple top turnip, diced
8 cups water
1/2 small cabbage, shredded
pinch of basil

pinch of thyme
pinch of fennel seeds
pinch of caraway seeds
1 large bay leaf
large pinch of sugar
salt and pepper, to taste
1/4 cup dried large lima or fava beans,
    soaked in water overnight, simmer
    in fresh water until almost tender
dill, for garnish
sour cream or yogurt, for garnish

- In a large pot, heat the olive oil over medium heat, add onion, reduce heat to medium-low and sauté for 8–10 minutes.
- Add the beets, carrots, tomato paste, and a little water and stew for 5 minutes.
- Add celery, parsnip, and turnip, and continue stewing 5 more minutes.
- Add water, bring to a boil, add cabbage, herbs and spices, and sugar. Reduce heat, cover, and simmer for 15 minutes.
- Add the beans and simmer another 10–20 minutes until the vegetables are very tender. Adjust the seasoning.
- Let cool at room temperature, half covered. Tastes best if refrigerated overnight and reheated. Serve with chopped dill and a dollop of sour cream or yogurt.

Quick Beet Soup

Mrs. Jesse Schneider

1 No. 2 can small whole beets
1 1/2 cans water
1 teaspoon salt
1/2 teaspoon onion salt

1/2 teaspoon garlic salt
1/8–1/4 cup sugar
3–4 tablespoons lemon juice
sour cream, optional

- Drain beets and add juice to small saucepan. Add water and bring to a boil.
- Add beets, seasonings, and lemon juice. Boil for 20 minutes.
- Grate beets when cool enough to handle.
- Whip in sour cream if desired, when ready to use.

Sweet and Sour Cabbage Soup

Karen R. Baron

2 pounds flanken
2–3 marrow bones, optional
1 large onion, sliced
2 teaspoons salt, optional
1/2 cup raisins

2 pounds cabbage
2 cans tomato soup
1/2 cup brown sugar
1 tablespoon lemon juice

- Place meat, bones, onion, and salt into a deep pot, and cover with hot water. Cook 1–1 1/2 hours, skimming when necessary.
- Meanwhile, shred cabbage and boil for 5 minutes. Drain and add cabbage to meat mixture. Add tomato soup, brown sugar, lemon juice, and raisins. Cook 1/2 hour or more until meat is tender. Serves 4.

Tomato Cabbage Soup

Mrs. Jordan Sandman

1 small head of cabbage
3/4 pound brisket and a marrow bone
1 onion, cut-up fine
salt and pepper

1 No. 2 can tomatoes
3 tablespoons sugar
3 tablespoons lemon juice, or small piece of sour salt

- Shred cabbage, rinse in hot water then in cold water.
- Put meat and bones in large pot with onion, salt and pepper. Cover with water and cook until meat is almost tender.
- Add cabbage and cook for 1/2 hour. Then add tomatoes, sugar, and lemon juice. Cook 15 minutes longer.

Harriet's Sweet and Sour Cabbage Soup
Harriet G. Tullman

Always comes out "great" — can be frozen.

1 soup bone, marrow
1/2 pound or more soup meat
1 medium-sized cabbage, cut-up or
    chopped
1 onion, chopped (or use onion powder,
    to taste)

1 jar of beets, grated or cut-up small
1 large can of tomatoes
3 tablespoons lemon juice
3 tablespoons brown sugar
salt and pepper, to taste

- Place bone and meat in large pot and cover with water. Bring to boil and "skim" fat off.
- Lower heat and add all ingredients except lemon juice and brown sugar. Cook 2 hours over low heat.
- Add lemon juice and brown sugar. Check for taste, adding more salt or pepper, if necessary. Continue cooking until sweet and sour.

Tomato-Bread Soup
Mike Andrews

Great light soup.

6 whole garlic
1 whole medium-sized onion
3 tablespoons vegetable oil
1/2 cup fresh basil, chopped
1 bunch chopped fennel (can substitute
    fennel seed)

6 fresh, diced tomatoes
2 cans whole tomatoes, crushed
4 cups chicken stock
4 cups large toasted croutons
salt and pepper, to taste

- Chop garlic and onion and sauté in oil in a large saucepan until golden in color.
- Stir in basil, fennel, diced tomatoes, and crushed tomatoes. Sauté for 5 minutes.
- Add chicken stock and simmer for 1/2 hour.
- 20–30 minutes before serving, add large croutons and salt and pepper.

Tomato Rice Soup

Lois Singer

1 28-ounce can ground and peeled
    tomatoes
3 cans water
4 stalks celery, thinly sliced
2 small white onions, diced
4 carrots, thinly sliced
4 tablespoons sugar
1 tablespoon salt

fresh ground pepper, to taste
3/4 teaspoon basil
1/4 teaspoon oregano
1/2 small zucchini, diced
1/2 small yellow summer squash, diced
4 handfuls rice
spinach leaves, optional

- Cook all ingredients except rice together for 1 hour.
- Add rice. Cook another 20–30 minutes. You may also add fresh spinach leaves when you reheat soup.

Hearty Tomato Soup

Karen Hodes Turk

3 cloves garlic, minced
1 cup choped onions
1/2 cup diced celery
1 tablespoon oil
2 16-ounce cans tomatoes, drained and
    diced
1 cup dry white wine

1/2 teaspoon sugar
1/2 teaspoon salt
8 ounces canned corn
1 16-ounce can tomatoes, chili style (this
    helps thicken/flavor)
1 cup chopped cilantro

- Sauté garlic, onions, and celery in oil in large saucepan.
- Add remaining ingredients in order, and simmer.

Gazpacho

Mrs. Haskell R. Gordon

A delightful summer soup.

4 cups peeled and chopped ripe tomatoes
2 cups peeled, seeded, and chopped
    cucumbers
1 cup diced green bell peppers
1/2 cup finely chopped sweet onion,
    sautéed in butter or olive oil
24 ounces tomato juice

1 slice white bread, crust removed
3 tablespoons wine vinegar
3 tablespoons olive oil
1/2 teaspoon pinch salt
1 clove garlic, minced
freshly ground pepper
sour cream, for garnish

- Combine half the tomatoes, cucumbers, green peppers, onions, and tomato juice in a glass or stainless steel bowl.
- Place all the remaining ingredients in a blender and blend until smooth.
- Combine the blended ingredients with the vegetables in the bowl, cover and chill for 4–6 hours or overnight.
- A dollop of sour cream may be added atop the soup. Serves 8.

Lentil Soup

Ruth Margolis

Parve, healthy, and luscious.

1 cup chopped celery
1 cup chopped carrots
1/2 cup chopped onion
2–3 tablespoons oil for sautéing
3 cloves garlic, minced
1 teaspoon salt
1 teaspoon cumin
1 teaspoon chili powder

1/2 cup chopped parsley and mint leaves
1/4 teaspoon pepper
rosemary, to taste
tarragon, to taste
basil, to taste
2 cups washed lentils
3 Telma vegetable bouillon cubes
10 cups water

- Sauté vegetables in oil. Add seasonings and stir to blend.
- Add the washed lentils, bouillon, and water and simmer for 1 hour. Serves 12.

Mom's Lentil Soup

Rachel Shabane

Middle Eastern version of old favorite.

1 bag of lentils
12 cups water
4 carrots, cut-up
1 onion, chopped
1 celery stalk, chopped
4 potatoes, cut-up

1/2 package fresh spinach
2 large tomatoes, cut-up
2 tablespoons oil
cumin, to taste
salt and pepper, to taste
2–4 teaspoons vinegar or lemon juice

- Mix all together except vinegar. Bring to boil and then simmer about 1 hour.
- Add vinegar or lemon juice and cook 15 minutes more. Serves many.

Russian Armenian Apricot-Lentil Soup

Zoe Ostrow

Delicious Soup

1 onion, chopped
2 cloves garlic, minced
1/3–1/2 cup chopped dried apricot halves
oil to sauté
1/2 teaspoon ground cumin
1/2 teaspoon thyme

1/2 cup rinsed red lentils
5–6 cups chicken broth
2 tablespoons tomato paste
pinch saffron, optional
oil as needed

- Sauté onion, garlic, and apricots in oil. Add cumin, thyme, and lentils, and stir.
- Add chicken broth and cook on low heat for 20 minutes. Add tomato paste.
- At this point, can be puréed in blender or food processor. Add lemon juice and/ or parsley to taste and adjust for other seasonings. Serves 6.

Hearty Pea Soup

Elaine Palley

1 onion, diced
2 tablespoons oil
1 bay leaf
1 teaspoon celery seed
1 cup split peas
1/4 cup barley
1/2 cup baby lima beans
10 cups water

2 teaspoons salt
1 dash pepper
1 carrot, chopped
3 stalks celery, diced
1/2 cup minced parsley
1 potato, diced
1/2 teaspoon basil
1/2 teaspoon thyme

- Sauté onion in oil until soft, with bay leaf and celery seed.
- Stir in peas, barley, and lima beans. Add 10 cups water and bring to boil. Cook 1 hour 20 minutes.
- Add salt and pepper, vegetables, and herbs and simmer 45 minutes. Add more water if necessary.

Pea Soup

Karen R. Baron

1/2 cup green peas
1/2 cup yellow peas
1 1/2–2 quarts water
3 stalks celery, sliced
3 carrots, sliced
1 onion

2 sweet potatoes, diced
2 white potatoes, diced
salt and pepper, to taste
1 tablespoon paprika
1 pound beef chuck, in pieces

- Place peas in large, tall pot and cover with water. Add all ingredients. Bring to boil and stir. Skim if necessary.
- Lower heat to slow boil. (Do **not** simmer or soup will be too thin.) Stir occasionally and cook about 4 hours until thick (can add more water for desired consistency). Discard onion when soup is cooked.
- Can be made with onion powder for low-sodium diet. Serves 8.

Black Bean Soup

Ann F. Sloane

Don't forget lemon juice — brings out all the flavor.

8 ounces black beans
6 cups chicken broth
1 tablespoon margarine
1 cup chopped onion, sautéed in butter or olive oil
1 cup shredded carrots
1 cup chopped celery

1 bay leaf
1 teaspoon salt
1 cup diced potatoes
1/2 teaspoon garlic powder
1/4 teaspoon pepper
3 tablespoons lemon juice

- Soak beans as directed on package and drain.
- In large deep pot, bring beans and broth to boil. Reduce heat and simmer 1 1/2–2 hours.
- In large skillet, melt margarine and sauté onions, carrots, and celery 3–5 minutes until softened.
- Add sautéed vegetables and remaining ingredients, except lemon juice, to beans and stir well. Simmer covered, 1 hour.
- Just before serving, stir in lemon juice, and garnish with sliced lemon, if desired. Serves 6.

Chatham Chowder

Gina Schultz

This is my friend's mother's recipe and it won second place in a chowder cooking contest.

5–7 tablespoons butter
3 medium-sized onions, sliced
5 medium-sized potatoes, diced
3–4 teaspoons salt
1/2 teaspoon pepper

3 cups boiling water
2 pounds haddock, skinned
1 quart milk, scalded
1 cup evaporated milk

- In Dutch oven, melt 4 tablespoons of butter. Add onion and sauté over low heat (do not brown). Add potatoes, salt, pepper, and boiling water.
- Lay fish, cut into large pieces, on top. Cover and simmer for 25 minutes or until potatoes are tender.
- Add scalded milk, evaporated milk, and 1–3 tablespoons butter. Heat through. Serves 6–8.

Fish Chowder

Mrs. Arthur Ringer

3 tablespoons margarine
²/₃ cup sliced onion
2 cups water
1 carrot, finely cubed
3 cups cubed raw potatoes

1 teaspoon salt
¹/₄ teaspoon pepper
2 pounds (lean) fish (clear meat)
¹/₂ teaspoon Accent
¹/₂ cup evaporated milk

- In large saucepan, melt margarine, and sauté onions until a light yellow color.
- Add 1 cup water and carrot and simmer for 10 minutes.
- Add potatoes, salt and pepper, fish, and 1 cup of water, and cook until the potatoes are soft and fish is cooked.
- Break fish into coarse flakes and add evaporated milk. If thinner consistency is desired, add more milk.

Asparagus and Wild Rice Soup

Margery Blonder

3 pounds asparagus
2 tablespoons margarine
1 large onion, coarsely chopped
8 cups water or vegetable broth
1 cup wild rice

1 cup light cream, (or for low-fat, use evaporated skim milk)
salt and pepper, to taste
a dash of nutmeg
a dash of ginger

- Cut off top 2 inches of asparagus and set aside. Cut up rest and coarsely chop.
- Melt margarine in large, heavy skillet. Add onion and chopped asparagus and cook over low heat until onion is translucent.
- Add 4 cups liquid, ¹/₂ cup wild rice and simmer for 45 minutes or until rice is tender.
- Purée through food processor, and set aside.
- Cut asparagus tops into ¹/₂-inch pieces and boil in rest of liquid. Cook for 2 minutes. Transfer with slotted spoon to another bowl.
- Add rest of rice and cook for 45 minutes or until tender.
- Heat all together. Add cream. Serve with nutmeg and ginger on top.

Cucumber Soup

Mansour Sadigh

2 cups peeled, seeded, and grated cucumber
1 pint buttermilk
½ cup half and half
1 large container plain yogurt
1 cup finely chopped walnuts

1 cup raisins
1 teaspoon dried basil
1 cup chopped scallions
½ teaspoon tarragon
salt and pepper

- Drain juice from cucumber. Mix cucumber with all ingredients and stir.
- If too thick add more milk or yogurt.

Heart Saver Soup

Ethel Gladstone

You can make this soup with just two of the beans. It is very delicious. Enjoy!

2 tablespoons olive oil
½ cup diced celery
1 cup diced onion, sautéed in butter or olive oil
1 cup diced carrots
2 pinches salt
⅔ teaspoon pepper
1½ tablespoons minced fresh basil
1½ tablespoons dried oregano
1½ teaspoons dried thyme

2 cloves garlic, minced
4½ cups basic vegetable stock
1 cup diced raw potatoes
1 cup cooked black beans
1 cup cooked Great Northern beans
1 cup cooked garbanzo beans (chickpeas)
½ cup lentils
½ cup green split peas
2½ cups tomatoes, peeled and chopped

- In a medium-sized soup pot, heat oil on medium-high. When hot, add the next 9 ingredients and stir.
- Add vegetable stock and potatoes. Bring to boil and simmer about 10 minutes.
- Purée ½ the black beans and half the northern beans and add to pot. Add remaining ingredients and simmer about 10 minutes.

Autumn Soup

Sandra Landau

This is a main course dish in the cold weather, served with bread and a salad. You should season, and make the soup thinner or thicker to your family's tastes. You can't go wrong.

1 small onion, chopped
2 tablespoons canola oil or margarine
1 large sweet potato, cut into cubes
2 large carrots, sliced into "pennies"
1 pound butternut squash, cut into cubes, or 1 can pumpkin
2 quarts chicken broth

$1/2$ teaspoon salt
2 teaspoons curry powder
1 teaspoon cinnamon
$1/2$ teaspoon nutmeg
1–2 tart (Granny Smith) apples, peeled, cored, and grated coarsely

- Sauté onion in a soup kettle in oil until limp.
- Add vegetables, salt, and chicken broth (do it in this order or the vegetables will splash into the broth and ruin your silk blouse). Simmer until vegetables are soft, abour 45 minutes.
- Stir in seasonings. Cool mixture, then puree in blender.
- Just before serving, add some grated apple to each bowl (optional). Serves 8.

Health Soup

Bea Comeh

Delicious! Freezes well! Large soup pot.

6 cups chicken broth
1 cup lima beans, soaked 3 hours
3 stalks celery, sliced
3 onions, sautéed
3 cloves garlic, minced
$1/2$ cup barley
1 large can plum tomatoes, drained and chopped

1 small can stewed tomatoes
1 tablespoon oil
3 potatoes, diced
$1/2$ cup red wine
handful green beans
cooked shells, optional
carrots, optional

- Add chicken broth to lima beans. Add rest of ingredients, except green beans. Simmer, covered 45 minutes and add green beans. May add thinly sliced carrots to the celery when cooking.
- Before serving, add small cooked shells, if desired. Serves 10–12.

Mushroom Barley Soup

Arleen Danford

¹/₂ cup pearl barley
2 tablespoons parve margarine
1 tablespoon oil for sautéing
1 pound mushrooms, stems and pieces,
    thinly sliced
6 carrot, thinly sliced

1 medium-sized onion, chopped
6 cups chicken stock
4 tablespoons chopped fresh dill
salt and pepper

- Place barley in bowl, cover with hot water, and let stand 20 minutes. Drain.
- Melt margarine and oil in pot. Add mushrooms, carrots, and onion, and sauté 5 minutes.
- Add barley, stock, dill, salt and pepper. Reduce heat from medium to low, cover, and cook 45 minutes. Serve hot. Serves 6.

Mushroom Scallion Soup

Toby Richmond

Very gourmet.

1 bunch scallions, chopped
4 tablespoons butter
4 teaspoons flour
4 cups George Washington light
    seasoning (4 packets)

4 cups boiling water
¹/₂ pound fresh mushrooms, cut-up
1 cup light cream

- Melt butter in sauté pan and sauté scallions until soft, not brown, about 10 minutes.
- Blend in flour. Stir in George Washington broth and let come to a boil with the scallions and flour. Simmer 20 minutes.
- Add mushrooms and cook 5 minutes more.
- Put soup and mushrooms in a blender and purée. Put back into a pot and reheat.
- Add cream and stir. Serve hot. If desired, slice additional mushrooms and stir in while heating. Serves 4–6.

Curried Corn Chowder

Arleen Danford

Very fast, easy, and delicious

¹/₂ cup butter
1 tablespoon curry powder
1 tablespoon chopped shallots
2 16-ounce cans creamed corn

1 16-ounce can corn niblets
2 cups medium cream, warmed
¹/₂ teaspoon dried rosemary
salt and pepper

- Melt butter in large pot. Add curry powder and shallots and stir until smooth.
- Add corn (drain the corn niblets), warmed cream and seasonings. Heat through.

Sweet Potato Vichyssoise

Rosalie Olds

1¹/₄ pounds sweet potatoes
1 cup sliced (lightly packed) scallions
2¹/₂ cups chicken stock

¹/₄ cup Farm Rich non-dairy creamer
1 tablespoon chopped chives
salt and white pepper

- Bake potatoes, cool, and scoop out pulp.
- Combine pulp, scallions, and 1 cup chicken stock in a large saucepan. Simmer 10 minutes stirring occasionally.
- Pour into food processor, add ¹/₂ cup more stock and purée until smooth.
- Return to saucepan and add remaining stock. Bring to a boil and reduce to simmer for 5 minutes. Add salt and pepper to taste. Refrigerate 24 hours.
- Beat non-dairy creamer and swirl into bowls of soup. Garnish with chives. Serves 4–6.

Cream of Squash Soup

Mari Seder

2 tablespoons onion, minced
1/2 teaspoon butter
1 teaspoon curry powder
1 hubbard squash, boiled and mashed or
    microwaved, or 1 can squash

1 can of parve chicken broth
1 can Carnation evaporated milk (can use
    skimmed evaporated milk)
yogurt (optional)

- Sauté onions with 1/2 teaspoon in small skillet. Add curry powder to onions
- Place onions in a food processor with mashed squash. Add broth and evaporated milk.
- Can be served cold or heated. Serve with a dollop of yogurt.

Curried Butternut Squash Soup

Nancy Seder

4 tablespoons margarine
2 cups finely chopped onions
4–5 teaspoons curry powder
3 pounds butternut squash (2 medium or
    1 large)
2 apples, peeled, cored, and chopped

3 cups chicken stock
1 cup apple juice
1 Granny Smith apple, shredded (garnish)
salt and pepper, to taste

- Melt margarine in pot. Add onion and curry powder and cook until tender, 25 minutes.
- Peel squash, scrape seeds, and chop.
- When onions are tender, pour in stock. Add squash and apples and bring to a boil. Reduce heat and simmer, partially covered, until squash and apples are tender, 25 minutes.
- Reserve liquid and transfer solids to a processor and process until smooth.
- Return puréed soup to pot, add apple juice and approximately 2 cups of liquid and process until soup is desired consistency. Season with salt and pepper.
- Simmer briefly to heat through. Garnish with shredded apple. Serve immediately.

Eggplant Soup

Lorraine Cotton

2 tablespoons margarine
2 tablespoons olive oil
1 medium-sized onion, chopped
2 cloves garlic, minced
1 pound ground beef
1 medium-sized eggplant, cubed
1 stalk celery

1 35-ounce can plum tomatoes, chopped
2 14-ounce cans beef broth
$^1/_2$ teaspoon sugar
$^1/_2$ teaspoon nutmeg
2 tablespoons parsley
$^1/_2$ cup small shells, uncooked

• Heat margarine and oil, and sauté onion, garlic, and beef, until beef loses its color.
• Add eggplant, celery, tomato, broth, and seasoning. Simmer for 30 minutes.
• Add shells and cook until tender.

Linda's Hearty Short Rib Soup

Mari Storm

Serve with a green salad and crusty bread.

1 pound white pea beans
1–2 packages short ribs
1 large can tomatoes, undrained
6 carrots, cut-up

4 or more potatoes, cut-up
1 cup brown sugar, or more, to taste
salt and pepper, to taste

• Boil beans in about 14 cups salted water for 1$^1/_2$ hours.
• Add meat and cook another 2 hours.
• Remove meat and debone. Add vegetables and cook until tender.
• Add sugar and meat which has been cut into small chunks. Cook about 10 minutes.
  Serves 12.

Hot and Sour Soup

Mike Andrews

6 cups chicken stock
2 tablespoons soy sauce
1/2 pound chicken, cut into 1/4-inch pieces
and diced
8 dried black mushrooms, soaked and cut
into julienne strips
3 slices gingeroot
3/4 teaspoon white pepper
1/4 cup rice wine vinegar

5 teaspoons cornstarch
5 tablespoons water
1/2 cup bamboo shoots
1/2 cup bean sprouts
1/2 cup soaked and shredded black fungus
(closed ears)
1 piece tofu, cut into 1/4-inch pieces
and diced

- Bring stock to boil and turn down to simmer. Add soy sauce, chicken, mushrooms, and gingerroot, and simmer for 10 minutes.
- Add pepper, vinegar, and thicken with cornstarch mixed with water. Taste for seasoning and add bamboo shoots, bean sprouts, black fungus, tofu, and simmer.
- Garnish with scallions and a few drops of sesame oil. If you like some spice, add some szechuan garlic and red chili paste to taste. Serves 8–10.

Eggs, Cheese, Rice,
and Pasta

Cream Cheese Kugel

Sue Seder

4 eggs
1 8-ounce package cream cheese
1/4 pound butter
1/2 cup sugar

1 1/2 cups milk
1 teaspoon vanilla
8 ounces noodles, cooked
graham cracker crumbs

- In mixer, beat eggs. Add cream cheese, butter, sugar, milk, and vanilla, and beat until the mixture has liquified.
- Combine the cheese mixture with cooked noodles that have been rinsed in warm water. Place in large shallow pyrex dish and sprinkle with graham cracker crumbs.
- Bake in a 350°F oven for 40 minutes.

Nellie's Noodle Pudding

Nellie Diamond

8 ounces medium-sized noodles, cooked
1/4 pound margarine, melted (save 2 tablespoons)
1/2 pint sour cream
1 pound cottage cheese

3 eggs, beaten
2 cups milk
1/2 cup sugar
1 teaspoon vanilla
cinnamon

- Mix noodles, margarine, sour cream, and cottage cheese. Pour in 9 x 13-inch greased pan and set aside.
- Pour eggs slowly over noodles.
- Combine milk, sugar, and vanilla, and pour over eggs
- Sprinkle cinnamon on top with remainder of melted margarine.
- Refrigerate overnight.
- Bake at 350°F for 1 1/2 hours.

Apricot Noodle Pudding

Marianne Baker

You'll always get compliments when you serve this.

1 16-ounce package noodles, cooked
1/4 pound melted butter
1/2 cup sugar
6 eggs, beaten
1/2 teaspoon salt
1 cup milk
1/2 pound farmer cheese
1 pound cottage cheese

1/4 pound cream cheese
drop cinnamon, optional

Topping:
1 12-ounce jar apricot preserves
1/2 cup brown sugar
1/2 cup slivered almonds

- Grease pyrex dish.
- Mix all ingredients except topping in the dish. Bake for 1/2 hour at 350°F.
- Mix the topping ingredients and spread on top and bake for an additional 1/2 hour. Serves 16.

Quick Noodle Kugel

Beverly Rice

Excellent and easy. Enjoy! Enjoy!

1/4 pound butter or margarine
8 ounces medium or wide egg noodles
    (uncooked)
4 eggs, beaten
12 ounces creamed cottage cheese
8 ounces softened cream cheese

1 teaspoon vanilla
2 cups milk
1/2 cup sugar
raisins (optional)
1 or 2 cups corn flake crumbs
cinnamon

- Melt butter in oven proof casserole.
- Mix noodles, eggs, cottage cheese, cream cheese, milk, sugar, and raisins together well. Sprinkle top with corn flake crumbs and bit of cinnamon.
- Bake at 350°F for 1 hour, or until done. Serves 6.

◻ Noodle Pudding

Mrs. Jacob D. Freelander

1-pound package broad noodles
1/4 pound butter or margarine
1 pound cottage cheese
    or
3/4 pound cottage cheese and
1/4 pound cream cheese
4 eggs
1 cup sour cream
3/4 cup milk
3/4 teaspoon salt

1/4 cup sugar
1/4 teaspoon cinnamon

Topping:
1/3 cup corn flakes, crushed
2 tablespoons sugar
1/4 teaspoon cinnamon

- Boil noodles according to directions, drain well, and add butter and cheese mixture.
- Add eggs, one at a time, mixing well after each egg. Add remaining ingredients, and blend well.
- Pour into a well-buttered, large pyrex dish or casserole. Top with mixture of corn flake crumbs, sugar, and cinnamon.
- Bake in a 350°F oven at least one hour.

Pineapple Noodle Pudding

Betty Greenberg

Wonderful! I've also made this noodle pudding with egg beaters, no-fat sour cream and no-fat cottage cheese. Also good!

6 eggs
1 cup sugar
1 pint sour cream
1 pint small curd cottage cheese
1/2 cup melted butter
1 20-ounce can crushed pineapple
    in juice

1 cup white raisins
1 pound medium noodles, cooked
2 large cans sliced peaches, drained
cinnamon, for topping
sugar, for topping

- Combine eggs, sugar, sour cream, cottage cheese, butter, pineapple, and raisins and add to noodles which have been cooked and drained. Pour into well buttered 9 x 13-inch pan.
- Place peaches on top of pudding. Sprinkle with cinnamon and sugar.
- Bake at 350°F oven for 1 hour and 15 minutes. Serves 18–24.

Eva's Noodle Pudding

Eva Sherman

Tastes like cheese pie!

8 ounces fine noodles
3 or 4 eggs
$^2/_3$ cup sugar
1 cup creamed cottage cheese
1 teaspoon vanilla

1 pint sour cream
2 teaspoons baking powder
$^1/_4$ cup melted margarine
1 8-ounce can crushed pineapple, drained
corn flake crumbs

- Cook noodles for 3 minutes. Drain.
- Beat eggs, add sugar, then cottage cheese, vanilla, sour cream, baking powder, melted margarine, and pineapple. Fold in cooked noodles.
- Place in a 8 x 12-inch greased pan. Sprinkle with cornflake crumbs.
- Bake in a 400°F oven for $^3/_4$ hour. Serves 10–12.

Note: Can all be mixed in an electric mixer.

Custard Noodle Pudding

Roma K. Josephs

Delicious and light.

$^3/_4$ cup fine pastina, cooked and drained
6 eggs
$^1/_2$ pound cream cheese
$1^1/_2$ pints sour cream

$^1/_4$ pound margarine, melted
1 teaspoon vanilla
4 tablespoons sugar
corn flake crumbs

- Mix together in a large bowl, all ingredients except cornflake crumbs and margarine.
- Melt margarine in a 9 x 13-inch pan. Pour off margarine into bowl, leaving enough to grease pan. Add ingredients to bowl and mix well. Sprinkle top with cornflakes.
- Bake at 325°F for at least 30 minutes. Remove when slightly brown. Serves 8.

Noodle Upside Down Pudding

Reva Thomashow

Very different.

1/2 cup light brown sugar
8 slices pineapple, drained and cut
    in half
1/4 cup margarine
1/4 cup granulated sugar
2 eggs

1/2 teaspoon cinnamon
1 tablespoon lemon juice
1 teaspoon lemon rind
1/2 cup white raisins
8 ounces medium noodles

- Grease 9-inch square pan. Sprinkle with brown sugar and add pineapple in a circle.
- Cream margarine, add granulated sugar, and mix well. Add eggs, cinnamon, lemon juice, rind, and raisins, and mix well.
- Cook and drain noodles. Rinse and add to a large bowl. Stir in egg mixture. Spoon over pineapple slices.
- Bake in a 350°F oven for 45–50 minutes. Do not let it get dry. Let stand 5 minutes on rack, loosen with spatula, and invert onto plate. Serves about 10.

No Cheese Pineapple Noodle Pudding

Sheree Pollock

8 ounces egg noodles
3 eggs
a dash of salt
3/4 cup granulated sugar
1/4 teaspoon cinnamon
1/4 pound margarine, melted

1 12-ounce can crushed pineapple in
    juice
1 large can sliced pineapple
1 jar marachino cherries, drained
brown sugar and cinnamon, for topping

- Cook noodles and drain well.
- Beat eggs and salt. Slowly add granulated sugar and cinnamon. Beat well.
- Add margarine, crushed pineapple with juice, and noodles, and mix well. Pour into 2-quart greased casserole.
- Place sliced pineapple and cherries on top and sprinkle with cinnamon and brown sugar.
- Bake at 350°F for 1 1/2 hours, uncovered. Serves 8–10.

Apple-Raisin Noodle Pudding

Marilyn M. Goodwin

My personal favorite kugel recipe!

12 ounces medium noodles, cooked
$^1/_2$ cup marargine, melted
$^1/_2$ cup orange juice
$^1/_2$ cup sugar
4 eggs, or the equivalent in egg substitute
$^1/_2$ cup golden seedless raisins
$^1/_2$ cup seedless raisins

$^1/_2$ teaspoon salt
1 21-ounce can apple pie filling
$^1/_2$ cup crushed corn flakes
3 tablespoons sugar
$^1/_2$ teaspoon cinnamon
juice of $^1/_2$ lemon

- Combine noodles, margarine, orange juice, sugar, and eggs in a large bowl and mix well. Stir in raisins, salt, and pie filling. Pour into a greased 9 x 13-inch baking dish.
- Mix corn flakes, 3 tablespoons sugar, cinnamon, and lemon juice in bowl, and sprinkle over pudding.
- Bake at 350°F for 1 hour. Note: Cover the baking dish with foil for the first half-hour of baking time to prevent the noodles from drying out on top. Serves 15.

Blintzes

Mae Montag

2 eggs
1 cup water
$^3/_4$ cup unsifted flour
salt, to taste

Filling:
$^1/_2$ pound cottage cheese
$^1/_2$ pound cream cheese
1 egg
cinnamon and sugar

- In a glass measuring cup (for easy pouring) beat eggs slightly with fork. Add water, flour, and salt. Strain. Consistency should be like heavy cream.
- Crumple waxed paper and rub it in butter. Using 2 fry pans at a time, heat pans and swish with butter.
- Pour just enough batter to cover the bottom of the pan. Cook until just set, and turn out onto dish towel. Set in stack when cool until all the batter is cooked.
- If temperature and consistency are correct, you should have one pan cooking and one pan filling all the time, but you must work quickly.
- Mix together ingredients for the filling. Spoon some filling in the middle of the cooked side of the "blettle," fold up, and fry just before serving. Fruit pie filling from the can may also be used for filling.

Blintzes (Cheese) Casserole

Rose S. Klein

6 cheese blintzes
3 eggs
3 tablespoons butter
1/4 cup orange juice

3/4 cup sour cream
1/2 teaspoon vanilla
1/8 teaspoon salt
1/8 cup sugar

- Grease an 8 x 8-inch pan. Place blintzes side by side.
- Mix balance of ingredients and pour over blintzes.
- Bake at 350°F for 45 minutes. Serves 6.

Ricotta Cheese Pudding

Lisa Honig

Filling:
1 1/2 pounds ricotta cheese
2 8-ounce packages cream cheese, at
    room temperature
2 eggs
1/4 cup sugar
3 1/2 tablespoons fresh lemon juice
1 teaspoon grated lemon peel
1 teaspoon grated orange peel

Batter:
1 cup flour, sifted
1 tablespoon baking powder
1 cup (2 sticks) butter, melted
1/2 cup sugar
3 eggs
1/4 cup milk
1 teaspoon vanilla
1/3 cup blanched slivered almonds
sour cream
strawberry jam

Filling:
- Beat all filling ingredients until blended.

Batter:
- Preheat oven to 300°F. Butter a 9 x 13-inch inch baking pan.
- Combine flour and baking powder in large bowl. Mix in butter, sugar, eggs, milk, and vanilla.
- Pour half of batter into prepared pan. Spoon filling over, gently spreading without mixing into batter. Pour remaining batter over filling.
- Bake until set, about 1 1/2 hours. Sprinkle with almonds. Cut into squares and serve warm, passing sour cream and jam separately. Serves 12.

Blintz Muffins

Ceril Glass

1 pound small curd cottage cheese
3 tablespoons sour cream
3 eggs
1/2 cup flour
1/4 teaspoon baking powder

1/4 cup oil
1 teaspoon vanilla
3 tablespoons sugar
1/2 stick melted margarine

- Combine all ingredients in a large bowl and beat until smooth.
- Pour into greased muffin tins, filling almost to the top of each muffin cup.
- Bake at 350°F for 35–40 minutes or until golden brown.
- Cool before removing from tins. To remove, go around edges with a knife or metal spatula. Can be served with sour cream and frozen sliced strawberries. Makes 12 large or 36 small muffins.

Cheese Pancakes

Mrs. John Beller

1/2 pound cottage cheese
1/2 cup sour cream
1/4 cup milk

1 egg
pinch of salt
1/4 cup flour

- Mix cheese, sour cream, milk, egg, salt, and flour.
- Form into pancakes and fry in hot butter.

☐ Blueberry Pancakes

Mrs. Aaron Krock

1 1/4 cups flour
2 1/2 teaspoons baking powder
2 tablespoons sugar
3/4 teaspoon salt

1 egg, beaten
1 cup milk
3 tablespoons butter, melted
1 cup fresh or frozen blueberries, drained

- Mix flour, baking powder, sugar, salt. Add beaten egg, milk, butter, and berries.
- Fry as for pancakes.

Oven Apple Pancakes

Doris C. Shairman

Delicious for brunch or lunch.

4 eggs, or equivalent in egg substitutes
1 cup milk
1 cup flour
1/2 cup sugar

1 tablespoon cinnamon
3–4 tart apples, cored, peeled, and cut
into 1/4-inch wedges

- Combine eggs, milk, and flour, and beat with a whisk or rotary beater until smooth.
- Combine sugar and cinnamon and toss with apples to coat.
- Grease or spray 2 9–inch pie plates. Put half of the apples in each pie plate. Pour half of the batter over apples in each plate.
- Bake at 375°F oven for 30–35 minutes or until light brown and set. Cut into wedges and serve hot. Serves 8.

Overnight French Toast

Doris Shairman

Excellent for brunch or lunch.

1 loaf French or Italian bread, or challah
4 eggs, or egg substitutes
¼ teaspoon baking powder
1 tablespoon vanilla
1 cup orange juice

1 20-ounce bag frozen whole strawberries
4 ripe bananas sliced
½–¾ cup sugar
1 tablespoon apple pie spice, (nutmeg, cinnamon, ginger, allspice)

- Cut bread into 8 thick slices.
- Combine eggs, baking powder, vanilla, and orange juice in 9 x 13–inch baking dish. Add slices of bread. Turn to coat both sides. Cover and refrigerate overnight.
- In morning, combine strawberries, bananas, sugar, and spices. Pour into another 9 x 13–inch greased baking dish. Top with prepared bread from other dish. Sprinkle with cinnamon and sugar.
- Bake at 450°F for 20–25 minutes. Serve with the fruit sauce over the slices. Needs no other syrup. Serves 4–8.

Varnitchkas

1 cup medium buckwheat groats
1 egg
salt

3 cups boiling water
1 tablespoon shortening
1 cup bow ties (egg noodles), cooked

- Put groats, salt, and egg in baking pan and mix until groats are slightly moistened. Roast in 350°F oven about 10 minutes, stirring once or twice until groats are brown.
- Add boiling water and cover pan. Cook until water is absorbed.
- Add shortening and bow ties and serve with meat gravy.

Chinese Rice

Carol Halsband

This is a basic recipe. Other ingredients can be added such as: bean sprouts, peas, meat, and chicken. This recipe differs from traditional Chinese in that the rice doesn't have to be cold.

2 eggs	6 cups cooked rice
1 teaspoon salt	1 small onion, minced
1 teaspoon rice wine or dry sherry	2–3 scallions, chopped
6 tablespoons cooking oil	

- Beat eggs with half of the salt and the rice wine.
- Pour oil in hot wok, stir in onion and cook until soft. Add egg mixture, scramble, and break into small pieces until quite dry.
- Add rice, the rest of the salt, and scallions. Stir constantly until ingredients are well blended and thoroughly heated.

Curried Brown Rice and Lentils

Gail Zarr

1–2 tablespoons canola oil	3/4 cup lentils, washed and picked over
1/2 onion, chopped	4 cups water
3 cloves garlic, pressed	2 vegetable bouillon cubes, optional
1/4 teaspoon ginger	salt, to taste
1/2 teaspoon turmeric	1/2 cup raisins or currants
2–3 teaspoons curry powder, to taste	1/4 cup sunflower seeds
1 cup brown rice, washed	1 medium- to large-sized apple, peeled and diced

- Heat 1 tablespoon oil in heavy-bottomed soup pot or Dutch oven and sauté onion with 1 clove garlic until pale.
- Add ginger, turmeric, and curry powder, and sauté a few minutes longer.
- Add more oil if necessary, then add rice and sauté 2 minutes more.
- Add lentils, water, bouillon cubes, salt, remaining garlic, raisins, and sunflower seeds, and bring to boil. Cover and simmer for 25 minutes.
- Add apple, cover, and simmer for another 10–15 minutes, until water is absorbed.
- Serve topped with yogurt if desired. Serves 6–10.

Minted Rice

Nancy Hodes

2¼ cups chicken bouillon
1 clove garlic, minced
1 cup brown rice
1 tablespoon finely grated lemon zest

2 tablespoons chopped fresh spearmint
2 tablespoons margarine
salt and pepper, to taste

- Bring bouillon and garlic to a boil. Stir in the rice, cover, and cook until the liquid is absorbed.
- Remove from heat, add the lemon zest, and let stand covered for 5 minutes.
- Stir in the spearmint, margarine, salt and pepper.

Persian Sweet Rice

Mansour Sadigh

6 tablespoons butter, or more if needed
2 cups peeled and finely slivered carrots
½ cup sugar
juice of 1 lemon
1 cup slivered orange peel

1 onion, coarsely chopped
saffron, to taste
1 cup chopped pistachios, optional
3 cups Persian rice (Basmati)

- Melt 3 tablespoons butter and sauté carrots.
- Add sugar and mix. Cook until melted and add lemon juice. Simmer 5 minutes.
- Boil 2 cups water, add orange peel, and boil 5 minutes. Drain and repeat procedure.
- Add orange peel to carrots.
- Sauté 1 onion in 3 tablespoons butter. Add to orange and carrots and mix.
- Add saffron (grind with a little sugar to make a powder) and pistachio nuts, if desired.
- Soak rice 1 hour in warm water mixed with 2 tablespoons of salt before cooking. Drain.
- Bring 8 cups of water to boil in large pot (should be about half full). Add drained rice and boil over medium-high heat until rice is half cooked (slightly swelled), and drain.
- Boil ½ cup of water and add 3 tablespoons of butter and let it melt.
- Layer 3 portions of rice and 2 portions carrot mixture in pot beginning and ending with rice. Poke holes for steam. Pour water and butter over rice.
- Cook on medium-high heat on stove until it starts to steam. Reduce heat to low, cover pot lid with a dish towel to absorb steam and cook ½ hour.

Persian Vegetable Rice

Mansour Sadigh

3 cups Basmati rice
2 tablespoons salt
2 cups chopped parsley
1 cup chopped dill

1 cup chopped scallions, greens only
1/2 cup chopped cilantro
2 cloves garlic, minced
4 tablespoons butter

- Soak rice 1 hour in warm water with 2 tablespoons salt. Drain.
- Boil 8 cups water in a large pot. Add rice and boil until half cooked and slightly swelled. Drain.
- Mix all chopped greens and garlic together.
- Boil 1/2 cup water and add butter to melt.
- Layer rice and greens (2 portions) beginning and ending with rice. Pour water and butter over rice. Poke holes in rice for steam.
- Put on high heat and cook until it steams. Reduce heat to low and cover lid with dish towel to absorb steam. Cook 1/2 hour on low.

Barbara's Orzo

Barbara W. Burwick

1-pound box of orzo
2 packages onion soup mix
1 stick (1/4 pound) butter or margarine

1 large can sliced mushrooms or sliced
    fresh sautéed mushrooms

- Cook orzo according to instructions on box. Drain but do not rinse.
- Add remaining ingredients to hot orzo. Stir to mix well.
- Can be eaten immediately or reheated.

Orzo with Spicy Broccoli, Cauliflower, and Raisins

Gail Zarr

3/4 cup orzo or pasta
1 tablespoon olive oil
1 pound onions, chopped
1 large clove garlic, minced
6 ounces broccoli florets, finely chopped
5 ounces cauliflower florets, finely chopped
1/4 teaspoon hot pepper flakes, to taste, optional

1/2 cup dry white wine
1/4 cup raisins
1/4 teaspoon salt, optional
freshly ground black pepper
2 ounces coarsely grated sharp Cheddar cheese

- Bring 2 quarts water to boil in a covered pot and cook orzo.
- Heat oil in nonstick skillet and sauté onions and garlic until onions begin to soften and take on color.
- Add broccoli, cauliflower, hot pepper flakes, wine, raisins, and salt and pepper to taste. Cover, reduce heat and simmer until vegetables are tender, about 10 minutes.
- Drain cooked orzo and mix with vegetables and cheese. Serves 2.

Safta Leah's Wheat Pilaf

Rachel Shabani

Great with roast chicken or turkey.

1 3/4 cups water
1 3/4 cups medium bulger
vegetable oil to sauté onion and fruit
1 onion, chopped
handful of raisins, chopped apricots, or chopped prunes and slivered almonds

1 teaspoon coriander
1/2 teaspoon cumin
1/2 teaspoon cinnamon
salt and pepper

- Bring salted water to a boil. Add bulger and simmer about 10 minutes until water is absorbed.
- Heat small amount of oil in large skillet and sauté onion. Add fruit, nuts, and seasoning, and stir until almonds start to brown. Add the bulger and mix all together. Serves 6–8.

Linguini with Broccoli Garlic Sauce

Freda Medoff

To use as side dish or main dish, add cooked chicken, cut into ¹/₄-inch pieces.

2 cups broccoli florets and stems
1 medium-sized onion, quartered
2 cloves garlic, peeled
4 teaspoons olive oil
6 ounces linguini
¹/₂ cup diced red bell pepper

2 teaspoons cornstarch
¹/₂ cup chicken broth
¹/₂ teaspoon dried oregano
¹/₂ teaspoon black pepper
2 tablespoons choped parsley

- Bring a large pot of water to a boil.
- Meanwhile place broccoli, onion, and garlic in food processor and process until coarsely chopped. Set aside.
- In a large, nonstick skillet over medium-high heat, warm the oil until hot but not smoking. Add chopped vegetables and cook 3–5 minutes, stirring, until onion browns.
- Add pasta to boiling water and cook al dente 7–9 minutes. Drain.
- Add bell pepper to vegetables in skillet. Cook stirring 2–3 minutes.
- Mix cornstarch, chicken broth, oregano, black pepper. Add to vegetables. Bring to a boil and cook 1–2 minutes until thickened.
- Serve linguine topped with the sauce and parsley. Serves 4.

Three Pepper Linguini

Harriet Lowe

Very Colorful! I tend to use more garlic and pesto.

2 tablespoons olive oil
1 large green bell pepper, coarsely chopped
1 large red bell pepper, coarsely chopped
1 large yellow bell pepper, coarsely chopped
2 large onions, chopped

2 cloves garlic, minced
1 cup canned Italian-style plum tomatoes, drained and chopped
9 ounces spinach linguini, freshly cooked
¹/₂ cup prepared pesto, or make your own grated Parmesan cheese

- Heat oil in heavy skillet over medium heat, add peppers, onions, and garlic, and sauté until soft, about 5–6 minutes.
- Stir in tomatoes and simmer about 7 minutes.
- Toss linguini with pesto. Spoon bell pepper sauce over. Sprinkle with parmesan cheese and serve. Serves 4.

Linguini and Vegetable Quick Stir

Jenique Radin

2 tablespoons margarine or butter
2 cups shredded zucchini
1 cup shredded carrot
1/2 cup chopped onion
8 ounces cooked linguini
4 ounces shredded mozzarella cheese
    (1 cup)

1/2 cup half and half cream or milk
2 tablespoons dry white wine
1/2 teaspoon salt
1/2 teaspoon garlic powder
1 tablespoon fresh chopped basil,
    (1 teaspoon dried leaves if fresh
    not available)

- In large skillet, melt margarine and add zucchini, carrot, and onion. Stir for 3 minutes.
- Add cooked linguini and remaining ingredients to the vegetables. Toss mixture until cheese is melted. Serve immediately.

Cheese Tortellini Alfredo

Harriet Lowe

1 small package frozen cut-up leaf
    spinach
1 10–12-ounce package fresh
    mushrooms, sliced

1 package frozen cheese tortellini
1 10–ounce container fresh alfredo sauce
2 tablespoons butter or margarine to
    sauté mushrooms

- Cook spinach as per package instructions. When cooked, let sit with liquid until ready to use.
- Sauté sliced mushrooms in butter or margarine on a low flame until softened, approximately 10 minutes. Let mushrooms sit until ready to use.
- Cook tortellini according to instructions and drain.
- Combine tortellini, spinach with liquid, mushrooms with liquid, and alfredo sauce. Serve immediately.

Spaghetti with Garlic, Oil, and Hot Peppers

Ina Sirk

1 pound spaghetti
1/2 cup plus 2 tablespoons olive oil
6 large cloves garlic, minced
1/2 teaspoon crushed red pepper flakes,
    or to taste

1/2 cup chopped flat leaf parsley
1/4 cup grated Parmesan cheese

- In large pot of water bring spaghetti to boil and cook until al dente. Drain.
- Meanwhile, in a large skillet, combine 1/2 cup olive oil, garlic, and red pepper. Cook over moderate heat until garlic turns golden but does not brown, 2–3 minutes.
- Add pasta to skillet with the sauce. Toss, add 2 remaining tablespoons oil, toss again, and cover.
- Let rest off heat for 1–2 minutes to absorb sauce. Add parsley and cheese and serve immediately.

Penne with Asparagus and Red Pepper

Ina Sirk

3 tablespoons butter or margarine
1 pound medium-sized asparagus,
    peeled, tough ends snapped, and
    stalks cut into 2–inch pieces
2 yellow peppers, charred, peeled, and
    diced
2 red peppers, charred, peeled, and diced

1 1/2 teaspoons minced garlic
1 1/2 cups parve chicken bouillon
1 tablespoon salt
1 tablespoon fresh thyme
3/4 pound penne
pepper
2/3 cup grated Parmesan cheese

- In a skillet, melt 2 tablespoons butter or margarine and add asparagus. Cook asparagus until tender and lightly browned, 5–7 minutes. Stir in the peppers and garlic, and toss 1 minute.
- Add chicken bouillon, bring to boil, and set aside.
- Cook pasta in 1 tablespoon salt until al dente. Drain.
- Return skillet to medium heat and add penne and fresh thyme, stir to combine, and cook 5–7 minutes, or until pasta is cooked through.
- Stir in remaining butter or margarine, and salt and pepper to taste. Add half the cheese, transfer to bowl, and sprinkle with remaining cheese, and serve

Puttanesca

Andrea Hersh Bartfield

A hearty vegetarian pasta dish with brilliant flavor! Wonderful! Wonderful!

8 cloves garlic, or to taste
olive oil
1 tablespoon capers
1 small can mashed anchovies
1/8 teaspoon crushed red pepper

2 tablespoons fresh chopped basil
10 large Greek olives (calamata)
2 large cans of chopped tomatoes
16 ounces thin spaghetti or pasta of
   your choice, cooked and drained

- Sauté garlic in olive oil in a large skillet.
- Add remaining ingredients and simmer to blend. Pour over cooked, thin spaghetti or pasta of your choice. Cover with 3 tablespoons of chopped parsley and Romano cheese.

Baked Spaghetti Pie

Barbara Robbins

Double the recipe for a larger amount of people.

8 ounces spaghetti, cooked and drained
2 tablespoons vegetable oil
2 large eggs, well beaten
1/2 cup grated Parmesan cheese

1 15–ounce container ricotta cheese
1 cup spaghetti sauce
1/2 cup mozzarella cheese
2 tablespoons grated Parmesan cheese

- Preheat oven to 350°F and grease a 10-inch pie plate.
- In large bowl, toss hot spaghetti with vegetable oil.
- In small bowl, combine eggs and 1/2 cup Parmesan cheese. Stir this mixture into the spaghetti.
- Pour this whole mixture into the pie plate and form into a crust. Spread ricotta cheese evenly over the crust, but not quite to the edge, and top with spaghetti sauce. Bake uncovered for 25 minutes.
- Top with mozzarella cheese, and bake for another 5 minutes, or until cheese melts. Remove from oven and sprinkle with remaining 2 tablespoons Parmesan cheese. Cool for 10 minutes before cutting into serving pieces. Serves 6–8.

Fish

Mom's Gefilte Fish

Lillian R. Silverman (Mother—Dora S. Cohen)

Delicious — can keep refrigerated for several days.

2 pounds each pike, whitefish, and buffel carp	6 onions, sliced
4 carrots, sliced	6 eggs
3–4 stalks celery, sliced	1 cup cold water
2 onions, sliced	4–5 teaspoons salt, to taste
1 parsnip, sliced	1 1/2–2 teaspoons white pepper
	4–8 tablespoons matzoh meal

- Have fish filleted, reserving parts.
- Place sliced carrots, celery, onions, and parsnips in bottom of a large pan.
- Add fish heads, skin, and bones and 6 sliced onions in about 1 quart water, together with 2 teaspoons salt and 3/4 teaspoon pepper. Bring to a boil.
- Grind or chop fish, adding onions and eggs alternately. Add water slowly to mixture as needed, together with matzoh meal, salt and pepper. Chop until very fine for a fluffy fish (most important).
- Moisten hands, shape into balls, and drop into boiling mixture.
- Cover loosely and cook over low heat 1 1/2 hours or so. Remove cover for last 1/2 hour. Taste fish stock and correct spices to taste.
- Cool fish before placing on platter or in bowl. Serve cold with fish stock that has jelled in the refrigerator. Serve with horseradish. Serves 12–20 people, depending on size of balls.

Kane's "Chrain"

Benson Kane

Commonly called horseradish.

1 horseradish root, approximately 12 inches long	5 drops liquid hot pepper sauce
3 fresh red beets, approximately 2 1/2 inches in diameter	1/2 teaspoon salt
	1/4 teaspoon garlic powder
1 pint white vinegar (for passover use cider vinegar)	1 pint pure cold water

- Soak horseradish root for 1/2 hour in cold water.
- Use vegetable brush to remove as much dirt as possible. Peel with vegetable peeler, making sure to peel with the grain.
- Cut root into 1-inch circles and cut up large end to approximately 1-inch pieces. Place in food processor and grind to almost the desired consistency.
- Peel beets, cut into 1-inch pieces, add to food processor, and grind mixture to desired consistency. Remove to large bowl while protecting eyes and nose from harsh fumes (can be done outside).
- Add vinegar, hot pepper sauce, salt, garlic powder, and water. More water can be added to dilute mixture to desired thickness.
- To make stronger, use additional gnarled end of another root. Store in refrigerator until needed.

All–in–One Company Fish Dish

Lois Lopatin

Easy and festive. Can be prepared early in the day and baked just before serving.

4 medium-sized white potatoes
1/2 pound mushrooms, sliced
2 tablespoons butter or margarine
1 teaspoon salt, optional
1/2 teaspoon pepper
paprika

1/2 cup white wine
1 1/2 cups sour cream
2 pounds fillet of sole (or other thinly cut white fish)

- Grease a 9 x 13–inch glass baking dish.
- Cut potatoes into 1/4-inch dice. Boil until firm (not soft), about 10 minutes. Drain potatoes and place in baking dish, covering the entire bottom of the dish. (You can cut the slices to fill in the spaces left by the rounded parts of the slices and/or you can overlap the potato slices.)
- Spread raw, sliced mushrooms over the potatoes. Dot with butter or margarine.
- Sprinkle with 1/2 of the salt and pepper, and then sprinkle with paprika. Pour wine over all.
- Using a rubber spatula or other wide instrument, spread half of the sour cream over the mixture.
- Cover sour cream with fish. You can overlap pieces to cover the entire surface of the dish.
- Sprinkle with rest of salt and pepper, cover with remaining sour cream.
- Sprinkle with paprika and bake 375°F for 1/2 hour. Serve immediately, using a large, square serving utensil so that each piece comes out of the dish whole. Just needs a green salad to complete the meal. Serves 8.

Spinach–Fish Casserole

Roberta Kunen

2 packages frozen spinach souffle, slightly defrosted
2 pounds any white fish
lemon juice

salt
1 box garlic or onion Tam Tam crackers
1 stick margarine, melted
paprika

- Spread spinach souffle on bottom of greased 9 x 13 x 2–inch baking dish.
- Lay fish on top of souffle. Sprinkle fish with lemon juice and a dash of salt.
- Crush the Tam Tams (I use my food processor) and mix with margarine. Spread mixture on top of fish. Dot with margarine and sprinkle top with paprika.
- Bake for 20–25 minutes at 400°F. Serves 6–8.

Fish in Tehinah

Mike Andrews

2 pounds fresh or frozen fillet of sole
juice of 1 lemon
1/2 teaspoon salt
1 onion, thinly sliced
2 tablespoons oil
1/2 cup pinenuts

Tehinah:
1/2 cup tehinah
1/2–3/4 cup water
juice of 1 lemon
1 teaspoon salt
1/2 teaspoon cumin
4 cloves crushed garlic
2 tablespoons parsley

- Soak fish in salt and lemon juice for 1 hour, drain, and pat dry.
- Combine tehinah ingredients in a small bowl to make thin tehinah.
- Put fish in a greased baking pan or ovenproof casserole.
- Sauté onions and pinenuts separately, and tranfer to absorbent paper.
- Sprinkle onions and pinenuts over the fish.
- Pour tehinah over fish and bake for 20 minutes in preheated 350°F oven.
- Remove from oven and sprinkle with parsley. Serve with rice and a vegetable.

Fish, Portuguese Style

Mike Andrews

4 sole or flounder fillets
salt and pepper
1 tablespoon butter
1/4 cup fish stock

1/2 cup dry white wine or water
1/2 cup canned tomatoes, drained
2 tablespoons minced parsley
2 tablespoons chopped onion or shallots

- Roll the fillets and secure them with toothpicks. Sprinkle lightly with salt and pepper.
- Rub a skillet with the butter and arrange the fillets in the pan.
- Pour the stock and wine over fish. Add the tomatoes, parsley, onions, and bring to a boil.
- Cover with aluminum foil and cook for 10–12 minutes, or until fillets are done, turning them once as they are cooking.
- Remove the fillets to a hot serving dish and cook the remaining sauce in the pan over high heat for 1 minute. Season the sauce with salt and pepper to taste, and pour over the fish. Serves 4.

Baked Stuffed Fish

Lorraine Cotton

¹/₄ pound margarine or butter
¹/₄ cup finely chopped onion
¹/₄ cup finely chopped pepper, red or green
1 small can mushrooms
4 plus tablespoons lemon juice
4 plus tablespoons dry vermouth

1¹/₂ cups crushed snack crackers (reserve 2 tablespoons for top)
8 pieces of fillet of sole
¹/₄–¹/₂ cup cheese crackers, crushed
paprika

- Melt ¹/₂ stick of butter in large pan and sauté onion and pepper until tender.
- Add mushrooms and enough lemon juice and wine to moisten, stir.
- Mix all crumbs and toss until well mixed.
- In buttered casserole, place fillet of sole, top side down, and fill with heaping table-spoon of crumb mixture on tail end. Roll.
- Melt remaining butter, 4 tablespoons of wine, 4 tablespoons of lemon juice, and pour over fish. Coat with paprika and reserved cracker crumbs. Refrigerate for ³/₄ hour before cooking.
- Bake for 40 minutes in a 350°F oven. Baste with juices, adding more if necessary.

One Dish Fish Dinner

Barbara Robbins

2¹/₂ pounds scrod or other white fish
³/₄ cup milk, approximately
3–4 celery hearts
1 medium-sized onion
4 carrots

1 medium-sized green bell pepper
¹/₂ cup margarine
4 all-purpose large potatoes
pinch salt and pepper
1 can condensed tomato soup

- Use large casserole dish.
- Wash the fish with cold water, pat dry, and soak in milk.
- Cut celery, onion, carrots, and green pepper into small pieces. and place in casserole dish.
- Melt margarine and pour over the vegetables.
- Slice the potatoes quite thin and place them over the vegetables. Add the salt and pepper.
- On top of all this, add the slices of fish, then pour the full can of condensed tomato soup over the whole dish.
- Bake at 375°F for approximately 1 hour. Serves 4–5.

Matanah Fish

Lois Sobel

Easy to make. Can be prepared the night before or same day.

10 serving-size pieces of haddock
2 sticks margarine
1 box of onion or garlic Tam Tam crackers

1–1½ cups Jason's seasoned bread crumbs
lemon juice

- Spray a 13 x 9 x 2–inch dish with Pam. Place fish in dish.
- Melt 1 stick margarine and drizzle over fish.
- Drizzle 1–2 tablespoons of lemon juice over fish.
- Mix Jason bread crumbs and crushed TamTam crackers together. Spread over fish (fish can also be coated with this mixture).
- Melt second stick of margarine and drizzle over fish. Drizzle another 2 tablespoons of lemon juice over fish.
- Bake in a 350°F oven for 20 minutes or until flaky. Serves 10.

Broiled Scrod with Red Onion and Dill

Ina Sirk

⅓ cup finely chopped red onions
¼ cup mayonnaise
1 tablespoon fresh lemon juice

2 teaspoons coarse Dijon mustard
2 tablespoons fresh dill
1 pound scrod or other firm white fish

- In small bowl, mix together first 5 ingredients.
- Arrange fish on foil–lined rack of a broiler pan.
- Broil fish for 2 minutes without sauce.
- Cover fish with sauce and broil for 5–7 minutes 3 inches from heat or until fish is lightly browned and flaky. Serves 4.

Marinade for Grilled Fish

Carolyn Phillips

4 limes, squeeze juice (save rind from 1 lime)
1/2 cup sesame oil
1/4 cup soy sauce

1/2 cup chopped scallions
4 thin slices fresh ginger
2 cloves garlic, pressed
Dijon mustard

- Combine above ingredients (excluding mustard) together in a large pan for marinating.
- Brush fish with mustard and grated lime rind on top of fish. Marinate fish for at least 1 hour before grilling.
- Grill fish approximately 8 minutes per side.

Broiled Bluefish

Evelyn Malkiel

Recipe excellent over any fish.

2 pounds bluefish
salt and pepper
melted butter or margarine
1/2 cup mayonnaise

1/4 cup grated Parmesan cheese
2 tablespoons chopped green onions
1 egg white, beaten

- Sprinkle fish with salt and pepper and brush with melted butter or margarine. Broil fish.
- Combine mayonnaise, Parmesan cheese, and green onion. Fold in beaten egg white. Cover broiled fish with mixture.
- Broil about 1–2 minutes, until topping is puffed and golden. Serve immediately. Serves 4.

Baked Salmon with Mustard Crumb

Rebecca Freedman

Delicious!

2 tablespoons and 1 teaspoon distilled
    white vinegar
2 tablespoons sugar
2 tablespoons Dijon mustard
1 teaspoon white mustard

$^1/_3$ cup vegetable oil
4 6–7-ounce salmon fillets
dried thyme
salt and pepper
1 cup fresh French breadcrumbs

- Preheat oven to 375°F.
- Place vinegar, sugar, and 2 mustards in blender.
- With machine running slowly, pour in oil and blend until medium sauce forms.
- Lightly grease 13 x 9–inch baking dish and arrange salmon skin side down in prepared dish.
- Season with dried thyme, salt and pepper. Spread mustard sauce over each fillet. Press bread crumbs onto salmon.
- Bake until topping is crisp and golden brown, about 18 minutes. Serves 4.

Salmon Steaks in Marinade

Doris Goff

$^1/_2$ cup orange juice
$^1/_2$ cup soy sauce
4 tablespoons peanut or vegetable oil
4 tablespoons ketchup

1–2 tablespoons honey
$^3/_4$ teaspoon ginger
1–2 teaspoons chopped garlic
4 salmon steaks, about 6–8 ounces each

- In large dish, combine all ingredients except salmon.
- Add salmon steaks, turning to coat with marinade. Cover and refrigerate 1 hour or more. Drain.
- Broil. Turn carefully, and broil other side. Serves 4.

Salmon with Vegetables

Renee Gould

4 potatoes, sliced and halved
1 large carrot, peeled and sliced
2 large leeks, white and pale green parts
    only, sliced
3 scallions, sliced
4 ounces peapods, halved
5 mushrooms, sliced

1/4 cup olive oil
1/4 cup soy sauce
1 tablespoon dried basil
2 tablespoons dried dill
4 6–ounce salmon fillets, skinned
1 lemon

- Preheat oven to 450°F.
- Steam potatoes and carrot 5–7 minutes in microwave. Transfer vegetables to a large bowl.
- Add leeks, scallions, pea pods, mushrooms, olive oil, soy sauce, basil, and dill, and toss.
- Place 1 sheet of heavy duty foil on a cookie sheet, spray with Pam, and place salmon on foil.
- Sprinkle with fresh lemon juice and spoon vegetables over salmon.
- Use another piece of foil to cover, tent, and seal tightly.
- Cook 30 minutes.

Sesame Salmon

Rebecca Freedman

Excellent.

2 salmon fillets, 3/4–inch thick
    (no skin or scales)
1/2 cup flour
1 egg
1/4 cup sesame seeds
1/4 pound butter
2 tablespoons white wine

Sauce:
1/4–1/2 cup white wine
1 1/2 tablespoons chopped ginger
2 tablespoons heavy cream
1–2 tablespoons diced scallions

- Dip 1 side of fillets in flour, then egg, and then sesame seeds.
- Clarify butter—melt stick of butter over low heat, spoon off top white layer (prevents the butter from burning).
- In clarified butter, sauté fish sesame side down over medium-high heat until brown. Flip and place in glass baking dish with wine.
- Bake in 375°F oven for 7 minutes.

Ginger Sauce:
- Combine wine, ginger, and cream. Reduce over medium heat. Add scallions. Serve sauce over salmon fillets. Serves 2.

Sweet and Sour Salmon

Irene Garber

3 onions, sliced in ⅛–inch rings
¼ cup oil (or more if needed)
1 cup ketchup
1 bottle chili sauce
1 jar sweet pickles cut into 1–inch cubes

drain and reserve 1 cup pickle juice
¼ cup vinegar
2 heaping tablespoons brown sugar
3 pounds salmon, cut into serving-
   size pieces

- Sauté onions in oil until just limp. Add remaining ingredients except salmon and simmer together a few minutes.
- Put salmon steaks on baking pans and pour sauce over the fish.
- Bake 375°F oven until salmon is done.

Great and Easy Salmon Loaf

Connie Sobel

It's real good, ask my seniors!

1 tall can red or pink salmon
2 eggs, beaten
1 cup milk

1 small can cut-up mushrooms, optional
1 can French fried onion rings

- Mix all ingredients together. Put into greased casserole.
- Bake at 350°F about 45–60 minutes. Serves 4.

⌂ Baked Salmon Loaf

Mrs. Samuel Robbins

1 large can of salmon
2 eggs, beaten
2 cups corn flakes, crushed
2 carrots, grated

$^1/_2$ cup milk
$^1/_2$ cup diced celery
1 onion, grated
salt and pepper

- Mix ingredients thoroughly in given order.
- Bake in greased casserole for 45 minutes in 350°F oven.

Salmon Strudel

Mildred Weiner

1 14–ounce can salmon
$^1/_2$ cup sour cream or yogurt
$^3/_4$ cup Crax crackers
$^1/_8$ cup melted margarine

$^1/_8$ medium-sized onion, chopped
1 tablespoon lemon juice
2 frozen puff pastry sheets
1 egg white

- Mix first 6 ingredients together.
- Follow directions for defrosting pastry sheet.
- Open pastry sheet. Spread $^1/_2$ the salmon mixture on $^1/_2$ of the pastry sheet. Leave $^1/_2$–inch from edge, fold sheet over, and seal edges.
- Repeat for second pastry sheet and remainder of salmon mixture. Put on cookie sheet with seams on the bottom.
- Brush each loaf with egg white.
- Place in 425°F preheated oven then turn oven down to 400°F. Bake 20–25 minutes. Makes 2 loaves. Serves 4.

Cioppino

A famous fish stew from San Francisco. Delicious with crusty bread.

1/4 cup olive or vegetable oil
1/2 cup parsley leaves
2–3 cloves garlic, peeled
1 medium-sized onion, quartered
1/2 medium-sized green pepper, cut into
    6 pieces
1 28–ounce can tomatoes, undrained
1 8–ounce can tomato sauce
2 cups water

1/2 cup dry sherry or white wine
1 tablespoon sugar
2 teaspoons salt
1/4 teaspoon marjoram
1/4 teaspoon oregano
1/4 teaspoon pepper
2 1/2 pounds fresh or frozen, boned
    white fish, cut in pieces

- In 4–quart saucepan heat oil over medium heat. Add parsley and garlic and sauté. Add onion and green pepper and sauté about 10 minutes, stirring occasionally.
- Stir in tomatoes, tomato sauce, water, wine, and seasonings. Cover and simmer over medium-low heat, 30 minutes.
- Add fish. Cook 5 minutes.
- Cover and simmer 5 minutes more minutes and salt to taste. Makes 8 1/2-cup servings.

80   *The Jewish Home Cookbook*

Meats

Stuffed Cabbage

Rebecca Meyer

2 cabbages
1 egg
1 cup sugar (equivalent of Equal can
    be used)
juice of 1 lemon
1 cup uncooked rice
1 cup tomato sauce
1 teaspoon salt
1/2 teaspoon pepper
2–2 1/2 pounds chopped meat

Sauce:
2 cans tomato sauce
1 cup water from boiled cabbage
1/2 cup sugar, equivalent of Equal can
    be used
juice of 1 lemon
1 carrot, cut-up
1 onion, cut-up

- Boil cabbage until leaves are soft. Separate leaves carefully, cool. Drain and reserve water.
- Mix egg, sugar, lemon juice, rice, tomato sauce, salt, and pepper into meat. Place a large spoonful at one end of a single cabbage leaf. Fold over edge of cabbage leaf to cover filling, tuck in sides, and then finish rolling.
- Prepare sauce by combining sauce ingredients in large sauce pan. Add rolled cabbage leaves to sauce and simmer for 2 1/2 hours stirring occasionally.
- Best made the day before serving. Serves 10–12 people.

Easy Stuffed Cabbage

Geraldine Feldman

Comes out perfectly flavored every time.

1 cabbage
1 cup cooked rice
1 pound ground beef
1/2 cup raisins
2 cans whole berry cranberry sauce

1 cup ketchup
2 tablespoons brown sugar
2 tablespoons vinegar
2 teaspoons prepared mustard

- Core cabbage and place in pot of boiling water. Simmer until leaves are soft. Separate leaves and set aside to cool.
- Mix cooked rice and ground beef.
- Place 2 tablespoons of meat/rice mixture on the edge of each leaf. Fold the sides and roll to create a small bundle.
- In a large pot combine the remaining ingredients. Add the cabbage rolls. Cover pot and simmer gently for 45 minutes.
- Even better the next day or after being frozen!
- For Passover, omit rice and use 1 cup of farfel made soft with 2 cups of boiling water.

Carolyn's Stuffed Cabbage

Carolyn Gordon

1 large head of cabbage

Sauce:
1 large can of whole tomatoes
2 onions, sliced
4 carrots, cut-up
about 6 ginger snaps
juice of 2 lemons

6 dried apricots
$1/2$ cup brown sugar
$1/4$ cup sugar
handful of raisins

Filling:
$1 1/2$ pounds ground beef
handful of rice

- Boil the cabbage to soften the leaves. Cut at core, and trim the main vein, and separate into leaves.
- Combine all sauce ingredients in a large pot and simmer.
- Add a little sauce to ground beef and mix in rice.
- Place large spoonful of meat/rice mixture onto edge of cabbage leaf. Fold over edge, tuck in sides, and roll tightly. Continue filling leaves until filling used up. Add cabbage rolls to pot with sauce.
- Cook about $1 1/2$ hours, cool, and freeze. When ready to use, spread out in flat pyrex dish and bake for about an hour, at 350°F.

Stuffed Rolled Cabbage with Cranberry Sauce

Mrs. Samuel Glick

Sauce:
1 can cranberry sauce
1 can tomato sauce
1 cup water
juice of $1/2$ lemon
$1/4$ cup sugar
$1/2$ cup seedless raisins

1 medium-sized head cabbage

Filling:
2 pounds ground meat
1 egg
3 saltine crackers (soaked and squeezed dry)
salt and pepper, to taste
1 medium-sized onion, grated
$1/4$ cup warm water, mixed with 1 tablespoon of catsup

- Simmer all sauce ingredients except raisins in roasting pan and let come to a boil. Add raisins, and simmer 5 minutes.
- Core cabbage and put in large kettle. Cover with boiling water and cook for about 10 minutes.
- Remove from stove and let cold water run through cabbage. Separate leaves.
- Combine all the filling ingredients. Place large spoonful of filling on edge of cabbage leaf. Fold over edge, tuck in sides, and roll tightly. Continue until filling is used up.
- After filling cabbage leaves, place in roasting pan with sauce and cook on top of stove, covered, for 1 hour.
- Then bake uncovered at 350°F for another hour.

Fran's Sweet and Sour Meatballs

Frances R. Berger

Wonderful hors d'oeuvre!

1 small box raisins
1 large can whole berry cranberry sauce
1 jar chili sauce
1/4 cup brown sugar
fill chili sauce bottle with water
2 pounds ground beef

1 egg
1/2–3/4 cup breadcrumbs
1/4 teaspoon pepper
1/4 teaspoon garlic powder
1 1/4 teaspoons salt

- Combine raisins, cranberry sauce, chili sauce, brown sugar, and water in a pot and bring to a boil.
- Mix together ground beef, egg, breadcrumbs, pepper, garlic powder, and salt.
- Make small meatballs and put into boiling mixture.
- Simmer for 1 hour. Then cover and bake in 350°F oven for 45 minutes. Serves 12.

Sweet and Sour Meatballs

Mrs. David B. Silverman

1 large (2 1/2-pound) can tomatoes,
    chopped
1/2 cup brown sugar
1/2 cup water
1/2 cup seedless raisins
1 pound ground meat, to which 1/2
    teaspoon pepper has been added

1 egg
1 slice white bread
1 large onion
juice of lemons

- Place tomatoes with juice, brown sugar, water and raisins in large sauce pan and simmer over low heat.
- Combine the meat, egg, slice of bread, and grated onion, and mix well. Make into small balls.
- Add to tomato mixture, cover and let simmer for 1/2 hour.
- Add lemon juice and continue to simmer for another 1/2 hour until sauce becomes thick.

Savory Meat Loaf

Rebecca Meyer

2 pounds ground beef
1 8–ounce can stewed tomatoes
1/2 cup chopped onions
1/4 cup chopped green pepper
2 eggs

2 teaspoons Worcestershire sauce
2 teaspoons salt
1/4 teaspoon black pepper
3 shredded wheat cereal biscuits, crushed

- Lightly but thoroughly mix together all ingredients.
- Shape into a loaf and place in a baking pan.
- Bake in a preheated oven at 375°F for about 1 hour until done. Makes 12 3/4-inch slices.

Sweet and Sour Meat Loaf

Sylvia Seligman

Wonderful to bring to a friend. Reheats well!

1 pound ground beef
1 onion, minced
12 crushed snack crackers
1/4 teaspoon black pepper
1/4 teaspoon salt
1 8-ounce can tomato sauce
1 egg, beaten

Sauce:
2 tablespoons vinegar
2 tablespoons brown sugar
1/4 teaspoon dry mustard
2/3 cup water

- In a 9-inch pie plate, mix together the beef, onion, crackers, pepper, salt, 1/2 can tomato sauce and the egg. Form into a round mound, 1-inch smaller than the pie plate.
- Mix together the remaining tomato sauce, vinegar, mustard and brown sugar and pour over loaf. Pour water around edge of loaf and bake in a 350°F oven for 1 hour.
- Cut into slices and serve with sauce from pie plate. Serves 6.

Tzimmes

Nancy Hodes

10 pounds frozen sliced carrot
3 pounds fresh yams, peeled
2 pounds flanken
3 pounds short ribs

1 medium-sized onion
1 cup honey
1 cup brown sugar
1 cup granulated sugar

- Put carrots, yams, meat, and onion in large stock pot and add just enough water to cover. Bring to a boil, and then skim carefully.
- Add the honey and brown sugar and simmer covered for ¹/₂ hour.
- Turn into a roasting pan, meat first and then carrots and yams, discarding onion. Sprinkle with white sugar. Add enough of the cooking liquid to fill ¹/₂ the depth of the pan.
- Bake at 325°F for at least 2 hours, carrots should be browned.
- Baste with the liquid, but do not stir. Taste and adjust the seasoning. Serves 25.

Prune Tzimmes

2 cups of water
2 pounds chuck or brisket
3 white potatoes, sliced
¹/₂ pound prunes

2 heaping tablespoons brown sugar
1 teaspoon salt
4 large sweet potatoes, sliced and kept in
    cold water until ready to use

- Boil water in roaster, add meat, and boil for about 1 hour.
- Place white potatoes and prunes around meat on bottom of roaster. Sprinkle with salt and sugar, cover, place in 350°F oven and roast for ³/₄ of an hour.
- Place sweet potatoes under white potatoes so they won't color and roast until meat is tender, about ¹/₂ hour. Baste with liquid occasionally. Very little gravy should remain when done and potatoes browned.
- The cover may be removed the last 15 minutes, if meat is not brown enough.

Easy Brisket

Rebecca Meyer

1 beef brisket
1 package dried onion soup mix
1 bottle chili sauce

1/2 cup brown sugar
water

- Cover brisket with all ingredients. Add water to cover.
- Cover with heavy foil and bake at 350°F for 2 1/2 hours or until meat is soft.

Harriet's Brisket

Harriet G. Tullman

Like Mom used to make.

4 pounds single-cut beef brisket
2 teaspoons salt
1/2 teaspoon pepper
1/2 teaspoon garlic powder
2 tablespoons oil
3 onions, sliced

1 1/2 cups boiling water
3 tomatoes, diced
3 carrots, cut-up
2 green bell peppers, sliced
4 potatoes, diced

- In large saucepan, sprinkle meat with salt, pepper, and garlic powder.
- Heat oil and sear meat on all sides.
- Add onions, water, and tomatoes. Cover and cook over low heat for 2 1/2 hours.
- Add carrots, green pepper, and diced potatoes, and cook approximately 30 minutes longer, until potatoes are soft.
- Meat slices much easier if taken out, allowed to cool, and then put back in saucepan to reheat.
- If you freeze this dish do not add potatoes until ready to serve. Parboil potatoes and then add after "sauce" is defrosted. Heat on medium for 15 minutes. Serves 8–10.

Shirley's Brisket

Shirley Kane

A delicious old fashioned meat and potatoes meal all done in advance. Freezes well for two months.

5–6 pounds fresh single brisket
1 package onion soup mix
¹/₂ cup ketchup

¹/₂ cup water
6–8 potatoes, cut into quarters
frozen kishke, optional

- Place meat, fat side up, in roasting pan with tight cover. Mix dry soup mix with ketchup and water and pour over meat. Cover tightly and roast at 325°F for 2¹/₂–3 hours, until soft.
- Remove meat from juices and when cool wrap tightly in foil and refrigerate overnight. Reserve meat juices and refrigerate overnight.
- Next day remove top fat and place meat in roast-and-serve pan with potatoes for 30 minutes at 350°F.
- Remove meat and slice on diagonal. Place meat in pan with juices. Add to cooked potatoes. Re-roast until heated through. Sliced kishke can be added while re-roasting.

Bar-B-Q Brisket

Minna Gregerman

This is how they serve brisket in Texas.

4–5 pounds well trimmed boneless
beef brisket
¹/₂ cup ketchup
¹/₄ cup vinegar
¹/₂ cup finely chopped onion

1 tablespoon Worcestershire sauce
1¹/₂ teaspoons liquid woodsmoke
flavoring
1 bay leaf, crumbled
¹/₄ teaspoon pepper

- Put brisket in ungreased roaster pan. Stir remaining ingredients together and pour over meat. Cover tightly.
- Bake at 325°F for 3 hours or until tender.
- Cut in thin diagonal slices across grain. Serve on a soft roll, with potato salad and cole slaw.

Sweet and Sour Brisket

Helen Rubin

Delicious. Serve hot or cold.

5–5½ pounds, single, flat cut beef brisket
salt and pepper
1 large onion, cut-up
1 cup pineapple juice

1 cup ketchup
3 tablespoons cider vinegar
3 heaping tablespoons dark brown sugar
2 teaspoons Worcestershire sauce

- Season meat with salt and pepper. Brown all sides under the broiler at 450°F .
- Combine the rest of the ingredients in a bowl to make sweet and sour sauce. Pour sauce over the meat. Cover with tin foil, punching a few holes in the foil to let steam out.
- Lower temperature to 350°F and cook until tender for 3–3½ hours, basting 2–3 times during cooking.
- After ¾ of an hour take off foil, turn oven to 450°F. The sauce will thicken. If sauce is watery, reduce by boiling. Serves 6.

Marcia's Brisket

Amy Sherman

Top of stove. Easy!

3–5 pounds brisket
lots of sliced onions
1 clove garlic, minced
¾ cup brown sugar

½ cup vinegar
1 cup ketchup
1 cup water
salt and pepper

- Spray large pot or frying pan with Pam. Sear meat and remove.
- Line pot with onions. Add meat and the rest of the ingredients that have been mixed together. Cover and simmer until meat is tender.

Carol's Brisket

Carol Halsband

5 pounds brisket
cooking oil
1 package onion soup mix
1 small can whole berry cranberry sauce

1 cup catsup
1 jar chili sauce
gingerale, to cover meat
carrots, cut into large slices, optional

- In a Dutch oven, brown brisket in oil on both sides. Add carrots. Add dry soup, cranberry sauce, catsup, chili sauce, and enough gingerale to almost cover meat and carrots. Cover and cook slowly until tender, about 3 hours. This is best when cooked ahead.
- Remove meat from sauce and cool. When ready to reheat, slice meat cold. Place in lasagna-type pan with sauce, cover with foil, and reheat in 350°F oven.

Zesty Beef Stew

Nancy Hodes

1 1/2 pounds stew meat
flour for dredging
1 medium-sized onion, cut into wedges
3 carrots, sliced thick
2 potatoes, cut into wedges
2 cloves garlic, diced
1 tablespoon lemon juice

1 teaspoon sugar
1 teaspoon Worcestershire sauce
1/2 teaspoon pepper
1/2 teaspoon paprika
1 small can chopped tomatoes
1/2 cup red wine
tomato paste to thicken

- Dredge beef in flour. In a Dutch oven, brown beef to seal in the juices.
- Add the rest of the ingredients except the tomato paste. Bring to a boil, then simmer for 2 hours.
- When half done, check to see if paste is needed to thicken sauce.

Chili

Bev Hurwitz

Can be made spicy or mild—to your taste.

2 pounds lean ground beef or turkey
1 cup chopped onion
1 cup chopped green bell peppers
1 cup sliced celery
2 cups (1 can) kidney beans, reserve
    liquid

2 16-ounce cans tomatoes, cut-up
1 6-ounce can tomato paste
2 tablespoons chili powder
1 tablespoon cumin
2 teaspoons salt

- In large pan, cook beef (or turkey), onion, green pepper and celery until meat is brown and vegetables tender.
- Drain kidney beans, reserving liquid. Add beans and remaining ingredients and cover and simmer 1^1/$_2$ hours.
- Thin with some reserved bean liquid, if desired. Serves 8.

Chinese Beef

Harriet Robbins

Reheats wonderfully! May be frozen.

2–2^1/$_2$ tablespoons vegetable oil
2 pounds shoulder steaks, cut into strips
1 clove garlic or garlic salt
1 dash pepper
^{1}/$_4$ cup soy sauce

2 tomatoes, cut into quarters
2 green peppers, cut into chunks
^{1}/$_2$ teaspoon sugar
2–3 cans of bean sprouts

- In large fry pan heat the oil, add beef, garlic, and pepper and fry until brown. Add the soy sauce and cook for 5 minutes.
- Add tomatoes, green peppers, sugar, and drained bean sprouts. Bring to a boil, cover, and reduce heat.
- Cook for 15 minutes.
- Serve on cooked rice or noodles. Serves 6.

Sukyaki

Don Hodes

The preparation of the ingredients is as important as the ingredients themselves.

1 pound shoulder steak
6–8 white mushrooms
2 stalks celery
2–3 cups washed and torn fresh spinach
1 large onion
6 scallions
1 small can sliced bamboo shoots

1 small can water chestnuts
2 tablespoons peanut oil

Sauce:
$^1/_3$ cup soy sauce
3 tablespoons sugar
$^1/_2$ cup cream sherry

- Put the meat in the freezer for about $^1/_2$ hour to firm it enough to be able to slice it very thin.
- Cut the mushrooms from top to stem, forming "T" shapes. Celery should be cut at an acute angle, very thin. Slice onions into very thin rings. Cut tip off the root end of the scallions, trim the tips, and halve lengthwise.
- Arrange the meat and all the vegetables on a large platter (presentation sets the mood).
- Mix ingredients for the sauce in small bowl.
- Heat the oil in a large wok over high heat. Brown the meat quickly on both sides.
- Sprinkle the sauce over the meat, stir once, add the vegetables. Stir gently to be sure that all ingredients are covered with the sauce. Lower heat and cook for 5 minutes more.
- Serve over oriental rice noodles and serve immediately.

Fajitas

Nancy Hodes

2 pounds London broil, cut in chunks
1 green pepper, cut into chunks
1 red pepper, cut into chunks
1 large onion, cut into wedges
flour tortillas

Marinade:
1 cup fresh lime juice (about 6 limes)
$^3/_4$ cup teriyaki sauce
$^1/_2$ cup Worcestershire sauce

- Combine ingredients for marinade in small bowl. Whisk until blended.
- Arrange steak and vegetables on skewers and place in a roaster pan. Cover with the marinade and refrigerate for at least 2 hours, turning occasionally. Can be broiled in the oven, but best when barbecued.
- Cook only until medium-rare. Serve with the tortillas.

Grilled Spicy Skirt Steak

Nancy Benjamin

1 tablespoon chili powder
1 teaspoon ground cumin
1 large garlic clove, minced
1 teaspoon coarse salt
2 teaspoons Worcestershire sauce

1 teaspoon sugar
3/4 teaspoon pepper
1 tablespoon vegetable oil
3/4–1 pound skirt steak or London Broil

- In a small bowl stir together chili powder, cumin, garlic, Worcestershire sauce, sugar, pepper, and oil and rub over all meat. Marinate meat in plastic bag overnight.
- Grill or broil steak until done and cut diagonally to serve. Serves 2.

Peppered London Broil

Jenique Radin

Marinade:
1/4 cup vegetable oil
3 tablespoons soy sauce
2 tablespoons white vinegar
1 tablespoon seasoned pepper
    (regular pepper can be used)
1 1/2 teaspoons garlic powder
    (powder, not salt)
1 teaspoon Italian seasoning

Beef:
2 pounds London Broil, trimmed

- Combine marinade ingredients in a plastic bag or a shallow dish.
- Add meat and refrigerate for at least 1 hour. The longer, the better. Occassionally turn meat in marinade.
- Grill or broil steak to desired doneness.

Beef Wellington

Nancy Hodes

5–6 pounds rolled delmonico roast
salt and pepper, to taste
1 pound mushrooms, finely chopped
2 tablespoons margarine
1 clove garlic, crushed

1/2 teaspoon dried thyme
1/2 teaspoon dried basil
1 package frozen puff pastry, thawed
1 egg

- Preheat oven to 425°F.
- Season beef with salt and pepper and place on rack in roasting pan.
- Bake for 20 minutes. Cool for 30 minutes.
- Sauté mushrooms in margarine to make a duxelle, add spices. Press the mixture onto the top of the roast.
- Put pieces of puff pastry together to make one large piece by moistening edges.
- Cover the roast with pastry tucking around sides and bottom to cover completely and trim to fit. Use scraps to form decorations.
- Place seam side down on a cookie sheet and bake 30–40 minutes.
- Ten minutes before it is done, brush pastry with an egg wash to make it shine. Allow to stand for 10 minutes before serving.

Veal Stew

Nancy Hodes

This gravy is also excellent for use in chicken pie or for hot turkey sandwiches.

2 pounds veal shoulder, cut in chunks
3 tablespoons flour
2 cloves garlic, minced
1 1/2 cups chicken bouillon or broth
1/2 cup white wine
bay leaves, thyme, parsley, to taste

12 small white onions
1 can small new potatoes
1 12-ounce package frozen green peas
1 can black olives, drained
1 sheet of puff pastry for crust

- Dredge the meat in the flour and garlic.
- Using a 6 quart saucepan, sear the meat on all sides, remove from pan, and set aside. Deglaze the pan with the bouillon and wine.
- Add the rest of the ingredients and return the veal to the sauce. Cover and simmer for 1 1/2 hours.
- Put in a deep ovenproof casserole, cover with puff pastry making at least 1 air hole, and decorate as you like.
- Bake at 400°F until the crust is brown, about 1/2 hour. Serves 4.

Potato Stuffed Veal Brisket

Mrs. Nathan Jacobson

41/2 pounds veal brisket
1 large onion
1 carrot
celery leaves
1 teaspoon salt
1/4 teaspoon pickling spice
1 tablespoon ketchup
1/2 cup water
paprika

Stuffing:
5 potatoes, grated
1 medium-sized onion, chopped
3 tablespoons chicken fat
2 eggs, beaten
1 teaspoon salt
pepper
1/2 cup matzoh meal

- Have butcher make large pocket in brisket.
- Put veal in roasting pan over onion, carrot, and celery leaves that have been cut up and placed on bottom.
- Grate 5 potatoes.
- Sauté 1 medium-sized onion in 3 tablespoons chicken fat. Add to potatoes with 2 beaten eggs, 1 teaspoon salt, pepper, and 1/2 cup matzoh meal. Mix ingredients together and stuff veal.
- Now add spices, salt, and ketchup to water and pour over brisket. Sprinkle with paprika.
- Cook on top of stove until this comes to a boil.
- Remove and place in 325°F oven until done, basting occasionally.

Roast Stuffed Veal Brisket

Mrs. Philip Lang

3 to 31/2 pounds veal brisket
clove of garlic
salt and pepper
2 rolls
2 eggs
2 teaspoons chopped parsley
1 small onion, minced

1 tablespoon chicken fat
1/2 pound fresh mushrooms, sliced
paprika
1 onion, sliced
1 green pepper, sliced
2 tablespoons soy sauce

- Have butcher make pocket in veal.
- Rub veal with clove of garlic, inside and out.
- To prepare stuffing, soak 2 rolls in cold water and squeeze dry. Season to taste with salt and pepper.
- Add 2 eggs, unbeaten, chopped parsley (2 teaspoons), and 1 small onion minced and sauted in 1 tablespoon chicken fat with 1/2 pound sliced fresh mushrooms.
- Mix together and stuff veal, sew up ends. Place in roasting pan and sprinkle with salt and paprika.
- Slice 1 onion and 1 green pepper over the veal. Mix 1/2 cup water and 2 tablespoons soy sauce, and pour over veal.
- Cover and cook on top of stove for about 1/2 hour, then bake in slow oven (300–325°F) until done.

☐ Baked Veal Chops with Mushrooms and Wine

Mrs. Walter Bieringer

When prepared (but not baked) the previous day, the flavor is improved.

8 large veal chops
2 pounds mushrooms
8 medium-sized onions
Marsala wine
salt and pepper

Accent
egg
crackers or bread crumbs
chicken fat

- Chop onions coarsely and brown in chicken fat.
- Sauté sliced mushrooms—add them to the onions along with at least $1/2$ cup wine. Add salt and pepper to taste. (About 1 teaspoon of Accent plus whatever salt is needed)
- Dip chops in beaten eggs, cracker or bread crumbs, and seasoning. Brown well in chicken fat.
- Into a casserole put a layer of the mushrooms, onion and wine mixture, half of the chops. Then repeat layers ending with vegetables on top.
- Cover and bake for $1^1/2$ to 2 hours in moderate 350°F oven.
- Very good served with sweet and sour cabbage or noodles.

Veal Marsala

Jayne Cohan

Good for company — can be made ahead!

2 pounds (pounded thin) veal
2 tablespoons flour
$1/2$ teaspoon salt
$1/4$ teaspoon pepper
1 clove garlic

3 tablespoons olive oil
$1/3$ stick margarine
1 pound sliced mushrooms
$1/2$ cup water
1 cup Marsala wine

- Lightly coat veal in mixture of flour, $1/4$ teaspoon salt, and pepper.
- Brown garlic in oil for 3 to 4 minutes. Remove from skillet and brown veal. When brown, place in baking dish.
- Add $1/3$ stick margarine to unwashed skillet, brown mushrooms for 4–6 minutes until golden brown, then add water, $1/4$ teaspoon salt, and wine. Scrape sides with a wooden spoon and bring to boil, then simmer for 2 minutes. Pour over veal. Bake for 30 minutes in 350°F oven, or refrigerate and bake when ready to serve. Serves 4.

Lamb Shish Kabob Marinade

Jody Garber

Marinade:
3/4 cup soy sauce
1/4 cup Worcestershire sauce
2 tablespoons dry mustard
1/2 cup wine vinegar

1/2 cup lemon juice
2 cloves garlic, minced
1/2 cup vegetable oil

2 pounds lamb

- Mix together all marinade ingredients.
- Add lamb and marinate at least 3 hours.
- To cook, broil or grill.

Honey Roasted Rack of Lamb with Herbs de Provence

Ina Sirk

3 1/2 tablespoons Herbs de Provence
1 tablespoon cracked black peppercorns
1 teaspoon salt
1 teaspoon ground cinnamon
1 cup fresh bread crumbs

1/3–1/2 cup honey
2 racks of lamb, about 2 pounds each,
    fully trimmed and "Frenched"
olive oil

- Preheat oven to 450°F.
- Combine Herbs de Provence, pepper, salt, cinnamon, and bread crumbs.
- Completely coat rack of lamb with honey. Cover with a generous layer of seasoned bread crumbs. Drizzle with olive oil.
- Arrange lamb on a rack over a roasting pan. Roast 20-25 minutes for medium-rare.
- Let meat stand for 5 minutes before carving between chops. Serves 3–4.

Glazed Corned Beef

Dinny Griff

Delicious—refrigerating the meat overnight reduces the shrinkage.

4–5 pounds pickled corned beef
1 onion
2 bay leaves
whole cloves

1 jar Manischewitz concord grape wine
1 12-ounce jar apricot jam
1 jar brown sugar

- Cook corned beef with onion and bay leaves 2–3 hours until done. Leave overnight in brine in refrigerator.
- Score corned beef and dot with whole cloves.
- Mix the wine, jam, and jam jar of brown sugar, and cook slowly for 20 minutes. Pour over scored meat.
- Bake 1 hour at 350°F. Baste. Serves 6.

Mom Maleman's Tongue

Gail Aframe

Our family legend!

1 beef tongue

Sauce:
1 small can crushed pineapple with juice
$1/2$ cup ketchup
2 tablespoons brown sugar
$1/4$ teaspoon garlic powder
$1/4$ teaspoon Accent seasoning
$1/4$ teaspoon black pepper

- Place tongue in cold water, boil until soft approximately 2 hours. When tongue is cool, peel and slice thin $1/4$-inch thick.
- Combine all sauce ingredients. Place tongue and sauce in casserole dish (sprayed with Pam), alternating layers.
- Bake at 350°F for $1/2$ hour until bubbling. Serves 8–10.

Tongue in Raisin Sauce

Nancy Hodes

This recipe was handed down to me from my mother-in-law, Nettie Hodes.

2 3–4 pound pickled tongues, cooked, skinned and cut into chunks

Raisin Sauce:
2 sweet onions, sliced
1 green bell pepper, diced
3 celery stalks, diced
enough oil for sautéing
1 large can of mushrooms

1 large can tomato sauce
1 large can tomato paste
2 cups water
1 cup slivered almonds
1 cup white raisins
$1/2$ cup brown sugar
3 tablespoons granulated sugar
juice of 2 lemons

- Sauté onions, pepper and celery until soft but not browned.
- Add the rest of the ingredients (except the tongue) and simmer for $3/4$ of an hour.
- Add the tongue and simmer for at least 1 hour. Adjust the sweetness.
- This freezes and reheats very well. Serves 8.

Sweet and Sour Tongue

Sandy Hersh

Stephen's favorite.

Sauce:
1 cup water
juice of 1 lemon
$1/4$ cup seedless raisins
$1/2$ cup brown sugar
$1/4$ cup vinegar
1 small onion, minced
4 large ginger snaps

1 beef tongue (not pickled)

- Bring all sauce ingredients to a boil, then simmer until the taste is pungent and sweet.
- If you double or triple the recipe, be careful of vinegar ($1/4$ cup for 4 tongues).
- Boil tongue until tender, but not overly so. Peel and slice into sauce.
- Gently simmer until perfect.

Poultry

Herb Roasted Chicken

Ina Sirk

4–5 pound chicken
salt and pepper
1 tablespoon margarine, at room
    temperature
4 sprigs thyme
3 tablespoons fresh parsley

1 tablespoon fresh tarragon
3/4 cup sliced carrots
3/4 cup sliced celery
1/2 cup sliced onions
2 cups chicken stock

- The day before cooking the chicken, salt and pepper it, inside and out. Cover and refrigerate overnight.
- Preheat oven to 425°F.
- Truss chicken legs and rub chicken with margarine. Place breast side down in a roasting pan and roast 30 minutes.
- Turn chicken onto back and place thyme, parsley, tarragon, carrots, celery, and onions in the pan. Continue cooking 35–40 minutes or until skin is brown. Check to make sure it is done. Allow chicken to rest 15 minutes before carving.
- Pour off fat from pan leaving vegetables and herbs in pan. Place pan over medium heat and pour in the chicken stock, as well as any juices accumulated on platter. Cook 4–5 minutes, scraping up browned bits.
- Carve chicken and serve with sauce and vegetables.

Grandma Palley's Chicken

Susan Sanders

It must be good for you. Jenny Palley lived to 95 years old!

1 onion, sliced
2 stalks celery, sliced
2 carrots, sliced
1 chicken, cut-up

salt
pepper
paprika
garlic, optional

- Preheat oven to 375°F.
- In the bottom of a roaster pan, spread onions, celery, and carrots. Place chicken on top and season to taste with salt, pepper, paprika, and garlic.
- Cover with tin foil and bake 1 hour. Remove foil, baste chicken, and reduce oven to 350°F for 1 hour. Remove when chicken is crisp and brown. Serves 4–5.

My Mother's Stuffing for Chicken

Simone Weinert

1 large Spanish onion, chopped
1 stalk celery, chopped
2 carrots, chopped
1 green pepper, chopped
1 4-ounce can mushrooms or 5 ounces
    fresh mushrooms, sliced

2 stack-packs Crax (low-salt) crackers
1 stack-pack saltines (low-salt) crackers
2 teaspoons cinnamon
2 tablespoons water

- Chop all veggies by hand or food processor.
- Crush crackers and mix with vegetables. Add cinnamon and water.
- Stuff mixture in chicken and roast.
- Stuffing can be frozen before cooking. Serves 8.

Bubby Sach's Stuffing

Sue Seder

1 stack snack crackers
6 handful rice crispies
1 large onion, chopped

1 egg
1/4–1/2 cup quick-cooking Quaker Oats

- Sauté onions in oil until light brown.
- Crush crackers with rolling pin and add onions to crackers.
- Crush rice crispies in your hands and add to mixture with egg and Quaker Oats.
- Add some water to make a consistency of slightly wet crackers.
- Stuff 1 6–8 pound roasting chicken and bake.

Stuffing For Chicken

Mrs. Philip (Nina) Cotton

12 Crax crackers
2 good fists full of corn flakes
3 heaping tablespoons of oatmeal
2 heaping tablespoons of Cream of Wheat
2 stalks celery, diced
1 medium-sized onion, diced

1 teaspoon sugar
½ teaspoon salt
⅛ teaspoon pepper
2–3 tablespoons vegetable oil

- Mix all ingredients thoroughly. Add vegetable oil and knead by hand. Use just enough oil to hold mixture together.
- Use to stuff 1 small chicken. For a 6–8 pound bird, I make at least twice the recipe.

"Gribines"/Rendering Chicken Fat

Lillian R. Silverman

Great appetizer for Shabbat meal.

Save up:
chicken fat
chicken skin, cut into small pieces

2 onions, cut into small pieces
giblets, optional

- Place fat and skin in pot on low heat. Cook until fat has turned to liquid.
- Add onions and cook until golden brown, mixing occasionally. Add giblets to melted fat.
- When done, strain fat and place in jar and refrigerate.
- Place golden skin and/or giblets in serving dishes and serve with raw cut-up onion. Serves 4.

Chicken Smash

Priscilla Jacobson

Truly a delicious and easy dish!

1/2 cup safflower oil
1/2 cup balsamic vinegar
3 tablespoons sugar
3 tablespoons ketchup
1 tablespoon Worcestershire sauce
1 tablespoon salt
2–3 medium-sized scallions, chopped

1 teaspoon salt
1 teaspoon dry mustard
1/2 teaspoon pepper
2 garlic cloves, minced
spritz hot pepper sauce
2 small, cut-up broiler-fryer chickens

- Mix all ingredients together except chicken.
- Place chicken in marinade overnight.
- Bake at 325°F one hour. Broil top to brown. Serves 6.

Chicken Marsala

Nancy Hodes

2 pounds boned and skinless chicken
    breasts
flour, mixed with garlic, salt, and pepper

oil for browning
2 pounds mushrooms, thinly sliced
1 cup Marsala wine

- Dredge chicken breasts in flour mixture. Sauté quickly.
- Place chicken in shallow baking dish, slightly overlapping the cutlets. Cover with a thick layer of the mushrooms. Can be prepared to this point and then frozen until needed.
- Pour enough Marsala wine over the preparation so that there is about an inch of liquid in the pan.
- Bake at 350°F for 35–45 minutes. Baste as it cooks so mushrooms do not dry out.

French Chicken in Orange Sherry

Ruth Medlinsky

4 chicken breasts
1 medium-sized onion, sliced
1/4 cup chopped green bell peppers
1 cup sliced mushrooms

Sauce:
1 cup orange juice
1 cup dry sherry
1/2 cup water
1 tablespoon firmly packed brown sugar
1/4 teaspoon pepper
1 tablespoon flour
2 teaspoons chopped parsley

- Place 4 chicken breasts on broiler pan, skin side up. Broil 2 inches from broiler rack for 10 minutes. Do not turn.
- Put chicken in shallow baking dish. Place onion, pepper and mushrooms on top of chicken.

Sauce:
- In saucepan, place orange juice, sherry, water, brown sugar, pepper, and flour. Blend well and cook over medium heat, stirring constantly, until sauce thickens and bubbles. Add 2 teaspoons chopped parsley.
- Pour sauce over chicken and bake at 375°F for 45 minutes, basting often. Serve over rice. Serves 4.

Vietnamese Chicken

Lilyan Spiegel

3 pounds chicken, cut into small pieces
1 jar apricot preserves

Marinade:
1/2 bottle soy sauce
1 medium-sized onion, minced
1 tablespoon sugar
1 teaspoon pepper
1 teaspoon ground ginger

- Combine marinade ingredients and marinate chicken for 24 hours.
- Drain marinade and mix with apricot preserves.
- Bake chicken in marinade mixed with preserves for 1 hour at 350°F, 1/2 hour covered and 1/2 hour uncovered, basting frequently. Serves 4.

Spicy Ginger Chicken

Cheryl Baskin

Very good.

¹/₄ cup whole blanched almonds
1¹/₂ tablespoons vegetable oil
¹/₂ pound skinless boneless chicken
    breasts, cut into bite-sized pieces
1 tablespoon minced fresh ginger root
4 green onions, cut into 1-inch pieces
¹/₄ teaspoon red pepper flakes

2 tablespoons water
1¹/₂ teaspoons cornstarch
1 tablespoon soy sauce
1 tablespoon sherry
1 tablespoon cider vinegar
2 teaspoons sugar

- In medium-sized skillet, stir fry almonds in ¹/₂ tablespoon oil for 5–7 minutes until golden. Remove with slotted spoon.
- Add remaining oil, chicken and ginger. Stir fry for 3 minutes. Add onion, almonds, and red pepper flakes.
- Combine with remaining ingredients. Stir water and cornstarch until dissolved. Add to pan. Cook, stirring until sauce thickens and coats chicken. Serves 2.

Oriental Soy Roasted Chicken

Barbara Rothstein

Delicious cold too! (If you have leftovers)

3–3¹/₂ pounds broiler/fryer chicken

Marinade:
¹/₃ cup low-sodium soy sauce
2 tablespoons canola oil
1 tablespoon sesame oil, toasted

1 tablespoon dry sherry, or white
    wine vinegar
2 cloves garlic, peeled and crushed
¹/₂ teaspoon grated fresh ginger root
2 teaspoons five-spice powder (may be
    purchased in natural food market or
    oriental market)

- Combine all ingredients. Rub the mixture inside and outside of the chicken.
- Marinate at least 3 hours or overnight in refrigerator.
- Roast in moderately hot 375°F oven for about 1¹/₄ hours or until tender. Serves 3–4.

Asian Chicken

Florence Katz

Absolutely mouth-watering—it's simple.

3 tablespoons canola oil (or other
  vegetable oil)
3½ pound frying chicken, cut into
  serving pieces or chicken parts, of
  your choice
1 bulb (not clove) fresh garlic, peeled and
  coarsley chopped

2 small dried hot peppers, optional
¾ cup distilled white vinegar
¼ cup soy sauce
3 tablespoons honey

- Heat oil in large, heavy skillet and brown chicken well on all sides, adding garlic
  and peppers when chicken is almost brown.
- Add remaining ingredients and cook over medium-high heat until chicken is done
  and sauce has been reduced somewhat, less than 10 minutes.
- If you are cooking both white and dark meat, remove white meat first, so it does not
  dry out. Watch carefullly so that sauce does not burn or boil away. There should be
  a quantity of sauce to serve with the chicken, and the chicken should appear slightly
  glazed. Serve wth Chinese noodles, pasta or rice. Serves 4.

Hawaiian Chicken

Sue Seder

Sauce:
1 can pineapple chunks, with syrup
1 teaspoon soy sauce
¼ teaspoon ginger
2 tablespoons cornstarch
1 chicken bouillon cube
¾ cup cider vinegar

1 chicken, cut-up
green pepper, chunked
tomatoes, chunked

- Drain pineapple. Reserve juice and add water to make 1¼ cups of liquid.
- Place juice and all remaining sauce ingredients in saucepan. Bring to a boil over
  medium heat for 2 minutes.
- Broil chicken pieces quickly to brown and put in pyrex dish.
- Pour sauce over and bake at 350°F for 30 minutes. Add vegetables and bake another
  30 minutes. Serves 4–6.

Tasty and Easy Baked Chicken

Ruth Ravelson

Nice served with rice pilaf

Marinade:
1 package onion soup mix
1 16-ounce can jellied cranberry sauce
5 ounces French salad dressing

6 large boneless chicken breasts

- Mix marinade ingredients and pour over chicken breasts. Refrigerate overnight.
- Bake next day uncovered at 350°F for 1 hour. Basting several times. Serves 6.

Honeyed Chicken

Harriet G. Tullman

I use an egg substitute in place of egg yolk.

1 egg yolk
$^1/_2$ teaspoon salt
$^1/_4$ teaspoon pepper
1 teaspoon paprika
2 tablespoons lemon juice

2 tablespoons soy sauce
2 tablespoons oil
$^1/_4$ cup honey
1 green bell pepper, chopped
1 chicken, quartered

- Beat all ingredients together. Except chicken.
- Dip each piece of chicken in sauce. Put in baking dish and pour remainder of sauce over all.
- Bake chicken for one hour in 350°F oven.

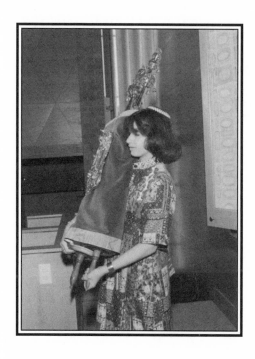

D and E's Sesame Chicken

Ethel Chaifetz

Delicious.

10 boneless chicken breasts
flour
4 eggs
2 tablespoons soy sauce
sesame seeds

parve breadcrumbs
garlic, to taste
salt, to taste
paprika, to taste
oil and sesame oil for frying

- Pound chicken. Dust chicken with flour.
- Mix eggs and soy sauce and dip floured chicken. Roll in sesame seeds, bread crumbs, spices, and place on tray and refrigerate.
- In heavy skillet, mix oils and quickly fry chicken on both sides.
- Freeze or refrigerate until ready to use.
- Bake in 350°F oven for 15–20 minutes. Serves 8–12.

Lemon Chicken

Toby Richmond

Can be made the day before and reheated. Great for large crowds.

4 chicken breasts
1/2 cup flour, mixed with salt and pepper
4 tablespoons margarine
1/2 cup white wine

1/8 cup fresh lemon juice, to taste
1 cup chicken broth
1/4–1/2 cup slivered almonds, toasted

- Pound chicken breasts.
- Put flour, salt and pepper in a bowl and coat breasts just before browning both sides in margarine.
- In a separate bowl, combine the white wine, lemon juice, and chicken broth. Pour liquid over the chicken and let it boil until nice and thick.
- Sprinkle toasted slivered almonds over it as you serve.
- If you want to make this in advance, boil chicken for only a couple of minutes. Put into pyrex dish and refrigerate.
- When you want to serve it, bake at 400°F for 20 minutes or so, basting it occasionally, until sauce is nice and thick. Serves 4.

Chicken Paprika and Dumplings

Mike Andrews

Pan to table—casual and delicious.

2 chickens, cut into eighths
flour for dredging, mixed with salt,
    pepper, and garlic powder
oil for frying
1 cup chopped onions
1/2 cup chopped celery
1/2 cup chopped mushrooms
1/2 teaspoon Worcestershire sauce
1/2 cup white wine

2 quarts (64 ounces) chicken broth
3 tablespoons paprika
1/3 cup tomato paste

Dumplings:
5 eggs
1 rounded cup flour
dash salt and nutmeg

- Dredge chicken pieces in flour seasoned with salt, pepper, and garlic. Brown chicken in oil in large braising pan. Remove chicken and set aside.
- Sauté onions, celery and mushrooms. Add Worcestershire sauce, wine, broth, chicken stock, paprika, and tomato paste. Bring to a boil.
- Add chicken and reduce to a simmer. Cook until chicken is done, about 30–35 minutes.

Dumplings:
- Mix eggs, flour, salt, and nutmeg together. Let rest 20 minutes.
- Bring water to a boil in a large pot. Drop egg mixture by tablespoon into boiling water. Cook 15 minutes.
- Drain and add to chicken, 5–10 minutes before serving. Dumplings will finish cooking in sauce. Serves 6–8.

Chicken Jubilee

Florence Medlinsky

Recipe must be made one day ahead for wine flavor to be good.

10 chicken breasts
1/2 cup margarine, melted

Sauce:
2 teaspoons salt
1/4 teaspoon pepper
1 teaspoon garlic salt
2 medium-sized onions, chopped

12 ounces bottled chili sauce
1 teaspoon Worcestershire sauce
1 cup water
1/2 cup raisins, optional
1/2 cup brown sugar
1 16-ounce can bing cherries, pitted and
    drained
1 cup sherry

- Brown chicken breasts in melted margarine.
- Combine all sauce ingredients, except cherries and sherry. Mix well.
- Pour well mixed sauce over chicken. Bake covered at 325°F for 45 minutes.
- Uncover, add 1 cup sherry and bing cherries. Cook uncovered for 15 minutes. Serves 10.

Tagine of Chicken with Prunes and Almonds

Ellen Berman Stone

Moroccan recipe.

2 tablespoons vegetable oil
1 medium-sized onion, finely chopped
1 chicken cut into pieces
1 cup chicken broth
1 1/2 teaspoons cinnamon
1/2 teaspoon ground ginger

1/4–1/2 teaspoon black pepper
1 pinch salt
1 cup pitted prunes
1 tablespoon honey
1 cup blanched almonds, lightly toasted

- In a deep skillet, heat oil, and sauté onion until tender. Add chicken to skillet and lightly brown.
- Mix broth with cinnamon, ginger, pepper, and salt and pour over the browned chicken. Simmer chicken for 30 minutes, turning pieces occasionally.
- Add prunes and honey, and mix with liquid. Cover skillet again and cook for 20 minutes.
- Transfer the chicken to large serving plate using a slotted spoon.
- Stir in one half of the almonds to prune sauce and then spoon the sauce over the chicken. Garnish the top with remaining almonds.
- To toast almonds, spread them on cookie tray. Heat in 350°F oven, stirring for 10 minutes. Serves 6.

Chicken and Chick Pea Stew

Rosalyn Ben-Chitrit

Tabika Bil "Houmus." This is a Libyan recipe (Jewish).

3/4 pound (1 1/2 cups) dried chick peas
1 3-pound chicken
1 tablespoon corn oil
2 pounds potatoes (approximately 5), peeled and quartered
1 large onion, chopped fine (approximately 1 cup)

1/2 cup flat-leaf parsley, chopped, rinsed under cold water and drained
2 3-inch cinnamon sticks
1 teaspoon salt, or to taste
2 cups water
1/4 teaspoon pepper
pomegranate seeds, for garnish, optional

- Soak chick peas in water overnight. Drain, peel off and discard skins.
- Cut chicken into eighths and remove loose skin and fat.
- Put all ingredients except pomegranate seeds, in a heavy pot and bring to a boil. Reduce heat to low, cover, and cook for 1 hour or as long as necessary to tenderize.
- Garnish with pomegranate seeds during the season when available. Serve warm over couscous or white rice. Serves 6–8.

Chicken with Cola

Helen Yaffe

You won't believe how good it is!

2 onions, cut into rings
3 tablespoons olive oil
1 teaspoon chopped garlic
6 skinless boneless chicken breasts

juice of ¹/₂ lemon
3–4 tablespoons brown sugar
1 can cola

- Sauté onions in olive oil with garlic until translucent. Place breasts on top. Pour lemon juice over chicken and sprinkle with brown sugar. Add cola.
- Cover and simmer until cola is absorbed. Serves 6.

Grilled Turkey Breast

Lisa Honig

2 shallots
¹/₂ cup orange juice
3 tablespoons olive oil
3 tablespoons chopped fresh rosemary,
    or 2 teaspoons dried
2 tablespoons balsamic vinegar

4 teaspoons grated orange peel
1 tablespoon honey
1 teaspoon salt
1¹/₄ teaspoon dried red pepper flakes
1 1³/₄ pound boneless turkey breast half,
    skinned

- Mince shallots in a food processor. Transfer to a zip lock plastic bag. Add rest of ingredients, except turkey breast. Seal and shake to mix.
- Flatten turkey breast until uniformly 1-inch thick. Place turkey in plastic bag with marinade and seal. Refrigerate at least 6 hours or overnight.
- Prepare barbecue.
- Grill turkey until meat thermometer registers 155°F in center of breast, about 10 minutes per side. Brushing turkey with extra marinade occasionally.
- Slice diagonally across grain and serve.

Turkey Rolls with
Sweet and Sour Cabbage

Irene Garber

2 pounds ground turkey
1 package onion soup mix
1 cup bread crumbs
3 eggs
1/4 cup hot water

Sweet and Sour Cabbage:
1 jar chili sauce
1 jar water
1 large can sauerkraut
1 cup brown sugar
1 can cranberry sauce

- Combine turkey, onion soup, bread crumbs, eggs, and water. Form meat balls and place in casserole.
- Combine chili sauce, water, sauerkraut, sugar, and cranberry sauce. Pour over meat balls.
- Bake in a 350°F oven for 1 1/2 hours.

Duck with Orange Glaze

Carol Halsband

An easy way to make a delicious duck

2 ducks, about 5 pounds each
garlic powder

Sauce:
1 12-ounce jar orange marmalade or
    apricot jam
1 tablespoon parve margarine
1 tablespoon dried parsley flakes
1 teaspoon powdered ginger
1 can mandarin oranges, drained

Duck:
- Clip wing tips from duck, trim excess fat, and sprinkle skin and cavity with garlic powder. In roasting pan with rack, bake at 350°F for 3 hours.
- Prick skin with long tyned fork every 30 minutes.
- Drain duck and cavity of excess fat and juices.

Sauce:
- To prepare sauce, combine all ingredients. Heat slowly until melted.
- Remove ducks to large jelly roll pan, brush on some of the sauce as a glaze. Place in 350°F oven until crisp.
- Serve sauce in separate bowl to spoon over duck.
- For a glamorous presentation, serve the ducks "au flambe." Serves 6–8.

Salads and Molds

Spinach Salad

Edith Ravelson

1/2 cup mayonnaise
2 teaspoons Dijon mustard
1/4 cup lemon juice
1/2 cup olive oil
1 tablespoon tarragon vinegar
1/2 teaspoon sugar
salt and pepper

1 package fresh spinach
2 hard-boiled eggs, grated fine
1/2 cup croutons
1 bunch scallions, chopped
6 ounces fresh mushrooms, sliced
1 small can mandarin orange sections,
    drained

- Mix mayonnaise, mustard, lemon juice, oil, vinegar, sugar, and salt and pepper together. Beat until smooth.
- Wash spinach, cut off ends, and toss to dry. Add eggs, croutons, scallions, mushrooms, and oranges.
- Add dressing or place in bowl on the side. Serves 4–6.

Goat Cheese and Raisin Salad

Myrna Kenney

1/2 head Boston lettuce
1 head red lettuce
1/2 head curly lettuce
1/2 cup pignola nuts
1 cup white raisins
1/4 pound Chevre goat cheese
1/4 pound Feta cheese

Dressing:
salt and pepper
1/3 cup balsamic vinegar
2/3 cup olive oil
1/4 cup fresh chopped basil, optional

- Mix all salad ingredients together. Combine dressing ingredients and toss before serving. Serves 6.

Mandarin Salad

Bea Comen

1/2 cup slivered almonds
3 tablespoons sugar
1/4 head each romaine, red leaf, and
    Boston lettuce
2 medium-sized stalks celery, chopped
1 tablespoon thinly sliced scallions
1 can mandarin oranges, drained

Dressing:
1/4 cup olive oil
1/2 teaspoon salt
2 tablespoons sugar
1 dash pepper
2 tablespoons vinegar
1 teaspoon snipped parsley

- Sauté almonds with sugar until coated and browning. Watch carefully so they don't burn. Set almonds aside to cool.
- Mix ingredients for dressing.
- Put greens, celery, scallions, and oranges in bowl. Add dressing and almonds, and toss to mix.

Spinach, Beet, and Onion Salad

Mike Andrews

Made with coriander cumin vinaigrette.

1/2 pound small fresh red beets, trimmed
1 tablespoon fresh lime juice
1/3 cup olive oil
1 teaspoon corriander seed, toasted and
    ground
1/2 teaspoon cumin seeds, toasted and
    ground

salt and pepper
1 pound fresh spinach leaves, stemmed
    and washed
1 small salad onion, thinly sliced

- Cook the beets in lightly salted, gently boiling water, for 15–20 minutes, or until they are done. Drain the beets and rinse under cold water.
- Peel and trim the beets and slice them 1/4-inch thick.
- Put the lime juice in a small bowl and whisk the olive oil into it. Add the coriander and cumin and season vinaigrette with salt and pepper.
- Toss the spinach and onion with about 2/3 of the vinaigrette.
- Arrange the salad on a platter or in a bowl with the beet slices over it. Drizzle the rest of the vinaigrette over the salad and serve. Serves 6.

24 Hour Salad

Eileen Levenson

Great for entertaining!

1 head lettuce
2 cups chopped celery
1 green bell pepper, chopped
1 small Bermuda onion, sliced

1 10-ounce package frozen peas,
    defrosted
1 cup sour cream
1 cup mayonnaise
1 package grated sharp Cheddar cheese

- Wash lettuce and chop into small pieces. Put in towel until dry and leave in towel in refrigerator overnight.
- In a large glass bowl, put half the lettuce on bottom. Next layer is celery, then a layer of pepper, layer of onions, layer of peas. Top with remaining lettuce. Mix sour cream with mayonnaise and spread on top of lettuce. Sprinkle with cheese.
- Let set 24 hours in refrigerator. Serves 10–12.

Romanian Eggplant Salad

Evelyn Ehrlich

May use for Passover. Ingredient amounts may be varied. May be frozen. When defrosted pour off excess liquid or add a few bread crumbs to absorb liquid.

1 medium-sized eggplant
1 medium-sized tomato, diced
1 medium-sized green pepper, diced
1 sweet onion, finely diced

juice of 1/2 lemon
4–6 tablespoons olive oil
1 teaspoon salt
1/8 teaspoon black pepper

- Prick eggplant with a fork a few times. Bake on brown paper bag at 350°F for 40–50 minutes until soft (or in microwave 12–14 minutes). When cool, peel off skin, drain off juice in colander. Chop finely.
- Add the rest of the ingredients and mix gently. Chill. Serves 4–6 on lettuce or 10–12 as appetizers on party bread.

Cucumber and Dill Salad

Reva Sher Weisman

This won a local contest several years ago.

4 cucumbers, peeled and thinly sliced
2½ teaspoons salt
⅓ cup white vinegar
2 tablespoons sugar, or more to taste
3 tablespoons cold water

¼ teaspoon fresh ground pepper
2 tablespoons finely chopped fresh
  dill weed
1 bunch scallions, thinly sliced

- Sprinkle the sliced cucumbers with salt and let stand for ½ hour.
- Combine the remaining ingredients and mix thoroughly. Pour over cucumbers.
- Refrigerate for a few hours to marinate before serving. Serve with a slotted spoon.
  Serves 6–8.

Vegetable Salad

Sylvia Davidson

1 8½-ounce can of tiny peas, drained
1 12½-ounce can white corn, drained
1 carrot, peeled and thinly sliced
1 cup thinly sliced celery
2–3 scallions, sliced

3 teaspoons sugar
1 teaspoon salt
½ teaspoon pepper if needed
¼ cup white vinegar
¾ cup oil

- Combine ingredients and marinate for 2–3 days before serving. Serve cold.
  Serves 8–10.

Claremont Salad

Vivian Sigal

Marinade:
3/4 cup vinegar
3/4 cup sugar
1/2 cup oil
4 tablespoons water
4 teaspoons salt

1 head cabbage, shredded
3 cucumbers (preferably pickling cukes),
    sliced thin
3 carrot, sliced thin
1 onion, sliced thin

- Combine marinade ingredients and pour over the shredded cabbage, sliced cucumbers, carrots, and onion. Cover and refrigerate.
- Let stand at least 12 hours. Drain excess liquid. Serves 8.

Fattoush

Mike Andrews

2 pounds tomatoes
2 pounds cucumbers
1 onion, finely chopped
4 tablespoons chopped fresh mint or
    1 tablespoon dried

juice of 2 lemons
1 tablespoon olive oil
salt and pepper, to taste
3 pita breads
3/4 cup yogurt, optional

- Finely dice tomatoes, and cucumbers.
- Add the onion, mint, lemon juice, oil, and spices.
- Slice the pita bread in half. Toast. Break into bite-sized pieces and add to salad before serving.
- Can be tossed well with yogurt before serving.

Herbed Tomato and Crouton Salad

Karen Hodes Turk

1¼ cups oil
3 cloves garlic
3 tablespoons red wine vinegar
1½ teaspoons Dijon mustard
½ cup fresh mint

½ cup chopped scallions
½ cup fresh parsley
salt and pepper
3 pounds tomatoes, chopped
5 cups croutons

- Mix first 8 ingredients for dressing and let sit to combine flavors.
- Add tomatoes and croutons just before serving.

Italian Bread Salad

Nancy Benjamin

Veggies:
3–4 large ripe tomatoes, cut into cubes
2 cucumbers, peeled, seeded, and diced
1 yellow pepper, julienned
2 tablespoons drained capers
½ cup pitted oil cured black olives,
    drained

Dressing:
⅔ cup olive oil
⅓ cup balsamic vinegar
½ cup shredded basil
salt and pepper
1 clove garlic, minced

Bread:
4 cups day old French or Italian bread,
    coarsely cubed

- Combine vegetables in large bowl and let sit 30 minutes.
- Add bread and toss with dressing.
- Wait 20–30 minutes before serving.

Chopped Salad

Lisa Honig

Vinaigrette:
6 tablespoons red wine or balsamic
  vinegar
2 tablespoons lemon juice
2 tablespoons minced garlic
1 tablespoon Dijon mustard
2 teaspoons dried oregano
$1/2$ teaspoon dry mustard
$1/2$ teaspoon sugar
1 cup olive oil
salt and pepper

Salad:
8 cups chopped iceburg lettuce
$1^1/4$ cups chopped seeded tomatoes
$2/3$ cup canned chickpeas, drained
$1/2$ cup chopped fresh basil
3 green onions, chopped
4 ounces mozzarella cheese
$1/4$ cup Parmesan cheese
1 can tuna

- In small bowl, whick together all vinaigrette ingredients except oil. Gradually whisk in oil.
- Season with salt and pepper to taste.
- Mix all salad ingredients together and toss with dressing.

Party Platter Salad

Jennifer Hodes Reich

Vegetables:
romaine or other leaf lettuce
snow peas
hearts of palm or white asparagus
artichoke hearts
roasted peppers
black olives
marinated mushrooms

Dressing:
$1/3$ cup oil
$1/3$ cup cider vinegar
$1/3$ cup water
2 tablespoons soy sauce
2 tablespoons minced onion
1 tablespoon honey
$1/2$ teaspoon dry mustard
minced garlic

- Arrange lettuce and vegetables on a large platter according to color and shape.
- Combine ingredients for the dressing, will stay fresh in a cruet for weeks.
- Salad can be put together in the morning, sprinkled with dressing, and served in the evening.

Armenian Vegetable Salad

Harriet Gordon

1 pound fresh green beans
1 7-ounce can black olives, drained
1 4-ounce can pimentos, sliced

1 bunch scallions, snipped
1 can of chickpeas
1 bottle of Catalina Salad Dressing

- Cut beans into 1-inch lengths. Combine all vegetables.
- Toss with dressing and marinate overnight.

Garbanzo Bean Salad

Margery Blonder

1 15-ounce can garbanzo beans, drained
1 cup sliced celery
1 cup chopped red bell peppers
1 small zucchini, sliced
1 tablespoon fresh parsley
$1/2$ teaspoon paprika

$1/2$ teaspoon ground cumin
dash red hot pepper
3 tablespoons sherry vinegar
1 tablespoon oil
1 large clove garlic, minced
salt and pepper, to taste

- Combine all ingredients in a large bowl. Toss and chill before serving.

Black Bean Salad

Lisa Solomon Hodes

Dressing:
¹/₃ cup lime juice
¹/₃ cup olive oil
fresh coriander
1 teaspoon salt
¹/₂ teaspoon red chili or a pinch of
    cayenne pepper

Vegetables:
1 15-ounce can black beans, rinsed and
    drained
1 11-ounce can corn niblets
2 medium-sized tomatoes, diced
1 red pepper, diced
1 green pepper, diced
¹/₂ cup chopped red onion

- Mix the ingredients for the dressing. Blend well.
- Add the vegetables. Allow to marinate for at least a few hours before serving.

Taco Bean Salad

Minna Gregerman

This is a favorite in our home!

1 #2 can pinto beans
1 small bottle Italian salad dressing
    (I use a red wine vinegar and oil)
1 medium-sized head lettuce

2 medium-sized tomatoes
2 tablespoons minced onion
1 cup grated mild Cheddar cheese
small bag corn chips, finely crushed

- Wash and drain pinto beans and marinate for several hours in dressing.
- Finely chop lettuce. Skin and finely chop tomatoes.
- Mix lettuce, tomatoes and onions with beans in large salad bowl. Spread cheese over salad.
- Just before serving, spread corn chips over top. Serves 8 or more.

Patio Potato Salad

Evelyn Ehrlich

Recipe uses no mayonaise - so safe for outdoors

2¹/₂ pounds boiling potatoes, peeled, and
    cut into ³/₄-inch cubes
4–6 tablespoons olive oil
3 tablespoons fresh lemon juice
2 tablespoons snipped dill
4–6 scallions, or a handful of chopped
    chives

1–2 onions, diced
¹/₂ cup each minced parsley and minced
    mint leaves
salt and pepper, to taste

- Boil potatoes in salted water. Test with a toothpick to determine if they are done.
- Mix oil and lemon juice and add to warm potatoes.
- Add the rest of ingredients and toss gently.
- Chill and taste, correct seasonings if necessary. If using dry herbs, use half as much.
  Serves 6.

New Potato and Green Bean Salad

Lisa Honig

Dressing:
¹/₄ cup balsamic vinegar
2 teaspoons Dijon mustard
2 teaspoons fresh lemon juice
1 clove garlic, minced
1 dash Worcestershire sauce
¹/₂ cup olive oil
salt and pepper

Salad:
1¹/₂ pounds small red-skinned potatoes
³/₄ pound green beans
1 small red onion, coarsely chopped
¹/₄ cup chopped fresh basil

Dressing:
- Whisk first 5 ingredients in meduim-sized bowl. Gradually whisk in oil. Season to taste with salt and pepper.

Salad:
- Steam potatoes until tender. Cool. Cut into quarters.
- Cook green beans in pot of salted boiling water until crisp, about 5 minutes. Drain. Transfer beans to bowl of ice water and cool. Cut beans in half.
- Combine beans, potatoes, onion, and basil in large bowl.
- Add dressing. Toss to coat. Serve at room temperature.

Kraut Salad

Florence Katz

Easy and a good side dish.

1 1-pound can or bottle of sauerkraut, drained
1 cup chopped celery
1 cup chopped onions

1 cup chopped green pepper
3/4 cup sugar
1/2 cup cider vinegar
1/2 cup salad oil

• Mix ingredients and let stand in refrigerator at least 24 hours or longer.

Cole Slaw

Mrs. Irving Kaplan

2 pound head of cabbage
3 medium-sized carrots
1 green pepper
1/4 cup chopped onions
1/2 teaspoon salt

1/4 teaspoon pepper
3 tablespoons sugar
2 tablespoons mayonnaise
1 1/2 tablespoons cider vinegar

• Shred the cabbage.
• Grate the carrots and pepper.
• Add all the ingredients together and mix well.
• Marinate for at least 3 hours. Mix again before serving.

Joyce's Coleslaw

Joyce Queen

Low calorie and most delish!

¹/₂ teaspoon Dijon mustard
2 tablespoons mayonnaise
3 cups shredded cabbage
3 tablespoons oil
¹/₃ cup vinegar, warm, not hot
1 teaspoon salt
freshly ground pepper

2 tablespoons sugar
1 tablespoon finely chopped onions
1 tablespoon chopped pimento
1 teaspoon celery seed
1 green pepper, sliced in rings
cherry tomatoes

- Mix Dijon mustard together with mayonnaise.
- In large bowl, toss cabbage with oil and vinegar. Add remaining ingredients, except green pepper and tomatoes and mix well. Cover and chill in refrigerator.
- Garnish with green pepper rings and cherry tomatoes. Serves 4.

Herbed Pasta Salad

Lisa Honig

1¹/₂ cups plain yogurt
³/₄ cup mayonnaise
1¹/₂ tablespoons white wine vinegar
³/₄ cup minced parsley
1 large red onion, quartered and sliced
    thin

¹/₂ cup fresh herbs, finely chopped
    (fresh basil and dill)
1¹/₂ pounds tricolor penne or fusilli,
    cooked, drained, and rinsed
salt and pepper

- Whisk yogurt, mayonnaise, vinegar, parsley, onion, and herbs.
- Mix pasta with dressing. Add salt and pepper to taste.
- May be made ahead of time. If pasta absorbs dressing, add 2–3 tablespoons of warm water and toss. Serves 12.

Fusilli Salad

Penny Shairman Sullivan

3/4 pound Feta cheese
1 pound tricolored pasta, cooked and
    drained
1/2 cup chopped onions
1/2 cup drained and chopped sundried
    tomatoes
1 cup pitted and chopped kalamata olives
3 cups thinly sliced spinach

1/4 cup chopped red bell peppers

Dressing:
1/2 cup olive oil
3 tablespoons red wine vinegar
1 clove garlic, minced, crushed
1/2 teaspoon salt and pepper, to taste

- Crumble Feta cheese over pasta. Add onion, tomatoes, olives, spinach, and red bell peppers. Toss.
- Combine dressing. Pour over pasta and toss.

Chinese Pasta Salad

Nancy Benjamin

1 pound angel hair pasta
4 tablespoons oil
1 bunch scallions, chopped
2–3 cloves garlic, minced

4 tablespoons soy sauce
2–3 tablespoons white vinegar
1 tablespoon sesame oil
1 teaspoon sugar

- Boil pasta until al dente. Drain and rinse briefly in cold water. Mix with 2 table-spoons oil.
- In a skillet, cook scallions and garlic briefly in remaining oil. Remove from heat and add the rest of the ingredients.
- Mix with the pasta. Refrigerate.
- May add red pepper slivers, sesame seeds, dry roasted peanuts, or chicken strips, if desired.

Chinese Chicken Salad

Irene Garber

Dressing:
$^1/_3$ cup vegetable oil
$^1/_3$ cup soy sauce
1 teaspoon dry mustard
2 tablespoons honey
2 tablespoons ketchup

1 head lettuce, shredded
$^3/_4$ cup chopped scallions
1 package or can crisp chow mein
    noodles
1 cup water chestnuts, drained and sliced
4 half chicken breasts, cooked, cooled,
    and thinly sliced

Dressing:
• Combine all dressing ingredients.

• On platter lay out lettuce, scallions, noodles, water chestnuts, and chicken breasts.
• Pour dressing over. Leftover dressing can be served on the side.

Chicken Salad

Sue Seder

3 whole chicken breasts
1 small can sliced pineapple
1 cup slivered almonds

1 cup chopped celery or scallions
$^1/_4$ –$^1/_2$ cup mayonnaise
salt and pepper

• Poach chicken. Cut into large chunks.
• Cut pineapple slices in $^1/_4$-inch wedges. Mix all ingredients together and season with salt and pepper. Use enough mayonnaise just to bind the salad together. Serves 6.

Cafe Danica Chicken Salad

Dinny Griff

You can buy Madras curry at health food stores and it really makes the flavor very special.

4 cups of cooked chicken, cut into chunks
2–3 apples, cut into chunks
3 celery stalks, cut into chunks
$^1/_2$–1 teaspoon Madras curry

$^1/_2$ cup mayonnaise
salt and pepper
$^1/_2$ teaspoon garlic powder

- Mix chicken, apples, and celery. Add Madras curry.
- Mix with mayonnaise, salt, pepper, and garlic powder to your personal taste. Serves 4–6.

Cranberry Jello Mold

Helene Shulman Chanson

1 package whole cranberries
1 No. 2 can pineapple tidbits, drained and
    reserved
2 cups liquid, juice from pineapple, and
    water

1 cup sugar
1 3-ounce package orange Jello
3 stalks celery, chopped
$^1/_2$ cup walnuts, chopped

- Cook cranberries with liquid and sugar for 4 minutes until they pop.
- Add Jello and mix well. Add the rest of the ingredients.
- Pour into a glass dish. Chill until firm. Serves 6.

"Simply Delish" Jello Mold

Lillian Glixman

1 large package black raspberry (or any red) Jello
3 cups boiling water
1 20-ounce can crushed pineapple

1 pound cottage cheese
1 container (8 ounces) frozen whipped topping

- Dissolve Jello in water.
- Add crushed pineapple and juice.
- Let this gel in refrigerator until shimmery.
- Then add cottage cheese and whipped topping.
- Mix well.
- Pour into lightly greased mold and chill until firm.
- Most attractive when unmolded on large platter and served with cantelope, honeydew, and watermelon squares around it.

Ruthie's Orange Sherbet Jello Mold

Mari Seder

2 3-ounce packages orange Jello
1 3-ounce package lemon Jello
1 pint orange sherbet

5 cups liquid (water and the juice from the mandarin oranges)
2 small cans of mandarin oranges

- Dissolve the orange and lemon Jello with 2½ cups of boiling water. Add sherbet, stir to dissolve.
- Add 2½ cups of cold water and mandarin orange juice. Add oranges.
- Pour into 6–8 cup Jello mold and chill until firm.

Ice Cream Jello Mold

Harriet Robbins

1 pint vanilla ice cream
8 ounces sour cream
2 3-ounce packages orange Jello
2 cups boiling water

1 small can crushed pineapple in juice,
   drained
1 large can fruit cocktail, drained

- Soften ice cream and mix with sour cream. Set aside.
- Dissolve Jello with 2 cups boiling water.
- Combine everything. Pour into molds. Chill until firm.

Lemon Mousse Jello Mold

Phyllis Sherwin

1 20-ounce can pineapple tidbits in juice,
   or crushed pineapple
5¼ cups liquid (reserved pineapple juice
   and water)

4 3-ounce packages lemon Jello
1 large can frozen lemonade concentrate
1 large container Cool Whip

- Drain pineapple, reserving liquid.
- Boil 5¼ cups liquid and dissolve lemon Jello, add frozen lemonade, and refrigerate until either partially gelled or very cold.
- Mix in pineapple and Cool Whip thoroughly. Mix all together and chill. Serves 12.

Confetti Jello Mold

Sara E. Miller

Parve

1 3-ounce package lime Jello
1 3-ounce package cherry Jello
1 3-ounce package orange Jello
3 cups hot water
1 1/2 cups cold water
1 cup pineapple juice

1/4 cup sugar
1 3-ounce package strawberry Jello
1/2 cup cold water
2 envelopes Dream Whip
1 cup Coffee Rich
1 teaspoon vanilla

- Prepare in a separate square pan for each color, the lime, cherry, and orange Jello, using 1 cup hot water and 1/2 cup cold water for each color. Refrigerate overnight.
- On the next day, heat pineapple juice and sugar until dissolved. Add strawberry Jello. Mix until disolved. Add 1/2 cup of cold water. Refrigerate until syrupy.
- Prepare Dream Whip by combining with Coffee Rich and vanilla using low speed on mixer. (Cool Whip may be substituted for Dream Whip if using with dairy.)
- Whip strawberry Jello mixture until foamy. Fold in Dairy Whip mixture.
- Cut 3 colored Jello into cubes. Put into bowl.
- Add Dream Whip mixture and fold together, lightly. Pour into large Jello mold. Refrigerate 3–4 hours.

Gazpacho Salad Mold

Sue Gotz

From my mother's recipe box — she was a great cook.

2 envelopes unflavored gelatin
2 cups tomato juice
1/3 cup red wine vinegar
1 teaspoon salt
dash hot pepper sauce

2 medium-sized tomatoes, peeled and diced
1 large cucumber, peeled and diced
1/4 cup red onions, finely chopped

- Soften gelatin in 1/2 cup tomato juice. Heat remining tomato juice and add gelatin mixture, stirring until mixed and gelatin has dissolved.
- Remove from heat and let cool. Refrigerate mixture until it thickens slightly.
- Add remaining ingredients and mix thoroughly.
- Pour into 1 1/2-quart mold. Refrigerate until firm.
- Unmold into platter lined with lettuce and decorate with fresh vegetables.

Zucchini Relish

Ruth Seder

10 cups chopped zucchini, sliced
4 cups chopped onion
1 sweet red pepper, chopped
1 green bell pepper, chopped
5 tablespoons salt
2 tablespoons cornstarch

5 cups sugar
2 teaspoons celery seed
2¹/₂ cups white vinegar
1 tablespoon tumeric
1 teaspoon black pepper

- Mix first 5 ingredients and refrigerate overnight.
- Drain–do not squeeze. Discard the liquid.
- Mix vegetables with remaining ingredients in pot and simmer 30 minutes.
- Pour into sterilized jars. Makes 5 pints.

Raw Berry Relish

Sandy Hersh

Simple, sweet, sour, and refreshingly delicious! A gift I've been proud to give.

2 whole lemons
1 pound cranberries, cut into pieces

1 cup (fresh or frozen) blueberries
2 cups sugar

- In food processor chop lemons coarsely.
- Add cranberries, chop fine.
- Add blueberries. Process to mix.
- Add sugar (1¹/₂ cups of sugar, then add additional sugar slowly to taste.)
- I usually double the recipe.

Vegetables

Very Baked Tomatoes

Eleanor Kunin

4 tomatoes, the riper the better (in
    season are best)
$^1/_4$ cup olive oil

2 large garlic cloves, peeled and minced
2 tablespoons fresh basil, chopped
salt and pepper, to taste

- Core tomatoes. Slice in half horizontally and place in baking pan, cut side up.
- Mix together oil, garlic, basil, and salt and pepper. Pour over the tomatoes.
- Bake at 325°F for 2 hours. The tomatoes will exude their juices and collapse, and
  then begin to carmelize. This is when they start to become delicious.
- Use a slotted spoon to serve. Serves 4.

Savory String Beans

Florence Gould

2 medium-sized onions, chopped
$^1/_4$–$^1/_2$ pound mushrooms, chopped
oil for sautéeing

2 pounds string beans
1 cup seasoned bread crumbs
1 cup Italian dressing

- Sauté onions and mushrooms in oil until golden brown.
- Cook string beans in boiling salted water until tender, but still crisp. Drain.
- Place beans, onions, mushrooms and bread crumbs in casserole. Add Italian dress-
  ing, mixing thoroughly.
- Just before serving, heat in a 350°F oven until warm. Serves 4–5.

Marinated Carrots

Sydell Israel

2 bunches of carrots, sliced and par boiled
1 can of tomato soup, undiluted
³/₄ cup sugar
¹/₂ cup oil

³/₄ cup vinegar
1 teaspoon Worcestershire sauce
1 teaspoon dry mustard
1 salad onion, sliced
1 green pepper, sliced

- Mix all ingredients together and marinate overnight in refrigerator.

Carrot Pudding

Selma Plotkin

This recipe is so good that I always double it.

1 cup flour
1 teaspoon baking powder
¹/₂ teaspoon baking soda
1 teaspoon salt

¹/₂ cup brown sugar
2 cups grated carrots
¹/₂ cup oil
2 eggs

- Sift together flour, baking powder, baking soda, and salt. Add brown sugar. Add other ingredients. Mix as with muffins, leaving a little lumpy.
- Use a well greased pan with hole in middle, such as a ring mold or bundt pan. When doubling recipe, use only ³/₄ cup oil.
- Bake at 350°F for 1 hour. Serves 6–8.

Artichokes, Roman Style

Mike Andrews

4 large artichokes
1/2 lemon
3 tablespoons chopped parsley
1/2 teaspoon mint

1 1/2 teaspoons chopped garlic
salt and pepper
1/2 cup olive oil
chicken stock

- Cut away outer leaves of artichokes. Scoop out center leaves and fuzzy core, using a melon ball cutter or spoon. Rub with lemon to prevent discoloration.
- Combine parsley, mint, garlic, salt and pepper, and rub 2/3 of this mixture inside artichoke bottoms.
- Arrange artichokes, stem up, in a heavy casserole. Sprinkle remaining parsley mixture over artichokes and add oil. Add enough chicken stock to cover 1/3 of artichokes.
- Cook covered over medium heat about 30 minutes, or until tender. Remove artichokes. Cook down remaining liquid 2/3 of the way.
- Serve lukewarm or room temperature with the reduced liquid. Serves 4.

Zucchini Pancakes

Florence Gould

Great hors d'oeuvres.

1/2 cup chopped onions
2 cups shredded zucchini
1 cup shredded carrots
2 eggs

1/2 cup flour
1 teaspoon salt
1/4 teaspoon pepper
oil, for frying

- Combine all ingredients together except oil.
- Heat oil in a large skillet. Drop mixture by tablespoonfuls into skillet. Brown on both sides.
- Serve with sour cream. Freezes well. Serves 4–6.

Low-Fat Zucchini-Spinach Squares

Lolita Baker

Yummy!

3 onions, chopped
5 cloves garlic
2 tablespoons oil
2 pounds zucchini
10 ounces frozen chopped spinach
3 eggs

1 cup bread crumbs
$1/2$ cup Romano cheese, or Parmesan
    cheese, grated
2 tablespoons dried basil
salt and pepper, to taste

- Brown chopped onion and garlic in oil.
- Steam zucchini for 6 minutes, drain well and chop.
- Drain defrosted uncooked spinach. Add remaining ingredients and mix well.
- Pour into greased 9 x 13-inch pan. Bake 45 minutes at 375°F. Serves 8 or more.

Zucchini in Pesto Sauce

Lolita Baker

6 small zucchini, sliced
3 tablespoons pine nuts or walnuts
2 fresh garlic cloves
2 teaspoons salt
2 cups fresh basil or 2 tablespoons dried
    basil with 1 cup fresh parsley

1 cup Parmesan cheese
$1/2$ cup olive oil
2 tablespoons butter

- Lightly salt zucchini and let drain for $1/2$ hour. Rinse and dry.
- Purée nuts, garlic, salt, basil, and cheese in food processor. Add oil.
- Stir fry zucchini in butter only until heated through. Toss with pesto. Voila!
  Serves 6.

Oriental Zucchini

Joy Goodwin

Great veggie.

1 pound zucchini (3 or 4), or more if
   desired
2 tablespoons salad oil
1 tablespoon soy sauce

1/4 teaspoon salt, if desired
sprinkle of pepper (1/4 teaspoon)
sesame seeds

- Wash zucchini and slice (do not peel) like cucumber, 1/4-inch thick.
- Heat oil in skillet, add zucchini and sauté about 2 minutes.
- Add soy sauce, salt and black pepper. Serve hot — sprinkle with lots of sesame seeds. Serves 4–6.

Potato Latkes

Cookbook Committee

Can be made ahead, but best when eaten right out of the pan.

4 large potatoes
1 large onion
2 eggs

1/4 cut matzoh meal
salt and pepper
oil, for frying

- Grate potatoes. Drain until all liquid is removed.
- Grate onion and add to potatoes.
- Beat eggs and add to potato mixture. Add matzoh meal. Season with salt and pepper to taste.
- Fill skillet to 1/4 inch with oil. Heat until very hot.
- Use large spoon to drop potato mixture into oil. Fry until very brown on one side, turn and finish. Drain latkes on paper towels.
- Can be frozen and reheated in 400°F oven.

Incredible Potato Latkes

Carole Dorris

Little fat is used in cooking these and they taste wonderful! They taste even better made in advance and reheated in oven.

4 potatoes scrubbed (peeling not
    necessary)
1 large onion
4–5 ounces mushrooms, chopped
2 eggs
1/2 teaspoon salt, or to taste

1/4 teaspoon pepper, or to taste
1/2 teaspoon garlic salt or 1/4 teaspoon
    garlic powder
2–3 scallions, sliced, including greens
oil, for frying

- Grate potatoes and onion.
- Add chopped mushrooms. Drain slightly. Add eggs and seasonings. Stir in scallions.
- Fry in a nonstick pan using approximately 1 teaspoon oil for first batch and as little as possible thereafter.
- Serve with sour cream and/or apple sauce. Serves 4–6.

Parmesan Potatoes

Lisa Honig

4 large potatoes, cut lengthwise into
    eighths
1/4 cup olive oil

1 teaspoon dried crushed red pepper
salt and pepper
1/2 cup freshly grated Parmesan cheese

- Preheat oven to 375°F.
- Place potatoes in roasting pan. Add oil and red pepper. Mix to coat. Season with salt and pepper.
- Bake until tender inside and crispy outside, about 1 hour, turning once. Sprinkle with Parmesan cheese.

Garlic Potatoes

Nancy Benjamin

1½ pounds red potatoes, cut in half
3 tablespoons olive oil
3–4 large garlic cloves, chopped

1 bunch scallions, sliced
3 tablespoons unsalted butter
salt and pepper, to taste

- Boil potatoes until tender. Drain.
- While potatoes are boiling, heat oil in heavy frying pan. Add garlic and cook over medium heat until garlic begins to brown. Add scallions and cook 1 minute more.
- Add butter and remove from heat. Swirl pan to melt butter.
- Mash potatoes with potato masher.
- Add oil mixture and stir to mix well with potatoes. Add salt and pepper to taste.
- Put potatoes in buttered baking dish and bake in 450°F oven for 10–15 minutes.

Potato Kugel

Lisa Solomon Hodes

If you make this recipe in a muffin tin, everyone gets their own crisp corner.

6 potatoes
ice water plus 2 tablespoons vinegar (to keep the potatoes white)
1½ teaspoons salt

1 large onion, finely chopped or grated
½ cup flour or matzoh meal
¼ teaspoon pepper
1 teaspoon baking powder

- Grate potatoes into bowl of ice water and vinegar.
- In another bowl, mix remaining ingredients.
- Turn potatoes into colander to drain. Add potatoes to batter.
- Turn into a well oiled 9 x 13-inch Pyrex baking dish. Bake in a 350°F oven for 1½ hours. If using a muffin tin, bake for 1 hour.

Authentic Russian Potato Kugel

Ethel Abramoff

A very forgiving recipe. More or less potatoes, more or less onions, more or less egg. It's still delicious. Has been authenticated by newly-arrived Russian cousins.

4–5 pounds raw potatoes	salt and pepper, to taste
2 onions, chopped	$1/2$ teaspoon garlic powder
2–3 tablespoons canola oil	paprika
4 eggs, well beaten	

- Boil unpeeled potatoes until soft.
- Meanwhile, sauté chopped onions until well done and beginning to brown.
- Peel potatoes and mash very well, adding onions and canola oil. Add eggs, salt and pepper, and garlic powder.
- Transfer to oiled baking dish, sprinkle with paprika. Bake at 350°F until crusty and brown on top.

Koo-Koo Sib-Zamini (potatoes)

Manouch Darvish

Excellent appetizer or side dish.

4 medium-sized potatoes	salt and pepper, to taste
3–4 eggs	$1/2$ teaspoon turmeric
1 cup brown raisins	olive oil
1 teaspoon flour	

- Cut up potatoes and cook until soft. Peel and grate potatoes.
- Mix in eggs, raisins, flour, salt and pepper, and turmeric.
- Heat olive oil in shallow frying pan. Add potato mixture and spread to form a large pancake. Cook over low heat for 15 minutes. Turn pancake and cook another 15 minutes. Turn the entire Koo-Koo over using a plate on top of the frying pan.
- Serve pie shape pieces as an appetizer or side dish. Serves 6.

Peach-Glazed Sweet Potatoes

Marylan Karsh

4 medium-sized sweet potatoes
    (2 pounds)
1/2 cup peach preserves

1/4 cup brown sugar
1 tablespoon lemon juice
1/4 teaspoon ground cinnamon

- Peel and cut sweet potatoes into 2-inch slices, cook.
- In skillet, combine preserves, brown sugar, lemon juice, and cinnamon. Heat until bubbly (in electric skillet 350°F).
- Add sweet potatoes. Cook and stir over low heat (220°F) until heated through and glazed, 10–15 minutes. Makes 4–6 servings.

Sweet Potato and Carrot "Tzimmes"

Florence Gurwitz

Great for Passover. (Tastes even better the next day.)

6 large sweet potatoes, peeled and
    quartered
1 bunch carrots, scraped and cut into
    1-inch pieces
3/4 cup dried apricots

1 cup orange juice
3/4 cup honey
1/2 teaspoon salt, or more to taste
1/2 teaspoon cinnamon
1/4 cup parve margarine

- Cook potatoes and carrots in boiling salted water to cover until tender but firm.
- Line a shallow 2-quart casserole with heavy duty foil.
- Drain vegetables and place in casserole with apricots. Stir gently.
- Mix orange juice, honey, salt, and cinnamon. Pour over casserole. Dot with margarine.
- Bake, covered with foil, in a preheated 350°F oven for 45 minutes. Serves 8.

Carrot and Sweet Potato Tzimmes

Esther Kamman

Very good!

1 pound carrots, cut in 1 inch pieces
6 sweet potatoes, peeled and quartered
$^1/_2$ cup pitted prunes
1 cup orange juice

$^1/_2$ cup honey
$^1/_2$ teaspoon salt
$^1/_4$ teaspoon cinnamon
$^1/_4$ cup margarine

- Cook carrots and sweet potatoes in boiling salted water until tender but firm.
- Drain and put in casserole with prunes.
- Stir gently.
- Mix orange juice, honey, salt, cinnamon and pour evenly over casserole.
- Dot top with margarine.
- Bake at 350°F for 40 minutes.
- Cover with foil for 30 minutes and bake uncovered for last 10 minutes. Serves 8.

⌂ Meatless Tzimmes

Mrs. Ellis Gordon

2 carrots, peeled and cut into chunks
3 cups cubed sweet potatoes
1$^1/_2$ cups soaked prunes
1 6-ounce can of frozen orange juice

1 can of water
$^1/_2$ teaspoon salt
2 tablespoons brown sugar, optional

- Place carrots and sweet potatoes in saucepan. Add remaining ingredients.
- Cover and allow to simmer until tender, about 1–1$^1/_2$ hours. Serves 4–6.

Squash Gourmet

Ann McDonald Kelly

Delicious — can be made a day ahead.

3 pounds Hubbard squash
2 tablespoons butter
1 cup sour cream

$^1/_2$ cup finely chopped onion
1 teaspoon salt
$^1/_4$ teaspoon pepper

- Cube and peel squash. I cook it in the oven, covered with foil, until soft.
- When cooked, I place it in food processor and add remaining ingredients.
- Turn into casserole and bake at 375°F for 30 minutes. Serves 8.

Yellow Squash Casserole

Evelyn Plotkin

You'll never believe it's squash!

3 pounds yellow squash, cubed	salt and pepper
1 cup Crax cracker crumbs	1 tablespoon sugar
1/2 cup margarine, melted	2 eggs

- Boil cubed squash in salted water for 20 minutes. Drain and mash.
- Add 1/2 cup crumbs, 1/4 cup of melted margarine, salt and pepper, and sugar.
- Beat the eggs and add to cooled mixture. Pour into casserole.
- Sprinkle rest of crumbs and margarine. Bake at 350°F for 1 hour. Serves 8–10.

Beets in Orange Sauce

Marilyn Wolpert

1 No. 2 can beets or 1 bunch of fresh beets	1 tablespoon flour
1 tablespoon butter	1/2 cup orange juice
2 1/2 tablespoons brown sugar	1 tablespoon orange rind

- If using fresh beets, peel and slice or julienne, and boil in water to cover until tender. If using canned beets, slice or julienne, and bring to boil in their own juice. Drain before adding sauce.

Sauce:
- Melt butter over low heat. Add sugar and flour, stirring well. Add orange juice gradually, stirring constantly, until smooth and thick. Stir in orange rind.
- Pour over hot, drained beets. Serves 4.

Corn Fritters

Ruth Medlinsky

1 17-ounce can Family Style corn, drain
    and reserve liquid
1 egg

2½ cups Bisquick
salad oil

- Heat 2–3 inches of oil to 375°F in heavy skillet.
- Pour liquid from corn into medium-sized bowl. Add egg and Bisquick mix. Stir until smooth. Fold in corn.
- Drop tablespoons of batter into hot oil. Fry to golden brown, turning once. Drain on paper towel.
- Serve hot with syrup. Makes 24 fritters.

Sweet-n-Sour Broccoli

Devy Pollock

Great as hors d'oeuvres too.

2 tablespoons white vinegar
2 tablespoons sugar
1 teaspoon salt

2 tablespoons sesame seed oil
sesame seeds, optional
1 pound broccoli florets

- Combine vinegar, sugar, salt and oil in Ziploc bag. Add broccoli and shake to coat well. Refrigerate overnight, shaking occasionally.
- Drain and place in serving dish with toothpicks. Sesame seeds can be added too. Serves many.

Vegetable Pie

Sandra Landau

Much better than pizza, and just as much fun (but you can't eat it with your hands!).

4 medium-sized red potatoes
2 tablespoons olive oil
1 teaspoon salt
1/4 pound Cheddar cheese, 1 cup grated
1/4 pound mozzarella cheese, 1 cup grated
1 medium-sized onion, separated into rings
1/2 large red pepper, cut into strips

8 large mushrooms, sliced
6 ounces frozen spinach, cooked until tender
2 large tomatoes, sliced , or about 8 sundried tomatoes, reconstituted and halved
Parmesan cheese
oregano

- Boil, then mash potatoes, leaving skins on. Mix mashed potatoes with olive oil and salt, then spread and pat down to cover bottom and sides of a jelly roll pan. Bake at 400°F until brown.
- Scatter grated cheese evenly over cooked potato shell.
- Sauté vegetables (except spinach and tomatoes) until limp, in a little olive oil, then spread all the vegetables, including spinach and tomatoes evenly over the shell. Sprinkle with Parmesan cheese and oregano (as much as you like of each).
- Bake 12 minutes at 400°F. Cut into squares for serving. Serves 3–6.

If you don't feel like preparing the potato shell, Italian flatbread, "Boboli," works very well, but makes fewer servings. You can experiment with various topping additions, such as anchovies — whatever your tastes and mood suggest.

Holiday Vegetable Casserole

Marsha Bernstein

For Passover — substitute 1 cup cake meal and 1/4 cup potato starch.

1 cup grated raw yams
1 cup grated apples
1 cup grated carrots
1 cup flour
1 teaspoon baking soda

1 teaspoon cinnamon
1 stick margarine, melted
3/4 cup sugar
dash of salt

- Combine grated yams, apples, and carrots. Add remaining ingredients.
- Put in greased 8-inch square pan. Bake covered in 325°F oven for 30 minutes. Uncover and bake at 350°F for 15 minutes more. Serves 8.

Roasted Ratatouille

Ina Sirk

1 red pepper, cored, seeded, and cut into thick strips

1 yellow pepper, cored, seeded, and cut into strips

3 or 4 small eggplants, stems trimmed, cut into thick strips

2 Belgian endive or small radiccio, cut into quarters

8 small red potatoes, cut into quarters

2 medium-sized Bermuda onions, peeled and cut into 8 wedges

2 each medium-sized summer and zucchini squash, cut into quarters lenghtwise

1/2 pound shitake mushrooms, stems removed

1/2 pound asparagus, tough ends trimmed and discarded

8 large cloves of garlic, peeled and halved

fresh rosemary

1/2–1 cup olive oil

salt and pepper, to taste

- Scatter vegetables in large roasting pan. Scatter rosemary and season with salt and pepper. Drizzle on enough olive oil to coat lightly.
- Preheat over to 500°F. Turn occasionally and bake 30–40 minutes until tender but firm.

Vegetable Casserole with Goat Cheese and Herbs

Lisa Honig

4 tablespoons olive oil

1 medium-sized onion, cut into 1/2-inch slices

1 medium-sized red bell pepper, cut into 1/2-inch strips

1/3 cup finely chopped garlic (16 cloves)

1/2 eggplant, peeled, thinly sliced

2 large zucchinis, thinly sliced

5 tomatoes, thinly sliced

salt and pepper

3 tablespoons chopped fresh herbs (thyme, oregano and parsley)

8 ounces soft goat cheese, crumbled

- Preheat oven to 350°F.
- Heat 2 tablespoons of olive oil in heavy large skillet over meduim heat. Add onion and red bell pepper slices and sauté until tender. Add half of garlic and sauté 1 minute.
- Spread mixture evenly on bottom of 9 x 13-inch glass baking dish. Arrange eggplant slices evenly over pepper and onion mixture then add zucchini and tomato slices. Season lightly with salt and pepper. Sprinkle with herbs and remaining garlic. Drizzle with remaining 2 tablespoons of olive oil.
- Bake until vegetables are tender and begin to brown. Baste with pan juices, about 50 minutes.
- Sprinkle crumbled goat cheese over casserole. Bake until cheese melts, 5 minutes.

Eggplant Pie

Lisa Cotton

Great as an appetizer or a main meal with salad.

¹/4 cup chopped onion
¹/4 cup chopped green bell peppers
¹/4 cup butter or margarine
3 cups eggplant, peeled, sliced, and
    quartered, ¹/4–¹/2-inch thick

4–6 ounces spaghetti sauce, or tomato
    sauce
9-inch pie pastry shell, frozen
1¹/2 cup shredded mozzarella cheese
¹/2 cup grated Parmesan cheese

- Sauté the onion and pepper in margarine until tender. Add the eggplant and tomato sauce. Cook about 15 minutes, stirring occasionally.
- Put half of the eggplant mixture into frozen pie shell. Pour 1 cup mozzarella cheese and all the Parmesan cheese over this. Then spread remaining eggplant mixture on top. Sprinkle with remaining mozarella cheese.
- Bake in a 400°F oven for 30–35 minutes. Slice in wedges. Serves 6.

Spinach Cheese Pie

Sandy Katz

This pie makes its own crust.

3 eggs or egg beaters' equivalent
1 package frozen chopped spinach,
    thawed and squeezed
1 16-ounce carton cottage cheese, small
    curd

3 tablespoons flour
8-ounce package Cheddar cheese,
    shredded
2 tablespoons margarine, melted
salt, to taste, optional

- Beat eggs. Add all ingredients to a bowl and mix well.
- Place in buttered or greased 10-inch pie pan and bake at 350°F for 1 hour or until light brown.
- Cut in slices and serve. Serves 6–8.

Spinach Casserole

Irene Garber

3 10-ounce packages frozen chopped
   spinach
1 8-ounce package cream cheese
1/2 cup butter
1/4 teaspoon salt and pepper
2 6-ounce jars marinated artichoke
   hearts, drained

1/2 cup bread crumbs
1/4 cup coarsely chopped walnuts,
   optional
1/4 cup grated Parmesan cheese

- Defrost spinach. Drain and squeeze dry.
- Melt butter with cream cheese over low heat and add to spinach. Season with salt and pepper.
- Slice artichoke hearts and place in shallow 9 x 12-inch casserole. Cover with spinach mixture. Top with bread crumbs, walnuts, if desired, and cheese.
- Bake in 350°F oven for 30 minutes. Serves 12.

Spinach Squares

Linda Goldstein

4 tablespoons butter
3 eggs
1 cup flour
1 cup milk
1 teaspoon salt

1 teaspoon baking powder
1–2 tablespoons chopped onion
20 ounces cooked spinach, drained and
   chopped, frozen can also be used
1 pound mild Chedder cheese, grated

- Preheat oven to 350°F.
- Melt butter in a 9 x 13-inch baking dish. Remove dish.
- Beat eggs. Add flour, milk, salt, and baking powder. Mix well. Add onion, spinach, and cheese. Spoon into baking dish. Make the ingredients level.
- Bake for 35 minutes. Let cool. Cut into bite-sized squares.
- This dish may be frozen. Defrost and reheat 12–15 minutes at 325°F or until hot.

Koo-Koo Sahbzi

Manouch Darvish

Vegetarian — excellent appetizer or side dish.

1 package parsley
1 bunch scallions
1/2 package spinach
3 eggs

salt and pepper, to taste
1/2 teaspoon turmeric
1 teaspoon flour
olive oil

- Wash and cut up vegetables in half-inch size pieces. Drain well.
- Mix eggs and blend with vegetables. Add salt, pepper, turmeric and flour.
- Cook in shallow fry pan with olive oil. Cook on low heat for 15 minutes on each side. You can flip the entire piece over using a plate on top of the frying pan.
- Serve pie shape pieces as a side dish. Makes 6–8 servings.

Auntie Karen's Black Bean Chili

Judy Freedman Fask

1 1-pound bag black beans
1/2 cup olive oil
2 large green bell peppers, chopped
2 large onions, chopped
1 tablespoon minced garlic
2 tablespoons cumin seeds
1 28-ounce can crushed tomatoes
Mrs. Dash seasoning

2 tablespoons paprika
1 teaspoon cayenne pepper
1 tablespoon sugar
1 tablespoon chicken soup mix
1/2 cup finely chopped Jalepeño pepper, drained
1 tablespoon cilantro

- Soak beans overnight. Drain beans and refill pot with beans and water. Cook until soft. Drain, reserving some water.
- Put olive oil in pot. Sauté peppers and onions. Add garlic and cumin seeds and sauté lightly.
- Add black beans and tomatoes. Add remaining ingredients. Let simmer, stirring occasionally.
- This can also be cooked in a crockpot. Serves 6–8.

Baked Beans

Hazel Benjamin

1 package white pea or navy beans
1/2 pound flanken or short ribs
1 medium-sized onion, peeled

Sauce:
1/2 cup molasses
1/4 cup brown sugar
1 teaspoon dry mustard
1/2 teaspoon pepper
1 teaspoon salt
1 cup water or tomato juice

- Put beans in large pot with water to cover. Bring to a boil and cook 2 minutes. Remove from heat and let stand 1 hour to soak.
- Drain beans. Place beans in bean pot with meat. Place onion in center of beans.
- Mix ingredients for sauce in a small bowl. Pour molasses mixture over beans and meat mixture just to cover. Place a "fat" piece of meat on top. Cover.
- Bake in a 300°F oven 5–6 hours, until brown and soft. If liquid is absorbed during baking add more water.

Stir-Fry Tofu

Eileen Levenson

1 clove garlic, minced
2 tablespoons freshly grated ginger
2 tablespoons peanut oil
1 green pepper, cut into strips
1 red pepper, cut into strips

2 stalks celery, diced
1 container extra firm tofu, cut into
    1-inch pieces
2 tablespoons lite soy sauce
1 teaspoon sesame oil

- Sauté in wok garlic and ginger 2–3 minutes in peanut oil. Add pepper slices and celery.
- Add pieces of tofu with lite soy sauce and sesame oil until tofu is heated thoroughly.
- Serve over rice. Serves 6.

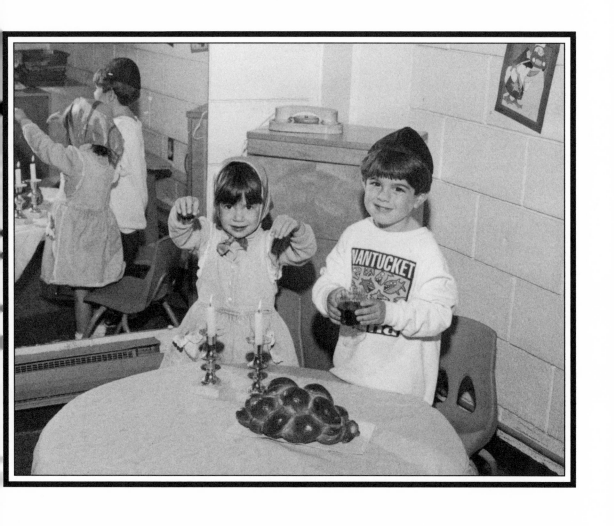

Breads, Muffins, and Coffee Cakes

Rebecca's Challah

Sophia H. Sheftel

Two large braided loaves.

2 packages dry yeast
$\frac{1}{2}$ cup sugar, plus 2 teaspoons
8 cups flour, approximately
$2\frac{1}{4}$ cups warm water 105°F–115°F
$\frac{1}{2}$ cup vegetable oil
2 tablespoons kosher salt, or 1
    tablespoon regular table salt

2 eggs, plus 1 egg white
1 egg yolk, plus 1 tablespoon water, for
    glazing
1 tablespoon poppy seeds for top,
    optional
1 baking sheet or 2 loaf pans, greased

Preparation:

- In a tall glass or 2-cup measuring cup put in yeast, 2 teaspoons sugar, 2 tablespoons flour, and $\frac{3}{4}$ cup warm water. Set aside until the liquid reaches the lip of the glass, proofing.
- In a large bowl, measure 4 cups flour. Add $1\frac{1}{2}$ cups warm water, $\frac{1}{2}$ cup oil, $\frac{1}{2}$ cup sugar, salt, 2 eggs and 1 egg white, and mix together thoroughly. When yeast is ready (about 10–15 minutes), add it to batter. Mix, and gradually add 3 more cups of flour. The dough will be rough, but will clean the sides of the bowl. If the dough continues to stick, add several sprinkles of flour.

Kneading: (8 minutes)

- Turn the dough onto a lightly floured surface. Knead with rhythmic motion 1-2-3 or push and turn and fold until smooth and elastic. Sprinkle with flour if dough continues to become sticky.

First Rising: ($1\frac{1}{2}$–2 hours)

- Place dough in mixing bowl. Grease top surface, cover bowl tightly with plastic wrap, and move to warm place (80–85°F) to rise. You can test if it has risen by poking a finger in it—the dent will remain.

Second Rising: ($1\frac{1}{2}$ hours)

- Punch down dough. If it is sticky, add $\frac{1}{2}$ cup flour, kneading to produce a soft dough. The kneading can be done right in the bowl. Knead only 2 minutes. Grease again and replace plastic wrap. Let rise until doubled in volume.

Shaping: (18 minutes)

- Punch down. Knead to press out bubbles. Divide the dough into 2 equal parts—divide each part into 3 pieces. Place under wax paper or towel and let rest for 5 minutes to relax dough. Roll each piece under the palms into a 10-inch roll. Place 3 rolls side by side and braid from center. Repeat with second piece. Set on baking sheet or in loaf pan.

Third Rising: (1 hour)
- Cover braids with wax paper. Set them in a warm place and allow to rise until double in bulk.

Baking: (350°F for 45–55 minutes for large challah; 35–40 minutes for medium-sized challah; 30–35 minutes for small challah)
- Preheat oven to 350°F. Combine the remaining egg yolk with the 1 tablespoon water. Brush each loaf and sprinkle a little sugar or poppy seeds if desired. Bake in oven until loaves are a lovely golden yellow. If they brown too quickly, cover with a tent of aluminum foil. Use a wooden toothpick to test. Insert it between the braids near the center of the loaf. If it comes out clean and dry, the loaf is done or until bottom sounds hollow when tapped.

Final Step:
- Remove challah from the oven. Use a spatula under the loaves to lift out. Cool on metal rack.

Challah

Gina Schultz

Very easy and tastes wonderful!

3 cups flour
3 tablespoons soft butter, divided into 4
    pieces
2 tablespoons sugar
1 teaspoon salt

1 package dry yeast
1/4 cup lukewarm water
1 egg, slightly beaten
1/2–3/4 cup lukewarm water

- In a food processor, process first 4 ingredients for 5 minutes. Blend yeast with water until dissolved–10 minutes.
- With processor running, add yeast mixture, then egg. In a slow stream add just enough water to form a loose ball. Stop processor.
- Form dough onto a floured surface and knead 9 or 10 times. Shape into ball and place in greased bowl. Cover, let rise until doubled.
- Punch down and turn onto floured surface. Form into ball and cover with bowl. Let dough rest for 15 minutes. Shape dough into loaf and let rise again.
- Brush with egg wash (1 egg yolk mixed with 1–2 tablespoons water). Bake at 375°F about 35 minutes.

Challah for Bread Machine

Marilyn Wolpert

Left-overs make great French toast!

2 1/2 cups white flour
1 teaspoon salt
2 tablespoons margarine or oil
1 tablespoon sugar

1 egg
5 1/2 ounces water
1 3/4 teaspoons yeast

- Place all the ingredients in the bread machine according to the instructions for your machine.
- Make on dough setting. Then let dough rest for 20–30 minutes in greased bowl.
- With string, cut into 3 equal sections and roll each section into a rope. Let rest 10 minutes.
- Braid and place into a small, greased loaf pan. Cover and let rise in a warm place for 45 minutes, or until doubled. Brush with beaten egg, sprinkle with poppy seeds. Bake at 400°F for approximately 30–45 minutes, or until done.

Garlic Bread

Jenique Radin

Bread Machine

1 cup plus 3 tablespoon tepid water
3 cups plus 2 tablespoons bread flour
1 cup plus $^1/_2$ tablespoon sugar
$^3/_4$ teaspoon salt
$^3/_4$ tablespoon butter, sliced into tiny pieces

1 tablespoon Parmesan cheese, finely grated
$1^1/_2$ teaspoons Italian seasoning
$1^1/_2$ teaspoons garlic powder
2 teaspoons active dry yeast
3 rounded teaspoons gluten*

- Place ingredients in the order your machine's manufacturer suggests. It is important to use exact measurements with all bread machine types. The recipe works well on the regular or rapid bake cycle.
- Serve warm for best flavor.

*Gluten can purchased in most health food stores. It is suggested for this recipe due to the cheese. Gluten allows for better bread structure.

Easy French Bread

Laura Glazier

For large bread machine.

$1^1/_2$ cups water
$3^1/_4$ cups white flour (King Arthur preferred)
$1^1/_2$ tablespoons sugar

$1^1/_2$ teaspoons salt
3 teaspoons gluten (can be bought in health food store).
3 teaspoons yeast

- Add ingredients in the order specified for your bread machine.
- Add yeast last and bake on regular cycle.

Broccoli Corn Bread

Hannah Aronovitz

This can be made for low fat diets.

1 10-ounce package frozen, chopped broccoli, thawed
1 8½-ounce package cornbread mix
3 eggs, (can use egg substitute)
1 medium-sized onion, chopped

1 cup Cheddar cheese, shredded (you can substitute low-fat cheese)
½ cup margarine or canola oil
½ teaspoon salt
¼–½ teaspoon garlic powder
¼ teaspoon ground red pepper

- Press broccoli between paper towels to remove excess water.
- Combine remaining ingredients and mix well.
- Stir in broccoli and spoon into greased 8-inch square pan.
- Bake at 375°F for 25–30 minutes until golden brown. Cool slightly and cut into 2-inch squares. Can be frozen and reheated—tastes best served warm. Makes 16 2-inch squares.

Nanny Fanny's "Babki"

Laura Glazier

It's the best - even though it takes all day!

2 packages yeast
1 cup sugar, plus 1 teaspoon
¾ cup warm milk
4 eggs, beaten
1 teaspoon salt
1 cup sour cream
¼ pound butter, softened
7 cups flour

Topping and Filling:
cinnamon
brown sugar
sugar
chopped walnuts
1 stick butter

- Mix 2 yeast packages with 1 teaspoon of sugar and ¾ cup warm milk. Set aside and let yeast rise, about 10 minutes.
- Mix eggs, 1 cup sugar, salt, sour cream together and then add butter and yeast mixture.Gradually add flour one cup at a time and knead well.
- Place mixture in an oiled dish and cover with waxed paper and damp cloth until doubles in size.
- Punch down and knead again Roll like a jelly roll and sprinkle cinnamon, brown sugar, sugar, walnuts and rub butter on it.
- Butter a large angel food cake pan and put walnuts, brown sugar and white sugar on bottom. Put jelly roll mixture around pan and let rise for couple of hours.
- Bake 350°F oven for 50 minutes.

"Bobke"

Ruth Lonstein

2 sticks butter or margarine	**Filling:**
1/2 cup sugar	3/4 cup sugar
3 large eggs	2 teaspoons cinnamon
3/4 cup warm milk	1 cup chopped nuts
1/2 cup sour cream	1 cup raisins
1 teaspoon vanilla	
2 packages active dry yeast	
4 1/2 cups flour	
1 teaspoon salt	

- Preheat oven to 350°F.
- Cream butter or margarine with sugar. Add eggs one at a time, beating well after each.
- Combine milk, sour cream, and vanilla, and add to creamed mixture. Beat well.
- Add yeast, and mix thoroughly.
- Combine 4 1/2 cups flour with salt and add 1/2 this mixture to above, beating at medium speed for 2 minutes. Stir in remaining flour by hand, forming a soft dough. Place in greased bowl, cover loosely, refrigerate overnight.
- Roll out on floured surface into 25-inch square. Mix ingredients for filling and spread on dough. Roll up jelly roll fashion. Cut roll into 6 sections and place in greased tube pan, standing each section cut side up, side by side.
- Cover with wax paper and let rise in warm place 1 hour. Bake at 350°F 45 minutes. Serves 18.

Yeast Coffee Cake

Gloria Thomashow

2 packages dry granulated yeast
½ cup very warm water
pinch sugar
3 large eggs
1 cup milk
2 sticks margarine
4 cups all-purpose flour

¼ cup granulated sugar
1 teaspoon salt

Filling:
1 cup sugar
1 tablespoon cinnamon, or more
raisins

- 10-inch tube pan, or angel pan that separates, greased.
- Dissolve yeast in very warm water with sugar. Set aside 10 minutes.
- Beat eggs by hand and set aside.
- Heat milk and margarine together until very warm and set aside. Margarine doesn't have to be completely melted.
- Mix together flour, sugar, salt. Add warm milk mixture, mix. Add beaten eggs, mix. Add yeast mixture and mix all together (loose mixture). Cover with plastic wrap and refrigerate overnight.
- Next day knead dough on floured board using more flour until smooth. Roll out into oblong shape, about 10-inch x 15-inches.
- Spread about 2 tablespoons soft margarine on dough. Sprinkle with raisins and sugar. Roll up tightly and cut into 8 or 9 parts.
- Place each part cut side up, into greased pan. Let rise covered about 1–1½ hours until dough reaches almost to top of pan.
- Bake in 350°F oven 45–50 minutes. Remove from oven, loosen sides—remove inner part only. Place on rack. Carefully loosen bottom but do not remove until cool. Then loosen bottom again. Invert or lift Bobke out carefully.

Criss-Cross Cheese Filled Coffee Cake

Jane Goldberg

Takes time but the effort is worthwhile.

Dough:
1/2 pound butter
1/4 cup milk
3 packages yeast
pinch of sugar
5 tablespoons water
5 cups flour
3/4 cup sugar
1 teaspoon salt
3 eggs and 1 egg yolk (save white for top)
1/2 pint sour cream

sugar for topping
slivered almonds, optional

Cheese Mixture:
2 pounds cream cheese
3/4 cup sugar
1 tablespoon orange juice
2 teaspoons freshly grated orange rind

Dough:

- Melt butter in milk. Let cool. Set aside.
- Dissolve yeast and sugar in water. Let stand until mixture bubbles.
- Place flour, 3/4 cup sugar, and salt in mixing bowl. Add eggs, yolk, and sour cream to flour mixture. Add cooled butter mixture to flour mixture and mix by electric mixer or dough hook until smooth texture, roll into soft ball. Refrigerate overnight (rising occurs in refrigerator.)
- Punch dough down. Cut chilled dough into 8 pieces. Roll out each piece to rectangle.

Cheese Mixture:
- Place all ingredients in bowl and beat together.
- Place cheese mixture down center of rectangle. Slice sides at right angle. Fold over so they will criss-cross and overlap with other side. Seal ends. Place on cookie sheet and let rise 1 hour.
- Brush with egg white and sprinkle with sugar, and slivered almonds if desired.
- Bake at 350°F for 30–40 minutes, or until brown. Makes 8 cakes in all.

Milchika

Sophie H. Sheftel

Anna Zitowitz's recipe. Excellent.

1 yeast cake (bakery type 2-ounce or
    2 packages dry yeast).
1/2 cup lukewarm water
9 cups flour, plus 1–1 1/2 cups more,
    if needed
1 cup sugar
2 cups milk
1/2 pound salted butter

2 teaspoons kosher salt or 1 teaspoon
    table salt
4 eggs, save some of yolk for brushing
1 cup sour cream
cinnamon and sugar
raisins
nuts

- Dissolve yeast in 1/2 cup lukewarm water together with 1 tablespoon flour and 1 tablespoon sugar taken from the allotted amount. Let rise to the top of a 2 cup measuring cup.
- While this is rising, scald milk, add butter, and stir until melted; then add salt, sugar, beaten eggs, sour cream and when cool enough, add the yeast mixture.
- To this add 9 cups of flour, 2 cups at a time and beat. If dough is too sticky, add 1-1 1/2 cups more of the flour for easy handling. This is a soft dough.
- Knead 8–10 minutes. Put in a warm bowl, cover with a towel, and place in a draft-free area. Let rise 1 1/2–2 hours. Test by poking with finger and if hole remains intact, punch down and allow to rise a second time for 1 more hour or until double in bulk. Do not rush rising.
- Form into buns, crescents or any desirable form, or make into a babke or roll in jelly roll fashion. Fill buns or roll with cinnamon, sugar, raisins and nuts, or any filling you desire. Let rise for 30–60 minutes.
- Brush with egg yolk to which 1 teaspoon of water has been added. Sprinkle top with sugar and cinnamon mixture. For pecan rolls use maple syrup with brown sugar and butter.

Baking Time:
- Buns, crescents and rolls, 400°F for 7 minutes, lower to 350°F for 10–15 minutes. Babke or Jelly roll: 400°F for 10 minutes, lower to 350°F for 15–20 minutes.
- In both cases, if the milchika is browning too quickly, make a tent of aluminum foil and put lightly over top and allow to continue baking for the allotted time.

Milchika Bulkies

Helen Yaffee

2 packages active dry yeast
$^1/_2$ cup warm water, 105–115°F
$^1/_3$ cup plus $^1/_2$ teaspoon granulated sugar
4–5 cups all-purpose flour
1 teaspoon salt
1 cup milk, scalded and cooled to 110°F
$^1/_3$ cup oil
2 eggs, at room temperature

Filling:
$^1/_2$ cup butter or margarine, softened
1 cup firmly packed brown sugar
$^1/_2$ cup granulated sugar
2 tablespoons cinnamon
$^1/_2$ cup golden raisins, optional

Icing:
1 cup confectioners' sugar, sifted
2 –3 tablespoons warm milk
1 teaspoon vanilla

- Dissolve yeast in water with $^1/_2$ teaspoon granulated sugar. Let stand 5 minutes.
- In mixing bowl combine 3 cups flour, remaining $^1/_3$ cup granulated sugar, and salt. At low speed, gradually beat in milk, oil, eggs, and yeast mixture. Beat until well blended. Beat in additional flour until dough pulls away from sides of bowl.
- On floured surface, knead dough until smooth and elastic, about 5 minutes. Place in a greased bowl, turning to grease top. Cover and let rise until doubled in bulk, about 1 hour.

Filling:
- In mixer bowl, beat all ingredients. Set aside.
- Preheat oven to 350°F. Grease 3 9-inch round pans.
- On floured board roll dough to 18-inch x10-inch rectangle. Spread with filling. Roll tightly from long side. Cut into 18 slices.
- Place 1 roll in center of each pan. Arrange remaining rolls (5) in a circle around center roll. Cover and let rise until doubled in bulk, 30–40 minutes.
- Bake 25–30 minutes until golden brown. Cool in pans 10 minutes, invert onto wire rack, invert again to cool.

Icing:
- In medium-sized bowl, whisk all ingredients until smooth. Drizzle over cooled rolls.

Miniature Coffee Rolls

Ruth Lonstein

1/2 pound shortening (1/4 pound butter, 1/4 pound margarine)
2 tablespoons sugar
pinch salt
2 beaten eggs
2 cups flour

1 yeast cake
1/4 cup warm water
mixture of cinnamon and sugar for topping
raspberry jelly
raisins and nuts

- Preheat oven to 350°F.
- Melt shortening. Add sugar, salt, eggs, flour, and yeast cake which has been dissolved in water. Cover dough and refrigerate overnight.
- Divide into 4 balls and roll out as for jelly roll in a mixture of cinnamon and sugar. Spread with jelly and mixture of raisins and nuts. Roll and slice in 1 1/2-inch slices. Place in greased miniature muffin tins.
- Bake at 350°F 20 minutes.

Coffee Rolls

Ruth Jacobs

8 ounces butter
1 pint sour cream
1 2-ounce yeast cake
5 eggs
7 cups flour
3/4 cup sugar

Filling:
melted butter
sugar
cinnamon
raisins

- Melt butter and remove from heat. Add sour cream, crumble in yeast, and allow to dissolve. Add eggs, one at a time, beating after each addition.
- Mix dry ingredients in a large mixing bowl, and make well in center. Pour liquid mixture into well and mix thoroughly. Add more flour if necessary.
- Place in refrigerator for a few hours or overnight.
- Divide dough into 4 parts, and roll out on floured board into rectangles. Brush with melted butter and sprinkle with filling. Roll up as jelly roll and cut into 1 1/2-inch or 2-inch slices. Place on greased pan and cover with towel to rise, until double in size.
- Bake at 375°F for 30 minutes, or until brown.

⌂ Baking Powder Coffee Buns

Mrs. William Aisenberg

2 cups flour
3 teaspoons baking powder
1/4 cup sugar
1/2 teaspoon salt
1/4 pound butter
1 egg

3/4 cup milk
1/2 cup sugar
1 teaspoon cinnamon
1/2 cup chopped nuts
1/4 cup yellow raisins

- Sift flour, baking powder, sugar, and salt. Cut in 1/8 pound butter with pastry blender.
- Beat egg, put in cup, and add milk. Add egg and milk to dry ingredients and mix.
- Turn out on floured board and with light hand roll dough into a rectangle, about 3/8-inch thick. Melt remainder of butter, spread on rectangle, sprinkle with sugar, cinnamon, chopped nuts, and yellow raisins. Roll as for jelly roll, cut into 1-inch slices, and place in greased muffin tins.
- Bake at 375–400°F until browned, from 15–20 minutes. Serves 12.

Gram's Hot Rolls

Emily R. Gerber

In memory of Bessie J. Schorr.

1 package hot roll mix
3 eggs, separated

Filling:
3 egg whites
1/2 cup sugar
cinnamon, to taste
raisins (optional)

- Mix 1 package of hot roll mix according to package directions. Set dough aside to rise for 1/2 hour.
- Beat 3 egg whites to form stiff peaks. Mix in 1/2 cup sugar. Roll out dough in long oblong shape.
- Spread egg white mixture over dough. Sprinkle cinnamon to taste. Adding raisins is optional.
- Roll dough the long way.
- Cut in 1/2-inch slices.
- Place slices cut side down into greased cupcake pans.
- Bake in oven 25 minutes at 350°F. Serves 18.

Blueberry Muffins

Lillian Glixman

6 tablespoons butter
1 1/4 cups sugar
2 large eggs
2 cups flour, unsifted
1/2 teaspoon salt

2 teaspoons baking powder
1/2 cup milk
1 pint blueberries
2 teaspoons sugar

- Preheat oven to 375°F.
- Cream butter and sugar very well. Add eggs one at a time and beat well.
- Sift flour, salt, and baking powder, and add to egg mixture alternating with milk.
- Remove 1/2 cup of berries and crush with a fork and add to batter by hand.
- Dry remaining berries thoroughly and fold into batter.
- Grease muffin tins well and place paper cups in each. Fill almost full. Sprinkle with sugar.
- Bake in 375°F oven 30 minutes or until brown. Cool 30 minutes. Serves 16.

Moist Bran Muffins

Lynn Freedman

1 cup milk
2 cups bran—do not use cereal
1/2 cup oil
3/4 cup honey
1 teaspoon baking soda, dissolved in 1 tablespoon water

2 teaspoons baking powder
1 cup flour
3/4 cup raisins, dates or cut-up prunes
1/2 teaspoon vanilla

- Soak bran in milk for 5 minutes.
- Add the rest of the ingredients in the order listed, mixing well. Do not overbeat.
- Spray muffin tins with Pam or use muffin papers, and fill to within 1/2-inch of the top.
- Bake in 350°F oven for 18–20 minutes. Makes 18 muffins.

Marvelous Muffins

Joy Goodwin

Very good! "Carrot Walnut Muffins"

1 1/2 cups flour
1/2 cup sugar
2 teaspoons baking powder
1/4 teaspoon salt
1/2 teaspoon cinnamon
1/2 teaspoon nutmeg

1/2 teaspoon ginger
1 cup chopped walnuts, optional
1/4 cup margarine or butter, softened
1/2 cup milk
1 egg
1/2 cup finely grated carrots

- Sift together first 7 ingredients. Toss walnuts into dry mixture.
- Cut in margarine (or butter). Add milk, egg, and grated carrot. Mix lightly—do not over mix. Pour into greased muffin tins until almost full.
- Bake in preheated 400°F oven for 15–20 minutes. Makes about 12.

Mock Doughnuts

Bev Hurwitz

1/3 cup shortening
1/2 cup sugar
1 egg
1 1/2 cups sifted flour
1 1/2 teaspoons baking powder

1/2 teaspoon salt
1/4 teaspoon nutmeg
1/2 cup milk
melted margarine
cinnamon and sugar

- Mix shortening, sugar, and egg thoroughly.
- Mix dry ingredients and add to above mixture alternately with milk.
- Fill small greased muffin tins 2/3 full.
- Bake at 350°F for 20–25 minutes.
- Dip in melted margarine, then a mixture of sugar and cinnamon. Makes 2 dozen.

Raisin Scones

Dorothy Kaplan

1³/₄ cups flour
¹/₃ cup sugar
1 teaspoon baking powder
¹/₂ teaspoon baking soda

²/₃ cup buttermilk
¹/₃ cup melted butter
¹/₃ cup raisins

- Combine dry ingredients.
- Add the remaining ingredients mixing just to combine.
- Grease a 10-inch x 15-inch baking sheet.
- Spoon dough into 6–8 equal mounds.
- Bake 18–20 minutes in a 400°F oven.

Zucchini Bread

Arlene Frem

3 eggs
2 cups sugar
1 cup vegetable oil
2 cups zucchini, peeled and grated
2 teaspoons vanilla
3 cups flour

1 teaspoon salt
1 teaspoon baking soda
¹/₄ teaspoon baking powder
2 teaspoons cinnamon
1 cup walnuts, chopped

- Beat eggs until light and foamy.
- Add sugar, oil, zucchini, and vanilla. Mix lightly, but well.
- Combine flour, salt, soda, baking powder, and add to mixture. Blend well and add cinnamon and nuts.
- Bake at 350°F in two 9 x 5-inch loaf pans, well greased, for 45 minutes. Cool on rack.

Poppy Seed Bread

Thelma Lockwood

Quick, easy, and out of the ordinary.

½ ounce poppy seeds, or 2 tablespoons
1 cup milk
1½ cups sugar
2 cups flour
2¼ teaspoons baking powder
¼ teaspoon salt

½ cup butter or margarine
½ teaspoon vanilla
2 eggs, slightly beaten
1 teaspoon sugar, optional
1 teaspoon cinnamon, optional

- Soak poppy seeds in milk for 1 hour.
- Sift sugar, flour, baking powder, and salt together.
- Cut in butter until crumbly. Add poppy seed mixture and mix for 2 minutes. Add vanilla and eggs and mix for 2 additional minutes. Pour into greased loaf pan. Add cinnamon and sugar to the top before placing in oven.
- Bake at 350°F for 1 hour.

Apricot Date Loaf

Edith Ravelson

Excellent sliced plain or spread with cream cheese.

3 eggs
1 teaspoon vanilla
¾ cup flour
¼ teaspoon baking soda
¼ teaspoon baking powder

dash salt
¾ cup brown sugar
2 cups whole dates
1 cup whole dried apricots
2 cups whole walnuts

- Preheat oven to 325°F.
- Beat eggs till foamy. Add vanilla.
- In another bowl mix together flour, baking soda, baking powder, salt, and brown sugar. Add dates, apricots, and walnuts. Mix well.
- Add eggs and vanilla. Press mixture into a greased and floured loaf pan.
- Bake 1 hour.

Date and Nut Bread

Mrs. Samuel Silverman

1 cup pitted dates, finely cut
1 teaspoon baking soda
1 cup boiling water
2 tablespoons butter
1 cup sugar

1 teaspoon vanilla
1 egg
1 1/2 cups flour
pinch of salt
1/2–1 cup chopped nuts, optional

- Combine dates, soda, and boiling water. Let stand.
- Cream butter, sugar, vanilla, and egg. Mix well.
- Sift flour with salt and add alternately with date mixture.
- Add nuts and blend.
- Bake in greased and floured loaf pan at 350°F oven for 1 hour.

Walnut Orange Nut Loaf

3 cups sifted all-purpose flour
4 teaspoons baking powder
1 teaspoon salt
1 cup chopped nuts, optional
1 egg, beaten

1 cup milk
2 tablespoons melted shortening
1/4 cup brown sugar
1/2 cup orange marmalade or apricot jam

- Sift flour, baking powder, and salt into mixing bowl. Add nuts.
- Mix egg with remaining ingredients. Add to flour and beat well.
- Pour into greased 9x5x3-inch pan. Let stand 20 minutes.
- Bake in moderate oven at 350°F for 65–70 minutes. Cool on rack.

Fruit Cake

Dorothy Kaplan

3/4 cup brown sugar
3/4 cup flour
2 cups chopped dates
2 cups diced apricots

2 cups broken walnuts
3 eggs
1 teaspoon vanilla

- Mix sugar and flour. Add dates, apricots, and walnuts.
- Beat eggs with vanilla and add to above mixture.
- Pour into greased and floured 13 x 3-inch bread pan.
- Bake in a 350°F oven for about 50 minutes.

Cranberry Bread

Irene Garber

2 cups flour
1 cup sugar
1/2 teaspoon baking powder
1/2 teaspoon baking soda
1/2 teaspoon salt
1 egg

3/4 cup orange juice
2 tablespoons melted butter
1 1/2 cups cranberries—coarsely chop
    about half, and leave half whole
1/2 cup nuts, coarsely chopped

- Mix all ingredients through butter until blended.
- Add cranberries and nuts.
- Bake in greased and floured loaf pan in 350°F oven for 1 hour.

Black Bottom Banana Bread

Mary Pulda

I like it even better than my original Banana Bread.

4 small ripe bananas
1 stick unsalted butter
2/3 cup sugar
3 large eggs
1/4 cup milk

1 cup cake flour
1/2 teaspoon baking powder
1 teaspoon baking soda
1/4 teaspoon salt
1 1/4 cups chocolate chips

- Place rack in center of oven and heat to 350°F. Grease a loaf pan and dust with flour. .
- Mash bananas in large mixing bowl.
- In another bowl cream butter and sugar. Add eggs and mix well. Add milk. Transfer to bowl with bananas.
- Add dry ingredients and chocolate chips with wooden spoon. Pour into loaf pan.
- Bake 55–60 minutes. Rest on rack for 10 minutes. Remove from pan and cool completely on rack. Wrap in foil and allow to rest at room temperature. Serves 8.

Ina's Banana Bread

Ina Sirk

2 ripe bananas, mashed
2 eggs, slightly beaten
1 3/4 cups flour, sifted
1 1/2 cups sugar
1/2 cup vegetable oil

1/4 cup plus 1 tablespoon buttermilk
1 teaspoon baking soda
1 teaspoon vanilla
1/2 teaspoon salt

- Preheat oven to 325°F. Grease and flour 9 x 5-inch loaf pan.
- Mix all ingredients in large bowl by hand. Pour into prepared pan and bake 1 hour and 15 minutes.

Banana Bran Bread

Ethel Chaifetz

1½ cups sifted all-purpose flour
2 teaspoons baking powder
½ teaspoon baking soda
½ teaspoon salt
¼ cup margarine, softened
½ cup sugar

1 large egg
1 teaspoon vanilla
4 small fully ripened bananas, 1½ cups
1 cup whole bran cereal
¼ cup chopped walnuts

- Preheat oven to 350°F.
- Thoroughly grease a 9 x 5 x 3-inch loaf pan and set aside.
- Sift dry ingredients together and set aside.
- In a large bowl, at high speed, beat margarine, sugar, egg, and vanilla until smooth, and fluffy and thoroughly combined.
- Peel bananas and mash until lumps are broken up. Add to the sugar mixture and stir until well blended.
- Add flour mixture, bran cereal, and nuts, beating until just smooth. Turn batter into prepared loaf pan.
- Place pan on center rack in oven and bake for 60 minutes until cake tester comes out clean. If necessary, bake a few minutes longer.
- Remove from pan to a wire rack and let stand until completely cooled. Serves 12.

Betty's Banana Bread

Nancy Shulman

Can be frozen or kept well wrapped in refrigerator for 1 week.

1 cup sugar
⅓ cup margarine, softened
2 extra-large eggs
1½ cups ripe bananas, mashed (3–4 bananas)
⅓ cup water

1⅔ cups flour
1 teaspoon baking soda
½ teaspoon salt
¼ teaspoon baking powder
½–1 cup chopped walnuts

- Preheat oven to 350°F. Grease bottom only of loaf pan, 8½-inch or 9 x 5-inch.
- Mix sugar and margarine together in mixer. Stir in eggs until blended. Add bananas and water, and beat 30 seconds.
- Stir in rest of ingredients, except nuts, until just moistened. Stir in nuts.
- Pour into pan. Bake until toothpick inserted in center comes out clean.
- Baking time: 8-inch pan 1¼ hours, 9-inch pan 55–60 minutes.
- Cool 5 minutes, loosen sides, remove from pan and cool completely on rack. Serves 8–10.

Banana Bread

Sarah Joseph Pulda

1/2 cup butter or margarine
1 cup sugar
2 eggs, beaten
4 bananas, mashed

1 3/4 cups flour
1/2 teaspoon salt
1 teaspoon baking soda
1 cup chopped walnuts

- Preheat oven to 375°F.
- Cream shortening and sugar together. Add beaten eggs and mashed bananas.
- Sift together flour, salt, and baking soda. Add to other mixture. Stir in chopped nuts.
- Grease and flour pan. Pour in batter and bake 45 minutes.

Banana Nut Cake

Mrs. Louis Pemstein

2 cups sifted flour
1/2 teaspoon baking powder
3/4 teaspoon baking soda
1/4 teaspoon salt
1/4 teaspoon nutmeg
1/4 teaspoon cinnamon
1/2 cup butter or shortening
1 1/2 cups sugar

2 eggs
1 teaspoon vanilla
1 1/4 cups mashed bananas
    (2 large or 4 small)
1/4 cup buttermilk
1 cup ground pecans or walnuts

- Sift together flour and all dry ingredients.
- Cream butter until soft, gradually add sugar, beating until light and fluffy. Beat in eggs 1 at a time. Stir in vanilla and mashed bananas.
- Add flour mixture alternately with buttermilk, beating until smooth after each addition. Fold in nuts.
- Bake in greased 9-inch tube pan at 325°F for 45–55 minutes. Cool.

Blueberry Poppy Seed Cake

Eileen Levenson

Cake:
1/2 cup sugar
1 stick margarine, softened
2 tablespoons grated lemon rind
1 egg
1 1/2 cups flour
3 tablespoons poppy seeds
1/2 teaspoon baking soda
1 8-ounce container of vanilla yogurt

Filling:
2 cups fresh or frozen blueberries
1/3 cup granulated sugar
2 teaspoons flour

Glaze:
1/3 cup confectioners sugar
1–2 teaspoons milk

- Beat sugar and margarine until light and fluffy. Add grated lemon rind and egg. Beat 2–3 minutes.
- Combine flour, poppy seeds, and baking soda. Add dry ingredients to butter mixture alternately with container of yogurt.
- Spread batter over bottom and up 1-inch of side of greased and floured 9-inch or 10-inch spring form pan making sure batter is 1/4-inch thick on sides of pan.
- If blueberries are frozen, thaw and drain on paper towel. Combine blueberries, flour, and sugar in bowl. Spoon filling over batter.
- Bake at 350°F for 45–55 minutes.
- Combine confectioners sugar and milk until glaze is drizzling consistency. Glaze on cool cake. Serves 8–10.

Blueberry Cake

Roseane Levine

Delicious!

2 cups blueberries
3/4 cup sugar
3 teaspoons butter
1 1/2 cups flour
1 teaspoon baking powder
1/4 teaspoon salt
3/4 cup milk

Topping:
1/3 cup sugar
1 teaspoon cinnamon
1 tablespoon cornstarch
1 cup boiling water

- Grease and flour an 8 x 12-inch glass pan and put blueberries on bottom.
- Cream sugar and butter.
- Sift dry ingredients.
- Add milk alternately with dry ingredients.
- Spread batter over blueberries.

Topping:
- Combine topping ingredients and sprinkle over cake.
- Pour boiling water over all.
- Bake for 1 hour at 350°F or 45 minutes in a glass pan.

Blueberry Coffee Cake

Ruth Ravelson

Delicious!

Cake Mixture:
1/4 cup margarine
1 cup sugar
1 cup sour cream
2 eggs
2 cups sifted flour
1 teaspoon baking soda
1 teaspoon vanilla

1 dash salt
2 1/2 cups blueberries
1/2 cup chopped nuts

Topping:
1/4 cup sugar
1 teaspoon cinnamon

Cake Batter:
- Cream margarine and sugar well. Add sour cream and mix well.
- Add eggs, flour, baking soda, vanilla, and salt. Beat well.

Topping:
- Combine 1/4 cup sugar and cinnamon.
- Pour 1/2 of batter into a greased tube pan. Spread 1 1/4 cups blueberries on batter. Sprinkle 1/2 of topping on blueberries.
- Add remaining batter and layer blueberries and topping. Sprinkle with nuts.
- Bake at 350°F for 50 minutes or until done. Serves 10.

Blueberry Tea Cake

Sue Seder

Freezes well!

2 cups sifted flour
2 teaspoons baking powder
1/2 teaspoon salt
1/4 cup butter
3/4 cup sugar
1 egg
1/2 cup whole milk
2 cups blueberries

Topping:
1/4 cup sugar
1/4 cup flour
1/2 teaspoon cinnamon
1/4 cup butter

- Sift together flour, baking powder, and salt.
- Cream butter and gradually beat in sugar. Add egg and milk and beat until smooth.
- Add dry ingredients and fold in blueberries.
- Spread in 9-inch square pan and sprinkle with topping.

Topping:
- Mix together all ingredients to a crumbly texture.
- Bake at 375°F for 40–45 minutes.

Rich Coffee Cake

Marjorie Bernstein

Best coffee cake ever!

Topping:
1/2 cup brown sugar
1 teaspoon cinnamon
2 tablespoons flour
1/2 cup chopped walnuts
1 cup chocolate chips

Cake:
1/4 pound butter
1 cup granulated sugar
1 teaspoon vanilla
2 eggs
2 cups cake flour
1 scant teaspoon baking soda
1 teaspoon baking powder
1 pinch salt
1 cup sour cream

Topping:
Mix the brown sugar, cinammon, walnuts, chocolate chips, and flour.

Cake:
- Cream butter. Add granulated sugar, vanilla, and eggs and beat.
- Gradually add dry ingredients, and sour cream. Put half the batter in a buttered pan. Sprinkle with topping. Repeat process.
- Bake in a greased tube pan for 55 minutes at 350°F. Serves 8–10.

⌂ French Coffee Cake

Mrs. David Silverman

2 1/2 cups flour
1/2 teaspoon baking soda
1 teaspoon baking powder
1 pinch salt
3 tablespoons cinnamon
1/4 cup brown sugar

1/2 cup walnut meats
1 cup butter
1 cup granulated sugar
3 eggs
1 cup sour cream
2 teaspoons vanilla

- Sift flour, baking soda, baking powder, and salt together.
- Combine cinnamon, sugar, and walnuts. Set aside.
- Cream granulated sugar and butter. Add eggs one at a time.
- Add the flour and sour cream alternately. Mix and beat well. Add the vanilla. Pour part of batter into spring form pan, sprinkle with cinnamon, brown sugar, and nut mixture.
- Add another layer of batter and sprinkle with mixture again and repeat until batter is used up, topping with nut mixture.
- Bake in 375°F oven for 45 minutes. Allow to cool for 15 minutes before removing collar from pan.

French Marble Coffee Cake

Mrs. Gladys Kaplan

This is my daughter's favorite pastry

$^1/_2$ pound butter
3 cups flour
3 teaspoons baking powder
2 cups sugar
3 eggs

3 teaspoons vanilla
1 cup Carnation evaporated milk
$1^1/_2$ squares semisweet chocolate or
$^1/_4$ cup chocolate bits, melted

- Mix first 4 ingredients together. Take $^1/_2$ cup of mixture and put aside.
- Add eggs, vanilla and milk and blend together. Place $^3/_4$ of batter in a greased 9 x 13 x 2-inch pan.
- Add melted chocolate to remaining batter and put on top of plain batter. Take a knife and marbelize it, then drizzle the $^1/_2$ cup mixture saved on top.
- Bake at 350°F for 45–65 minutes.

The Best Coffee Cake

Nancy Benjamin

$^2/_3$ cup brown sugar
$^1/_2$ cup white raisins
$^1/_2$ cup chopped walnuts
3 tablespoons unsweetened cocoa powder
2 tablespoons cinnamon
2 teaspoons instant coffee powder
$^3/_4$ cup unsalted butter, softened
$1^3/_4$ cups granulated sugar

2 teaspoons vanilla
3 eggs
3 cups sifted all-purpose flour
$1^1/_2$ teaspoons baking powder
$1^1/_2$ teaspoons baking soda
$^1/_2$ teaspoon salt
2 cups plain yogurt

- Combine first six ingredients in a bowl.
- Cream butter in large mixer bowl. Add granulated sugar. Beat until light and fluffy, about 5 minutes. Beat in vanilla. Add eggs, one at a time beating well after each.
- Sift dry ingredients together. Add flour mixture a third at a time alternately with yogurt. Beat just until mixed.
- Grease and flour bundt or tube pan. Alternate batter a third at a time with raisin mixture, ending with batter.
- Bake in a 350°F oven until wooden pick inserted in cake is clean, about 1 hour.

Desserts

Apple Crisp

Ina Sirk

4–6 cups MacIntosh apples
sprinkling of orange juice

Topping:
1 cup sugar
³/₄ cup flour
¹/₂–1 teaspoon cinnamon
¹/₄ teaspoon nutmeg
¹/₂ cup butter, softened

- Butter 7 x 11-inch baking dish.
- Combine sugar, flour, cinnamon, nutmeg, and butter to make a crumb topping.
- Peel apples and cut into large slices. Place in prepared baking dish.
- Sprinkle with orange juice and then with crumb topping.
- Bake at 375°F for 45 minutes.

Easy Apple Crisp

Pearl Treister

Easy and delicious!

8 apples, peeled and sliced (or other fruit
    can be combined)
1 cup sugar (¹/₂ cup granulated and
    ¹/₂ cup brown)

1 teaspoon cinnamon
1 box yellow cake mix, dry
1 cup chopped nuts
1¹/₂ sticks margarine

- Mix apples with sugar and cinnamon and place in 9 x 13-inch greased pan. Pour cake mix over apples. Sprinkle with nuts. Add margarine, diced, on top of mixture.
- Bake in 350°F oven for 30–40 minutes, until apples are soft. Serves 10–12.

Cranberry Apple Crisp

Frieda Rosen

5 cups peeled and sliced apples
    (6–7 sliced on the thick side)
1 1/2 cups fresh cranberries
1/3 cup granulated sugar, less if desired
1/2 cup flour

1/2 cup brown sugar, less if desired
1 teaspoon cinnamon
1/4 cup butter or margarine
chopped nuts, optional

- Grease a 9-inch square pan.
- Layer apples and cranberries in pan. Sprinkle with granulated sugar as you layer .
- Mix flour, brown sugar, and cinnamon in separate bowl. Cut in margarine or butter with pastry cutter until texture is crumbly. Sprinkle topping over cranberry and apple mixture in pan. Add chopped nuts on top if desired.
- Bake in 350°F oven for 45 minutes. Serve with Cool Whip, whipped cream, or ice cream if desired. Serves 8–9.

Apple or Peach Crumb Crisp

Lois Edinberg

Crust:
1/2 cup butter, softened
1/2 cup sugar
1 1/2 cups flour, sifted
pinch salt
3/4 cup walnuts, crushed and set aside
    for later

Apple Filling:
5 cups apples, peeled and cut into small
    pieces
2 tablespoons cornstarch
1/2 cup sugar
3/4 teaspoon cinnamon

Peach Filling:
4 cups fresh peaches
2 tablespoons cornstarch
1/4 cup sugar
1 tablespoon lemon juice

Crust:
- Crumb together butter, sugar, flour, and salt with pastry blender. Set aside 3/4 cup.
- Press remaining crumbs into bottom and 3/4 inch up side of 9-inch spring form pan. Put in refrigerator.

Filling:
- Combine ingredients and mix. Arrange over crumb shell.
- Bake 425°F for 20 minutes and 450°F for 10 minutes.
- Sprinkle with nuts and 3/4 cup of crumbs that were set aside.
- Return to oven at 425°F for 20–30 minutes until shell is brown. Serves 8–10.

Apple Cinnamon Coffee Cake

Karen Taylor

4 cups peeled, finely chopped MacIntosh apples
1/4 cup apple juice
1 1/2 cups all-purpose flour
1 1/2 cups whole wheat flour
1 1/2 teaspoons cinammon
1/4 teaspoon salt
1/2 cup margarine, softened

1 cup granulated sugar
2 large eggs
4 large egg whites
1/4 cup orange juice
1/4 cup skim milk
2 1/2 teaspoons vanilla
3 tablespoons firmly packed brown sugar

- Preheat oven to 275°F. Coat a 10-inch tube pan with cooking spray.
- Combine apples with apple juice in medium-sized bowl.
- In another bowl, combine flours, cinnamon, and salt.
- Beat margarine and granulated sugar in large bowl until light and fluffy. Beat in whole eggs then egg whites one at a time.
- Combine orange juice with milk and vanilla and add alternately with dry ingredients.
- Spoon 1/3 batter in pan. Spoon on 1/2 apple mixtue. Layer with 1/3 batter, the remaining apples and batter. Sprinkle top with brown sugar.
- Bake 1 1/2 hour or until toothpick comes out clean.

Mother's Apple Cake

Joyce Queen

The Best! Delish with ice cream or frozen yogurt.

2 eggs
1 cup sugar
1 cup oil
1 teaspoon vanilla
1 teaspoon salt, little less

2 teaspoons baking powder
3 cups flour
4–5 pounds apples
1/2 cup cinnamon and sugar
1 cup apricot jam

- Beat eggs, sugar, oil, vanilla, and salt together. Add baking powder and flour and mix well.
- Peel and thinly slice the apples. Mix them with cinnamon and sugar to taste.
- Spread a 9 x 13-inch pyrex dish with 1/2 the dough. Spread apple mixture on top and cover with apricot jam. Crumble remaining dough on top.
- Bake in a preheated 350°F oven until brown, approximately 50–60 minutes. Makes 9–12 squares.

Aunt Betty's Apple Cake

Roslyn Schorr Ritz

Delicious!

Filling:
3 pounds apples, peeled and sliced
1/2 cup sugar and cinnamon

Dough:
1 cup sugar
1/2 cup shortening
1 teaspoon baking powder
2 1/2 cups cake flour
2 eggs (egg beaters can be substituted)
1/2 teaspoon salt

- Cream sugar and shortening. Combine baking powder and flour and add to shortening (mixture will be thick).
- Press 1/2 the dough in bottom and sides of well greased pan or pyrex dish with the back of a spoon or by hand. Pour in apple mixture. Cover with the remaining dough. Sprinkle sugar and cinnamon on top.
- Bake for 1 hour at 350°F.

Apple Cake

Lois Sobel

It is very easy to make and a hit with our guests!

1 1/3 cups flour
2 1/2 teaspoons baking powder
1/2 teaspoon salt
4 tablespoons margarine (1/2 stick)
1 cup sugar, plus 1 tablespoon
1 egg
1 teaspoon vanilla

2/3 cup orange juice
5–6 apples
1 tablespoon cinnamon
 finely chopped walnuts, optional
cinnamon and sugar for top

- Sift together flour, baking powder, and salt,
- In large bowl, beat margarine, 1 cup sugar, egg, and vanilla. After this is creamy, add dry ingredients and orange juice.
- Place 1/2 the batter into a greased 8 x 8-inch pan.
- Slice and peel apples, layer on top of batter, and top with cinnamon and 1 tablespoon sugar.
- Add the rest of the batter. Sprinkle top with cinnamon and sugar (and walnuts if desired).
- Bake at 350°F for 45–50 minutes.

Spiced Apple Cake

Nancy Schulman

Smells great, tastes wonderful!

1 cup vegetable oil
3 extra large eggs
2 cups sugar
3 cups flour
1 teaspoon salt
1 teaspoon baking soda
2 teaspoons cinnamon

2 teaspoons ground nutmeg
1 teaspoon allspice
1 teaspoon cloves
1 cup walnut meats
3 cups peeled and chopped apples
1 teaspoon vanilla
1 teaspoon lemon juice

- Preheat oven to 350°F. Lightly grease 10-inch bundt pan.
- Beat together oil, eggs, and sugar.
- Sift together flour, salt, baking soda, and spices. Add to first mixture.
- Add nuts, apples, vanilla, and lemon juice. Mixture will be thick.
- Bake for 1 hour and 5 minutes. Cool in pan for 10 minutes, then on wire rack until completely cooled. Serves 8–10.

Scotch Apple Pie

Mrs. Ben Cohen

8 apples
1 1/2 cups brown sugar
1 cup flour

1/4 teaspoon salt
1/2 cup butter
3/4 cup nuts, chopped

- Pare and slice apples, arrange in pyrex pie plate, and add 1/2 the brown sugar.
- Mix remaining ingredients together and spread over the apples, pressing down around the edge.
- Bake in moderate oven at 350°F for 1 hour. Serve with hard sauce or ice cream.

Apple Upside Down Pie

Marcia Wolfson

Easy and delicious!

½ stick margarine
½ cup brown sugar
pecans, slightly toasted
2 ready-made pie crusts
8 large apples, Gravenstein's are best

3 tablespoons granulated sugar
2 tablespoons flour
juice of 1 lemon
2 teaspoons flour

- Melt margarine in the bottom of a 9-inch pie plate. Stir in brown sugar and pat to cover the bottom.
- Place pecans, flat side up, in concentric circles over brown sugar mixture. Place 1 pie crust over nuts.
- Pare and slice apples, and mix with granulated sugar and 2 tablespoons flour. Sprinkle lemon juice.
- Fill pie plate and top with other crust. Crimp edges. Cut steam vents.
- Put on baking sheet to prevent juices splattering. Bake at 350°F on bottom shelf of oven until brown.
- Turn upside down into 10-inch quiche dish. Serves 8.

Swedish Apple Pie

Mari Storm

From Jeanne Perry's Mother

6 apples
4 tablespoons sugar
1 teaspoon cinnamon
¾ cup butter or margarine, melted

1 cup sugar
1 cup flour
1 egg, beaten
1 pinch salt

- Fill 9-inch pie plate with sliced and peeled apples. Sprinkle with 4 tablespoons of sugar and cinnamon.
- In small bowl combine butter or margarine, 1 cup sugar, flour, egg, and salt. Pour this mixture over apples.
- Bake at 350°F for 45 minutes or until brown. Serves 6–8.

Easy Apple Dessert

Lilyan Bachrach

5 large apples, preferably Granny Smith
1/2 cup sugar
1 teaspoon cinnamon

Batter:
1 large egg
1/2 cup sugar
6 tablespoons margarine or butter, melted
   and cooled
1 teaspoon vanilla
3/4 cup white flour
1/4 cup chopped nuts, optional

- Quarter, peel, and thinly slice apples to almost fill a butter 8- or 9-inch square pan.
- Mix sugar and cinnamon together and sprinkle between layers of sliced apples.

Batter:
- In a small bowl, using a fork, beat egg and add sugar. Add margarine and vanilla. Gradually add flour and nuts.
- Spread the batter over the apples.
- Bake for 50 minutes in a 350°F oven until brown on top.

Apple Cheese Torte

Irene Garber

Crust:
1 cup butter
2/3 cup sugar
2 cups flour
pinch salt

Filling:
4 cups apples, peeled and sliced as for pie
1/3 cup sugar
1/2 teaspoon cinnamon

Mixture to Pour Over Crust:
8 ounces cream cheese
1/4 cup sugar
1 egg
1 teaspoon vanilla

Crust:
- Mix ingredients in food processor until blended.
- Press into 9-inch springform pan on bottom and 1–2 inches up the sides.

Mixture to Pour Over Crust:
- Combine cream cheese, sugar, egg, and vanilla, and beat until smooth. Pour over crust.

Filling:
- Combine apples, sugar, and cinnamon and place on cream cheese mixture.
- Bake in 400°F oven for 10 minutes, reducing heat to 350°F for 50 minutes or until apples are soft.

Pumpkin Crunch Custard

Roseanne Levine

If you like pumpkin pie, you'll love this!

Custard:
3 large eggs
1 16-ounce can solid-pack pumpkin
1 12-ounce can evaporated skim milk
³/₄ cup firmly packed brown sugar
1 teaspoon vanilla
2 teaspoons pumpkin pie spice
  or the following three spices
1 teaspoon ground cinnamon
¹/₂ teaspoon ground ginger
¹/₂ teaspoon ground allspice

Topping:
3 tablespoons firmly packed brown sugar
2 tablespoons flour
¹/₄ teaspoon ground cinnamon
4 teaspoons cold butter or margarine, cut
  into small pieces
¹/₃ cup pecan pieces

- Heat oven to 325°F.
- Whisk eggs in large bowl. Add the remaining custard ingredients and mix until blended. Pour into ungreased baking dish.
- Bake for 45 minutes until the sides of custard start to set.
- Meanwhile, prepare the topping. Mix sugar, flour, and cinnamon. Cut in butter until mixture is crumbly. Stir in pecans.
- Remove custard from oven and sprinkle with topping. Bake for 35–40 minutes longer until knife inserted in center is clean.
- Cool on wire rack. Serves 8.

Pumpkin Chiffon Pie

Barbara W. Burwick

Um Um Good!

Crust:
1²/₃ cups gingersnap crumbs
¹/₄ cup butter, melted
¹/₄ cup sugar

Filling:
1 cup canned pumpkin
4 egg yolks
¹/₂ cup sugar
1 cup milk

¹/₂ teaspoon salt
¹/₂ teaspoon ginger
¹/₄ teaspoon ground nutmeg
1 teaspoon cinnamon
2 tablespoons butter
1 envelope unflavored gelatin, softened
  in ¹/₄ cup of cold water
4 egg whites
¹/₂ cup sugar

- Combine crust ingredients and press into bottom and sides of a 9-inch pie plate.
- Cook pumpkin on top of double boiler for 10 minutes. Add egg yolks, sugar, milk, salt, ginger, nutmeg, cinnamon, and butter, stirring until custard consistency.
- Remove from heat and add gelatin. Chill.
- When mixture begins to thicken, fold in egg whites, stiffly beaten with ¹/₂ cup sugar. Pour mixture in crust.
- Chill or freeze. Serve topped with whipped cream.

Pumpkin Roll

Ellen Martin

Serves up as a nice desert, always want more.

3 eggs
1 cup granulated sugar
²/₃ cup canned pumpkin
2 tablespoons lemon juice
²/₃ cup flour
1 teaspoon baking powder
2 teaspoons cinnamon
¹/₂ teaspoon nutmeg
1¹/₂ teaspoon ginger
crushed walnuts
confectioners' sugar

Filling:
2 3-ounce packages of cream cheese
1 cup confectioners' sugar
¹/₄ cup margarine
1 teaspoon vanilla

- Beat 3 eggs for 5 minutes, gradually adding 1 cup of sugar.
- Mix in pumpkin and 2 tablespoons lemon juice.
- Mix together in separate bowl, flour, baking powder, cinnamon, nutmeg, and ginger. Fold into pumpkin mixture.
- Grease and flour jelly roll pan. Spread crushed walnuts in pan and pour batter over.
- Bake at 350°F for 30 minutes.
- Invert baked roll onto paper. Spread with confectioners' sugar and roll up. When cooled, fill with filling.
- To prepare filling, beat cream cheese, sugar, margarine, and vanilla until well blended.
- When cake is cooked, unroll, spread with filling, and roll up.

Fruit Torte

Judy Fask

Great for Passover.

7 tablespoons butter, at room temperature
¹/₂ cup granulated sugar
2 eggs
³/₄ cup ground almonds
pinch salt

Filling:
8 ounces cream cheese
2 tablespoons sour cream
1–2 tablespoons confectioners' sugar (use granulated sugar for Passover)
lemon juice, to taste

Topping:
fresh fruit: i.e. kiwi or strawberries
¹/₄ cup seedless raspberry preserves, melted
¹/₄ cup apricot preserves, melted

- Preheat oven to 375°F. Place waxed paper on bottom of cake pan.
- Combine butter and granulated sugar. Beat until fluffy.
- Beat in eggs, one at a time. Then blend in amonds. Spread in pan.
- Bake for 20–25 minutes. Cool. Invert onto plate.
- To prepare filling blend cream cheese, sour cream, confectioners' sugar, and lemon juice. Spread over torte shell.
- Spread melted raspberry preserves on top. Layer with fresh fruit. Spread melted apricot preserves on top.

My Favorite Compote

Ruth Short

Can also be served at Passover.

3/4 cup sugar
2 cups water
1 pound pitted prunes
1/2 pound dried apricots

2 lemons, sliced very thin
2 tablespoons honey
handful chopped nuts, optional

- Boil sugar and water for about 5 minutes. Add fruit and cook slowly until soft. Add lemon, honey, and nuts and cook in covered pot for another 5–10 minutes. Remove from heat and cool
- When cool, pour into container.
- Let set 1 or 2 days to thicken. Serves up to 12 when served over cake/ice cream.

Fruit Sorbet

Judy Fask

Great for Passover.

1–2 egg whites
10 ounces frozen fruit, raspberries or
   strawberries, slightly defrosted

1 ripe banana, mashed
1/4 cup sugar

- Beat egg whites until stiff. Add thawed fruit. Add banana. Add sugar gradually.
- Put in container to freeze. Thaw about 15 minutes before serving.

Outrageous Cheesecake

Phyllis Spool

Excellent. Make the day before you want to use it.

Crust:
23 Hydrox cookies, crushed
1/3 cup butter, melted
1/4 cup light brown sugar
1 teaspoon cinnamon

First Layer:
2 pounds cream cheese
1 1/4 cups granulated sugar
2 tablespoons flour
4 extra large eggs
2 egg yolks
1/3 cup whipping cream
1 teaspoon vanilla
16 Hydrox cookies, crushed

Second Layer:
2 cups sour cream
1 teaspoon vanilla
1/4 cup granulated sugar

Third Layer:
1 cup whipping cream
8 ounces chocolate chips
1 teaspoon vanilla

Crust:
- Combine ingredients for crust and press into bottom of 10-inch springform pan.
- Bake at 350°F for 8 minutes.

First Layer:
- Beat cream cheese at low speed. Add sugar and flour.
- Beat in eggs and yolks one at a time until smooth. Stir in cream and vanilla. Pour half over crust.
- Take cookies and sprinkle over cream cheese mixture. Pour rest of cream cheese mixture over cookies.
- Bake at 425°F for 15 minutes. Reduce temperature to 225°F for 50 minutes more.

Second Layer:
- Beat sour cream, vanilla, and sugar together.
- Spread on top of cake and bake 7 more minutes.
- Immediately put in refrigerator covered with plastic wrap.

Morning of Serving — Third Layer:
- Heat whipping cream until almost boiling. Add chocolate chips and melt until smooth. Add vanilla.
- Remove from heat and stir until smooth.
- Refrigerate until thick, 30–35 minutes.
- Take cheesecake out of refrigerator and remove from pan.
- Spread chocolate mixture over top. Refrigerate until ready to serve.

Refrigerator Cheese Cake

Mrs. Louis P. Pemstein

Filling:
4 eggs, separated
1 cup sugar
1 cup milk, heated
2 envelopes plain gelatin
³/₄ cup cold water, to soak gelatin
1¹/₂ pounds cream cheese
1 teaspoon vanilla
¹/₂ pint heavy cream, whipped

Zwieback Crust:
¹/₂ package Zwieback
3 tablespoons sugar
1 tablespoon cinnamon
3 tablespoons melted butter

Filling:
- Mix egg yolks, sugar, and hot milk in double boiler and cook until thickened. Add gelatin dissolved in cold water and let cool.
- Soften cheese in mixer. Add vanilla and egg mixture. When smooth fold in whipped cream.
- Fold in stiffly beaten egg whites. Pour into lined spring form pan and place in refrigerator.

Crust:
- Roll Zwieback fine, mix with sugar, cinnamon, and melted butter.
- Line springform pan with Zwieback mixture.
- Fill with cheese mixture and cover with chopped nuts, or sprinkle with small amount of Zwieback mixture, or decorate as desired.

Key Lime Cheesecake

Harriet Lowe

Beautiful Presentation!

Crust:
1½–2 cups fine graham cracker crumbs
2 tablespoons sugar
⅓ cup butter or margarine, melted

Filling:
2½ 8-ounce packages cream cheese, softened
¾ cup sugar
1 cup sour cream
3 tablespoons flour
3 large eggs
¾ cup key lime juice
1 teaspoon vanilla
a few drops of green food coloring, optional

Crust:
- In a bowl, stir together the crumbs and the sugar and add the butter. Mix well. Pat the mixture evenly onto the bottom and ½-inch up the side of a 9- or 10-inch springform pan. Bake crust at 375°F for 8 minutes. Let pan cool.

Filling:
- In a bowl, beat cream cheese and sugar until mixture is smooth. Then beat in the sour cream, flour, and eggs, one at a time, beating well.
- Add the lime juice, vanilla, and food coloring, and beat the mixture until it is smooth. Pour the filling over the crust.
- Bake the cheesecake in 375°F oven for 15 minutes. Reduce temperature to 250°F and bake the cheesecake for 50–55 minutes more, or until the center is barely set.
- Let the cheesecake cool on a rack and chill it, covered, overnight. Remove cheesecake from pan and transfer to cake stand.
- Pipe whipped cream into rosettes on the cheesecake. Garnish the cheesecake with lime slices and mint sprigs. Serves 14.

Chocolate Swirl Cheesecake

Sandi Cutler

1 6-ounce package chocolate chips
½ cup sugar
1¼ cups graham cracker crumbs
2 tablespoons sugar
¼ cup butter, melted
2 3-ounce packages cream cheese,
    softened

¾ cup sugar
½ cup sour cream
1 teaspoon vanilla
4 eggs

- Preheat oven to 325°F.
- Combine over hot (not boiling) water chocolate chips and ½ cup sugar. Heat until chocolate chips are melted and mixture is smooth. Remove from heat.
- In a small bowl, combine graham cracker crumbs, 2 tablespoons sugar, and butter, and mix well. Pat firmly into a 9-inch springform pan, covering bottom and 1½-inch up sides. Set aside.
- In a large bowl, beat cream cheese until light and creamy. Gradually beat in ¾ cup of sugar. Mix in sour cream and vanilla extract. Add eggs, one at a time, beating well after each addition.
- Divide batter in half. Stir melted chocolate mixture into first half. Pour into crumb lined pan. Cover with plain batter. With a knife, swirl plain batter with chocolate batter to marblize.
- Bake at 325°F for 50 minutes or until only a 2–3-inch circle in center will shake. Cool at room temperature. Refrigerate until ready to serve. Serves 6–8.

Kahlua Milk Chocolate Cheesecake

Lisa Honig

Crust:
½ cup graham cracker crumbs
2 tablespoons firmly packed light brown
    sugar
¼ cup butter, melted
1 teaspoon vanilla

Filling:
12 ounces cream cheese, at room temperature
½ cup granulated sugar
3 egg, at room temperature
7 tablespoons whipping cream
2 tablespoons Kahlua
3 ounces milk chocolate, coarsley chopped

Crust:
- Preheat oven to 300°F.
- Combine crumbs and brown sugar in bowl. Stir in butter and vanilla. Press into bottom of 8 x 1½-inch round cake pan.
- Bake 10 minutes.

Filling:
- Use electric mixer to blend cream cheese and sugar until smooth.
- Beat in eggs, one at a time. Gently mix in 3 tablespoons cream and Kahula. Pour into crust.
- Melt chocolate over double boiler with 4 tablespoons cream. Stir until smooth.
- Drizzle spiral pattern on top of filling. Stir with spoon to get marble effect. Don't over stir.
- Set in larger baking pan. Pour water into baking pan, ½ way up the side of the cheesecake pan.
- Bake until firm, 55 minutes. Serves 12.

☐ Cream Cheese Pie with Apricot Glaze   *Mrs. Samuel Lopatin*

Crust:
14 small Zweiback, crushed
$1/8$ pound butter
$1/4$ cup sugar
1 teaspoon cinnamon

1 pound cream cheese, at room
    temperature
$1/2$ cup sugar
2 whole eggs
1 teaspoon fresh lemon juice
1 teaspoon vanilla
$1/2$ cup sour cream
2 tablespoons sugar
stewed dried apricots, slightly sweetened
1 tablespoon cornstarch

- To prepare the crust, melt butter in 10-inch pie plate. Mix in the crushed Zweiback, sugar, and cinnamon. Press onto bottom and sides of pie plate.
- To prepare the filling, beat cream cheese in electric mixer. Gradually add $1/2$ cup sugar, the eggs, one at a time, lemon juice, and vanilla. Beat for fifteen minutes.
- Pour cheese mixture into Zweiback crust, and bake in a 350°F preheated oven for 20 minutes. Take out and rest on rack.
- Turn up heat to 400°F.
- Beat sour cream and sugar until frothy, pour over the baked cheese pie, and bake for 5 minutes. Take out and let cool.
- Drain juice from stewed apricots and reserve $1/2$ cup. Mix 1 tablespoon cornstarch with reserved juice, stir until smooth, boil until thick, and let cool.
- Placed drained apricots over top of pie and pour the cooled cooked apricot juice over top. Refrigerate.

Cheese Pie   *Lois Edinberg*

Very easy and delicious.

Crust:
$1 1/4$ cups graham cracker crumbs
1 tablespoon sugar
6 tablespoons butter, melted

$1 1/2$ pounds cream cheese
3 eggs
1 teaspoon vanilla
$3/4$ cup sugar

Topping:
$1/3$ cup red currant jelly
3 teaspoons lemon juice
dash allspice
dash cinnamon
1 10-ounce package frozen strawberries

- Mix ingredients for crust and place in bottom and a little up the sides of 9-inch springform pan.
- Beat cream cheese, eggs, vanilla, and sugar for 10 minutes until well mixed. Pour over crust.
- Bake at 350°F for 40–50 minutes. Top will crack when done — don't worry.

Topping:
- Combine ingredients for topping, heat and spoon over pie. Serves 8–10.

Edith's Baked Alaska

Mari Seder

A hit with Alaska's pioneering Senator Gruening on a vist to Worcester.

1 sponge, white, or pound cake
creme de cocoa, optional
1 quart coffee or maple walnut ice cream
1 quart vanilla ice cream
1 quart chocolate ice cream
slivered almonds

Meringue Topping:
4–5 egg whites
pinch of cream of tartar
1/4 cup sugar
1/2 cup white corn syrup
1 teaspoon vanilla

- Line bottom of a 10-inch pie plate with a 3/4-inch layer of cake. Sprinkle with creme de cocoa.
- Add layers of the varioius ice creams, sprinkling more creme de cocoa and slivered almond between the layers. Place in freezer.

Meringue:
- Make meringue by beating egg white and cream of tartar until peaks stand up firmly.
- Slowly add sugar and corn syrup and continue to beat until very stiff, about 10–15 minutes. Add vanilla.
- Remove ice cream from freezer. Mound meringue over the ice cream, completely covering it.
- Place in a 450°F oven for 3 minutes. Watch carefully.
- Put back in freezer.
- Serve with hot fudge, raspberry, or strawberry sauce. Can be made a few days in advance. Serves 16.

Baked Alaska

Ellen Stone

This pie is as beautiful as it is delicious. Serve with a hot fudge sauce.

1 1/2 box chocolate wafer cookies
2 tablespoons cinnamon and sugar, mixed
1/4 cup butter, melted
1/2 gallon coffee ice cream
1/2 gallon chocolate ice cream
1 pint rasberry sherbet

Topping:
4 egg whites
1/4 cream of tartar
6 tablespoons sugar

- Crush the cookies into small crumbs. Toss with cinnamon and sugar and then with butter. Line a 10-inch pie plate with the crumbs. Press down the crumbs with a spoon.
- Allow ice cream to soften. Smooth the coffee ice cream into the pie plate. Top with rasberry sherbet and then with chocolate ice cream. Freeze overnight.
- Add topping the next day and freeze again before serving.

Topping:
- Beat the egg whites until light and frothy. Add the cream of tartar. Beat until the whites are stiff enough to hold a peak.
- Beat in the sugar until the meringue is stiff. Pile the meringue lightly on the pie covering all edges.
- Place pie on a lined cookie sheet for overflow. and bake in a preheated oven 425°F degrees for 4–5 minutes until lightly browned. Serves 8.

Brownie Ice Cream Pie

Harriet Lowe

Rich but delicious!

1 package of brownie mix
10 ounces Hershey's milk chocolate bars
    with almonds

³/₄ pint heavy cream
¹/₂ gallon ice cream
slivered almonds

- Prepare brownie mix according to package directions or make your own recipe. Press brownies into bottom and sides of a 9- or 10-inch pie plate (do not use them all). Freeze.
- In a double boiler, melt chocolate bars. Remove from heat and add ³/₄ pint heavy cream, not whipped. Mix by hand until cream is totally incorporated and mixture is chocolately. Pour mixture into brownie crust and freeze overnight.
- Slightly soften ¹/₂ gallon of your favorite ice cream (I like coffee) and spoon ice cream over frozen mixture. Smooth out. Use about ³/₄ of the half gallon.
- Sprinkle pieces of leftover brownie over ice cream. I also put slivered almonds on top. Freeze.
- Take out of freezer before serving to soften slightly before serving.

Hot Fudge Ice Cream Pie

Gina Schultz

Crust:
1/4 cup finely chopped walnuts, optional
1 1/4 cups chocolate wafer crumbs
3 tablespoons sugar
6 tablespoons butter, melted

Hot Fudge Sauce:
1 cup sugar
3/4 cup unsweetened cocoa powder
1 teaspoon instant coffee powder
1 cup whipped cream
1/4 cup butter

Filling:
1 quart vanilla ice cream, softened
1 quart chocolate ice cream, softened
1/2 cup whipping cream, whipped

Garnish:
chopped walnuts, optional
maraschino cherries

Crust:
- Combine nuts, crumbs, and sugar, and mix well. Pour melted butter over mixture and toss lightly until well blended.
- Press mixture into bottom and up sides of 9- or 10-inch pie plate. Cover with plastic wrap and chill 30 minutes.

Sauce:
- Combine sugar, cocoa, and instant coffee in saucepan. Add 1/2 cup whipping cream and blend to smooth paste.
- Add remaining cream, blending well. Cook over medium heat, stirring constantly, until sugar is completely dissolved.
- Add butter and cook until mixture is smooth and thickened, 5–8 minutes. Keep warm.

Filling:
- Spread 1/2 of softened vanilla ice cream evenly over crust and freeze. Drizzle 1/2 of the fudge over the top and return to the freezer to firm.
- Remove from freezer and spread with remaining vanilla ice cream.
- Scoop balls from chocolate ice cream and arrange over vanilla layer. Drizzle with remaining hot fudge.
- Spoon whipped cream into pastry bag filled with star tip and pipe rosettes around scoops.
- Decorate with nuts and cherries. Serve immediately. Serves 10–12.

Sponge Cake I

Mariam Zieper

5 extra large eggs, separated
3 tablespoons cold water
1 cup sugar
1 teaspoon almond extract or lemon
    flavoring

1 1/2 cups flour
1 teaspoon baking powder
1/2 cup boiling water
1/2 teaspoon cream of tartar

- Beat egg yolks and cold water together. Add sugar and almond extract and beat about 5 minutes.
- Sift flour and baking powder together and add alternately with boiling water. Beat well.
- Beat egg whites and cream of tartar until stiff.
- Fold into egg yolk mixture.
- Bake in ungreased tube pan at 350°F oven for 60 minutes. Turn upside down to cool. Serves 12–14.

Sponge Cake II

Bobbie Hirshberg

I use this cake plain or to make strawberry shortcake, one of my family's favorites.

6 jumbo or 7 extra large eggs
1 cup sugar
1 cup sifted cake flour
1/3 cup cold water

1 teaspoon lemon extract
1 teaspoon vanilla
1/2 teaspoon cream of tartar
1/2 teaspoon salt

- Separate eggs and beat yolks in a small mixer bowl until thick and lemon colored. Beat sugar into the yolks gradually.
- Slowly add flour alternately with water beating well each time. Add flavorings. Put aside.
- In a large mixer bowl, place egg whites, cream of tartar, and salt. Beat until stiff peaks form. Pour batter into an ungreased 10-inch tube pan.
- Bake at 325°F for about 1 hour. Cool upside down. Loosen from form by cutting around with a sharp knife.

⌂ Gingerbread

Mrs. Bernard Pines

1 1/2 cups flour
1 teaspoon cinnamon
1 teaspoon soda
1 teaspoon ginger
1/4 pound butter, melted

1/2 cup sugar
1/2 cup molasses
1 egg, well beaten
1/2 cup boiling water

- Sift together all dry ingredients.
- To melted butter, add sugar, molasses, and beaten egg. Beat well.
- Add sifted dry ingredients, then finally the boiling water.
- Bake at 350°F for 40 minutes in 8-inch square pan.

Honey Cake I

Thelma Lockwood

Excellent — light — freezes well.

3 1/2 cups flour
2 1/2 teaspoons baking powder
1 teaspoon baking soda
1/2 teaspoon salt
1 teaspoon cinnamon
1/2 teaspoon ground cloves
1/4 teaspoon ginger
1 cup sugar

3 eggs, separated
1/4 cup oil
1 1/3 cups honey
1 1/3 cups warm black coffee
1 teaspoon vanilla
1/4 teaspoon cream of tartar
almonds, lightly toasted, for garnish

- Mix dry ingredients and sift into mixing bowl.
- Make a well and add egg yolks, oil, honey, coffee, and vanilla. Beat until blended and smooth.
- Add cream of tartar to egg whites and beat until stiff.
- Gently fold first mixture into egg whites, blending with a rubber spatula. Do not beat or stir.
- Pour batter into ungreased 10-inch tube pan and garnish with almonds.
- Bake in 350°F preheated oven for 50–60 minutes.
- Cake is done when it springs back when lightly touch with a finger. Invert pan to cook. Remove after cooling.

Honey Cake II

Bertha Allen

Very Good

3½ cups sifted flour
1 teaspoon baking powder
1 teaspoon baking soda
1 teaspoon ground cinnamon
1 teaspoon ginger
½ teaspoon allspice

½ teaspoon cloves
4 eggs, separated
1 cup sugar
⅓ cup oil
1 pound jar honey
1 cup gingerale

- Sift together flour, baking powder, soda and spices.
- Beat egg yolks, sugar, oil, and honey until light and thick. Add gingerale a little at a time to mix. Add dry ingredients.
- Beat egg whites until stiff and fold into batter.
- Bake in greased tube pan at 350°F oven for about 65 minutes until brown. **Cool up! Do not Invert!**

"Lekkach"

Zoe Ostrow

Honey cake for Rosh Hashana. Mother Tanya's recipe passed on by Tante Frumke.

1 pound honey
1 pound sugar (2 cups)
5 eggs
5 cups flour
2 teaspoons baking powder
1 teaspoon baking soda
¼ teaspoon nutmeg
¼ teaspoon ginger
½ cup whiskey

½ cup strong coffee
½ cup oil
2 cups almonds, dipped in flour
1⅓ cups gold raisins, dipped in flour
sugar
sliced almonds for top of cake

- Mix together honey, sugar, eggs, flour, baking powder, baking soda, nutmeg, ginger, whiskey, coffee, and oil.
- Stir in 2 cups of almonds and raisins that have been dipped in flour.
- Divide batter between 2 buttered loaf pans. Sprinkle batter with sugar and sliced almonds.
- Bake at 350°F for ½ hour or until golden brown. Serves 24 or more.

Spice Cake

Harriet Paige

2 cups coffee
1 cup raisins
2 cups sugar
4 tablespoons vegetable oil
2 teaspoons cinnamon
1 teaspoon cloves
1 teaspoon allspice

3 eggs
1 teaspoon baking soda
1 tablespoon water
3 cups flour
2 teaspoons baking powder

- Boil coffee, raisins, sugar, oil, cinnamon, cloves, and allspice for 10 minutes. Cool.
- Beat eggs, add spice mixture, and mix again.
- Add baking soda dissolved in water.
- Add flour and baking powder and mix well.
- Grease a 9 x 13-inch pan. Pour in mixture.
- Bake in 350°F oven for 35 minutes.

Ilse's Sewurzstallen

Lolita Baker

No fat, little cholesterol — spicey and yummy!

4 eggs
1 cup sugar
1 jigger brandy
2 cups flour
1 teaspoon cinnamon
1/2 teaspoon cloves
1 teaspoon nutmeg
1/2 cup chocolate bits

1/2 cup candied fruit peel
1 cup raisins
1/3 cup candied ginger, chopped, if
 available
1/2 cup nuts
extra flour to dust fruits and nuts

- Beat eggs and sugar until foamy. Add brandy.
- Add dry ingredients. Add chocolate. Add fruits and nuts that have been dusted with flour.
- Pour into greased loaf pan. Bake 1 hour at 350°F.

Desserts **203**

Coconut Pound Cake

Nancy Benjamin

1 pound unsalted butter, softened
2 cups sugar
6 eggs
2 cups flour
7 ounces flaked coconut
1 teaspoon coconut extract
1 teaspoon vanilla extract

Glaze:
1 cup sugar
1/2 cup water
1 teaspoon coconut extract

- Cream butter and sugar until light and fluffy, about 5–10 minutes.
- Add eggs, one at a time, beating well after each.
- Add 1 cup flour and just mix.
- Mix 1 cup flour with coconut. Add to butter mixture. Add flavorings and mix just until well blended.
- Bake in a 350°F oven in a greased and floured Bundt pan for 1–1 1/4 hours until it tests done.

Glaze:
- Combine sugar, and water in saucepan. Simmer 10 minutes. Remove from heat and add coconut extract.
- Pour syrup evenly over warm cake when it comes out of oven. Let the cake sit to absorb syrup 10–15 minutes. Unmold.

Aunt Pearl's Cake

Barbara W. Burwick

1/2 pound butter
3 cups sugar
6 eggs
3 cups flour
1/4 teaspoon baking soda
1/4 teaspoon salt

1 cup sour cream
1/2 teaspoon rum flavoring
1 teaspoon orange extract
1/2 teaspoon lemon extract
1 teaspoon vanilla
1/2 cup apricot brandy

- Cream butter and sugar. Add eggs one at a time. Beat well.
- Sift flour, soda and salt.
- Combine sour cream with flavorings and brandy.
- Add sour cream mixture alternately with flour mixture to butter and sugar mixture. Mix until well blended.
- Bake at 350°F for 70 minutes.

7-UP Cake

Lois Lopatin

3 sticks butter or margarine
3 cups sugar
5 eggs

2 cups flour
2 tablespoons lemon extract
³/₄ cup 7-UP soda, non-diet

- Cream butter and sugar for 20 minutes.
- Add eggs one at a time.
- Add flour slowly.
- Add lemon extract.
- Fold in the soda.
- Pour into a well greased 12 cup bundt pan.
- Bake in 325°F oven for 60–90 minutes.

Black Bottom Pie

Mrs. Maurice Jaffee

¹/₂ cup sugar
1 tablespoon cornstarch
2 cups milk, scalded
4 egg yolks, beaten
1 6-ounce package semisweet
    chocolate bits
1 teaspoon vanilla

1 baked 9-inch pie shell
1 tablespoon (1 envelope) unflavored
    gelatin
¹/₄ cup cold water
4 egg whites
¹/₂ cup sugar
1 cup heavy cream, whipped

- Combine sugar and cornstarch. Slowly add scalded milk to beaten egg yolks. Stir in sugar mixture. Cook in top of double boiler until custard coats spoon.
- To 1 cup of the custard, add the chocolate pieces. Stir until chocolate is melted. Add vanilla.
- Pour into bottom of cooled, baked pie shell. Chill.
- Soften gelatin in cold water, add to the remaining hot custard. Stir until dissolved. Chill until slightly thick.
- Beat egg whites, adding sugar gradually, until stiff peaks form. Fold into custard-gelatin mixture.
- Pour over chocolate layer and chill until set. Garnish with whipped cream and decorate with grated bitter chocolate.

Variation: 3 tablespoons of imported white rum may be lastly folded into custard if rum chiffon pie is desired.

Heavenly Pie

Mrs. Elias S. Grace

Make this a day before using. Great for Passover.

1 cup sugar
1/4 teaspoon cream of tartar
4 egg whites
3 tablespoons coconut shredded, optional
4 egg yolks

1/2 cup sugar
3 tablespoons lemon juice
1 tablespoon grated lemon rind
1/8 teaspoon salt
1 pint heavy cream

- Preheat oven to 275°F.
- Sift l cup sugar with cream of tartar.
- Beat egg whites until stiff peaks are formed. Slowly add sugar, beating well. When stiff and glossy, spread in a well-greased 9-inch pie plate, making bottom 1/2-inch high with sides l-inch. Sprinkle with coconut, if desired.
- Bake 1 hour. Cool.
- Beat egg yolks slightly in double boiler, then stir in 1/2 cup sugar, lemon juice, grated rind, and salt. Stir over boiling water until thick, about 8–10 minutes.
- When cool add l cup cream, whipped. Blend into custard filling. Pour into meringue shell. Refrigerate for 24 hours.
- Garnish with unsweetened whipped cream and strawberries, or use your imagination. This freezes beautifully.

Lemon Meringue Pie

Mrs. S. Gilbert Davis

1 baked 9- or 10-inch pie shell
6 eggs
1 cup sugar
juice of 2 lemons
grated lemon rind, optional

Meringue:
4 egg whites
1/3 teaspoon cream of tartar
8 tablespoons sugar

- Separate eggs, hold 2 whites aside.
- Beat yolks. add sugar gradually. Add lemon juice. Cook in top of double boiler until thick. Cool.
- Beat 2 egg whites, fold in, and pour into shell.

Meringue:
- Beat egg whites with cream of tartar until frothy. Gradually beat in sugar, a little at a time. Continue beating until stiff and glossy.
- Pile meringue onto filling, being careful to seal meringue to edge of crust. Swirl or pull up points for decoration.
- Bake at 400°F for 8–10 minutes. Let cool, away from drafts. Serves 8–10.

Banana Cream Pie

Ruth Seder

1 baked pie shell

Filling:
½ cup sugar
5 tablespoons flour
¼ teaspoon salt

2 cups milk
2 egg yolks
1 tablespoon butter
½ teaspoon vanilla
3–4 bananas, sliced

- Stir to combine sugar, flour, and salt. Put in top of double boiler, over simmering water. Add milk and cook stirring until thick. Cover and cook 10 minutes, stirring occasionally.
- Add egg yolks slightly beaten and beat till smooth. Cook 1 minute longer. Remove.
- Add butter and vanilla. Cover and cool.
- Slice bananas to cover pie shell in 1 layer. Cover with filling, another layer of bananas, and end with filling.
- Refrigerate. Top with whipped cream.

Southern Pecan Pie

Nancy Shulman

1 cup sugar
1 cup dark corn syrup
¼ teaspoon salt
1 tablespoon flour
2 extra large eggs

1 teaspoon vanilla
1 tablespoon butter, melted
2 cups pecan halves
1 unbaked 9-inch pie shell

- Preheat oven to 300°F.
- Beat together sugar, syrup, salt, flour, and eggs. Add vanilla, butter and pecans. Pour into unbaked pie shell.
- Place rounded sides of pecans up on top of pie.
- Bake at 300°F for about 1 hour until filling is set.

Pecan Pie

Mrs. Samuel O. Chandler

4 eggs
1 cup white sugar
1 cup dark Karo Syrup
1/2 teaspoon salt
1 tablespoon flour

3 tablespoons butter, melted
2 teaspoons vanilla
1 1/2 cup pecans
1 unbaked 9-inch pie shell

- Beat eggs well.
- Add sugar, Karo, salt, flour, butter, vanilla, and nuts. Mix well.
- Pour into unbaked pie shell and bake 55 minutes in a 350°F oven.

Continental Chocolate Torte

Mrs. Franz Meyersohn

3 ounces semisweet chocolate bits
1 tablespoon strong coffee
1 cup granulated sugar
7 eggs, separated
2 cups walnut meats, finely ground
  currant jelly

Frosting:
1/4 pound sweet butter
1 cup confectioners' sugar
1 egg yolk
3 ounces semisweet chocolate bits,
  melted
2 tablespoons strong coffee
2 tablespoons rum
  currant jelly

- Melt chocolate bits in coffee.
- Beat sugar and egg yolks, add melted chocolate and about 3/4 of the walnuts.
- Fold in stiffly beaten egg whites and the remaing walnuts.
- Butter and dust with flour a 9-inch springform pan and pour batter in.
- Bake in 350°F oven for about 50 minutes.

Frosting:
- Cream butter and sugar. Add egg yolk.
- When well creamed, add other ingredients and cream again. If frosting is too soft, refrigerate until it can be spread.
- After cake is cool, remove from pan and cut into 2 layers. Spread 1 layer with currant jelly and frosting. Place other layer on top and repeat this procedure, also spreading sides of cake with frosting.

The Jewish Home Cookbook

Cherry Chocolate Cake

Reva Thomashaw

Innovative

2 cups flour
³/₄ cup sugar
³/₄ cup canola oil
2 eggs
2 teaspoons vanilla

1 teaspoon baking soda
1 teaspoon cinnamon
1 can cherry pie filling
1 6-ounce package chocolate chips
1 cup chopped nuts

- Preheat oven to 350°F.
- In large bowl, put all ingredients except pie filling, chocolate chips, and nuts. Mix well. Mixture will be thick.
- Mix pie filling, chocolate chips and nuts and fold into batter.
- Pour into greased and floured 10-inch tube pan.
- Bake 1 hour or until done. Cool and remove from pan. Serves 10–12.

Chocolate Chip Cake Squares

Susan Starr

¹/₄ pound margarine
1 cup sugar
2 eggs
1 cup sour cream
1 teaspoon vanilla
2 cups flour
1¹/₂ teaspoons baking powder
1 teaspoon baking soda

Topping:
¹/₂ cup sugar mixed with 1 teaspoon cinnamon
6 ounces chocolate chips

- Cream margarine, sugar, and eggs. Add sour cream, vanilla, flour, baking powder, and baking soda. Batter will become very thick.
- Spread ¹/₂ the batter in greased 9 x 11-inch pan. Sprinkle with ¹/₂ the sugar mixture and ¹/₂ the chips. Spread the rest of the batter. Sprinkle the rest of the sugar and chips.
- Bake at 350°F for 30 minutes.

Ida and Ruthie's Hershey Cake

Mari Seder

Never fail — moist — easy!

1 cup sugar
¹/₄ pound butter
4 eggs
1 teaspoon vanilla

1 can Hersey's syrup
1 cup self-rising cake flour
nuts, optional
chocolate chips, optional

- Cream sugar and butter. Beat in one egg at a time. Add vanilla and Hershey's syrup. Add flour. Add nuts and/or chocolate chips if desired.
- Bake in a lightly greased and floured 11 x 9 x 2-inch pan, 350°F oven for 30–35 minutes. Cut into squares.

Never Fail Chocolate Cake

Sylvia Levy

This was my mother's recipe and was always most popular!

¹/₂ cup butter
1¹/₂ cups sugar
2 egg
2 squares unsweetened chocolate, melted
2 cups cake flour
¹/₂ teaspoon salt

¹/₂ cup milk
¹/₂ cup sour cream
1 teaspoon vanilla
1 tablespoon vinegar
1 teaspoon baking powder
1 teaspoon baking soda

- Cream butter and sugar.
- When well creamed, add the eggs, and beat only a minute or 2. Add melted chocolate.
- Combine flour and salt. Combine milk and sour cream.
- Add flour mixture and milk mixture to creamed mixture alternately, beating slowly. Add vanilla.
- Measure the vinegar into 1 tablespoon measuring spoon holding it over the cake mixture. Put the teaspoon of soda into the vinegar. It will foam up. Add to batter.
- Have 2 well buttered and floured 9-inch round cake pans ready. Pour cake mixture evenly into 2 pans.
- Bake ¹/₂ hour in 325°F oven.
- Frost between layers when cooled and over top and sides with either chocolate or vanilla icing. Serves 10–12 depending on size of serving.

Chocolate Sponge Roll

Mrs. Maurice Corbin

6 tablespoons flour, sifted
6 tablespoons cocoa
1/2 teaspoon baking powder
1/4 teaspoon salt
4 egg whites

3/4 cup sugar
4 egg yolks
1 teaspoon vanilla
confectioners' sugar
whipped cream or ice cream for filling

- Sift flour, cocoa, baking powder, and salt together.
- Beat egg whites stiff, gradually adding the sugar.
- Beat egg yolks until thick and light colored. Add vanilla.
- Fold yolks into whites carefully, then fold in the flour mixture. Pour into a buttered jelly roll pan that has been lined with waxed paper.
- Bake in a 400°F oven for about 12 minutes.
- Turn out onto a towel which has been covered with confectioners' sugar. Remove waxed paper and roll cake gently.
- Cover with towel until cool, then unroll cake and spread with a cup of sweetened whipped cream. Save some to cover up. Reroll and keep in refrigerator until serving time.
- Instead of the whipped cream, you can take about 3/4 of a quart of coffee ice cream, softened a bit, and spread on the roll. Reroll and put in freezer.
- Serve with a chocolate sauce — it's delicious.

Choc-o-Date Dessert

Annette McDonald Kelly

12 crushed chocolate sandwich cookies
1 8-ounce package cut pitted dates
3/4 cup water
1/4 teaspoon salt
2 cups tiny marshmallows

1/2 cup chopped walnuts
1 cup heavy cream, whipped
1/2 teaspoon vanilla
walnut halves

- Reserve 1/4 cup cookie crumbs. Spread remainder into a 10 x 6 x 1 1/2-inch baking tin.
- In saucepan, combine dates, water, and salt. Bring to boiling and simmer 3 minutes. Add marshmallows and cool.
- Add nuts, whipped cream, and vanilla and stir.
- Pour into baking tin and top with crumbs and walnuts. Chill overnight.

Chocolate Truffle Cake

Carol S. Glick

Very delicious and rich!

1/2 cup water
1 1/3 cups sugar
8 ounces semisweet chocolate chips
4 ounces unsweetened chocolate

1/2 pound sweet butter
5 extra large eggs, at room temperature
1 tablespoon vanilla

- Combine water with 1 cup sugar in 2-quart saucepan. Bring to a boil over high heat and cook about 4 minutes.
- Add both chocolates. Add butter, stirring until all is melted.
- Beat eggs with remaining sugar until pale yellow and trippled in volume, about 15 minutes.
- Reduce speed to low and add chocolate mixture, beating only until mixed. Add vanilla. Do not over beat.
- Grease a 9-inch cake pan and then add parchment paper that has been cut in a circle to fit. Grease again. Using a rubber spatula, turn batter into the pan. Set in a large pan and pour boiling water around it.
- Bake 25 minutes at 350°F. Test by inserting knife.
- When cool, sprinkle powdered sugar on it. Serves 10–12.

Melissa's Italian Cake

Melissa Benjamin

1/2 cup dried currants
1/2 cup rum
12 ounces semisweet chocolate bits
1 ounce bitter chocolate, chopped
2 sticks sweet butter
1/4 cup water
6 large eggs, separated
1 1/3 cups sugar
1 teaspoon almond extract

1 teaspoon vanilla extract
1/2 teaspoon salt
1/2 cup flour
1 1/3 cups ground almonds

Glaze:
1/2 cup semisweet chocolate
1 stick unsalted butter

- Combine currants and rum and let macerate for 15 minutes.
- Melt the chocolate and butter with water over low heat, stirring until the mixture is smooth.
- Beat the yolks with the sugar in mixer until the mixture is thick and pale.
- Stir in the extracts, salt, flour, almonds, currant mixture, and chocolate mixture until well mixed.
- In another bowl beat the whites until they hold stiff peaks.
- Stir 1/4 of whites into chocolate mixture then fold in the remaining whites.
- Pour the batter into a greased 9-inch springform pan fitted with parchment paper over the bottom and 1/2-inch up the sides (or use a 9- or 10-inch cake pan which has been greased and floured).
- Bake in 350°F oven 45–50 minutes until it is just set in the middle. Let cool and turn out of pan.

Glaze:
- Melt the butter and chocolate over low heat stirring until smooth. Pour glaze over the cake smoothing it on top and sides. Decorate it with toasted slivered almonds, if desired.

Coconut-Carrot Cake

Nancy Benjamin

4 eggs
2 cups sugar
1½ cups oil
2 cups flour
2 teaspoons baking powder
1½ teaspoons baking soda
½ teaspoon salt
2 cups grated carrots
1 cup crushed pineapple (8½ ounces), drained

1 cup chopped nuts
3½ ounces flaked coconut
2 teaspoons vanilla

Cream Cheese Icing:
4 ounces cream cheese
3 tablespoons unsalted butter, at room temperature
1½ cups confectioners' sugar
1 teaspoon vanilla extract

- Preheat oven to 350°F.
- Beat eggs and sugar until frothy. Add oil and beat.
- Sift dry ingredients together and add to mixture. Add remaining ingredients and mix until well blended.
- Bake 2 greased 9-inch pans for 45 minutes until tests dry. Unmold and cool.

Cream Cheese Icing:
- Mix cream cheese and butter in mixer until well blended.
- Sift in sugar and mix until fully incorporated. Add vanilla.
- Frost cooled cake.

Halsema — Yogurt Cake

Lorraine Lonstein

Greek recipe.

2 eggs
1½ cups quick-cooking Cream of Wheat
1½ cups sugar
½ cup butter, melted
1 16-ounce carton plain yogurt or sour cream
juice of ½ lemon
½ teaspoon baking soda

Syrup:
1½ cups sugar
1¼ cups water
juice of ½ lemon
lemon rind

- In a large bowl, beat eggs well.
- Combine the Cream of Wheat and sugar. Add to eggs along with the butter, beating well. Reduce mixer speed and gradually add yogurt.
- Combine lemon juice and baking soda and add to batter.
- Bake in a greased 13 x 9-inch baking pan at 375°F for 25–30 minutes or until golden brown.

Syrup:
- While cake is baking, combine all ingredients in a saucepan and gently boil for 10 minutes.
- Remove lemon rind and discard.
- Drizzle cooled syrup over warm cake. Cover tightly to steam, about 1 hour.
- May be served with whipped cream and sliced strawberries, peaches, or blueberries. Serves 24.

Eclair Ring

Roberta Kunen

It takes about two hours to defrost after freezing.

1 stick butter or margarine
1 cup water
1 cup flour
4 eggs

Filling:
2 packages instant vanilla pudding mix
2¹/₂ cups milk
1 teaspoon vanilla
1 pint heavy cream

- Melt butter in boiling water. Add flour all at once.
- Cook on low heat, stirring constantly, until the mixture forms a ball that doesn't separate. Remove from heat and cool.
- Add eggs one at a time. Beat until smooth after each egg.
- Drop by spoonfuls on a greased cookie sheet to form a ring.
- Bake at 450°F for 20 minutes.
- Cool, cut in half, and then fill.

Filling:
- Beat pudding, milk, and vanilla until it thickens. Refrigerate.
- Whip cream and fold into pudding.
- Fill ring and refrigerate (I freeze it until firm).
- Top with hot fudge before serving. Serves 8–10.

Tiramisu

Ellen Regent

2 egg yolks
¹/₄ cup sugar
¹/₂ cup low-fat milk
¹/₄ cup Kahlua or other coffee liqueur
2 tablespoons espresso coffee, brewed or made with instant

1 12-pack of small ladyfingers
1 ounce semisweet chocolate, grated
2 teaspoons cocoa powder
4 ounces softened cream cheese
³/₄–1 cup whipping cream, whipped

- In top of double boiler, combine egg yolks, sugar, and milk, stirring with a whisk during cooking, until slightly thickened.
- Set pot over ice water to cool, for about 15 minutes.
- Combine liqueur and coffee in a pie plate. Dip ladyfingers into liquid on each side to absorb, set aside.
- Combine chocolate and cocoa powder. Set aside.
- When milk mixture has cooled, fold in cheese, then whipped cream.
- Divide and layer ingredients in goblets, square dish, or dessert dish of your choice as follows: 1/3 cream mixture, 1/2 the chocolate, 3 ladyfingers each, remaining cream mixture, and remaining chocolate.
- Cover and chill 2 hours or overnight.

Lemon Jello Trifle

Barbara Robbins

1 6-ounce (or 2 3-ounce) box lemon Jello
2 cups boiling water
juice of 2 lemons (or 5 tablespoons
    lemon juice)
16 ounces of 7UP — be sure 7UP is
    not flat

8 ounces Cool Whip
Mandarin oranges, optional
sliced strawberries, optional
kiwi fruit, optional

- Add 2 cups boiling water to Jello. Add lemon juice and 7UP to the Jello. Refrigerate in large bowl for 2 hours.
- Take out and beat with electric mixer for 5 minutes.
- Fold in Cool Whip and put entire mixture in a large trifle bowl. Refrigerate overnight to set properly.
- As an option, after this is set, it can be garnished on top with Mandarin oranges and/or sliced strawberries, and kiwi fruit. Serves 12.

⌂ Baked Custard

Mrs. Max Cohen

3 eggs
$1/2$ cup sugar
1 teaspoon vanilla

$1/2$ teaspoon salt
1 pint milk, scalded

- Beat eggs, adding sugar gradually. Add vanilla and salt. Slowly add scalded milk.
- Pour into custard cups, set in pan two-thirds full of warm water.
- Bake in moderate oven (350°F) for 30–40 minutes. Test with a silver knife. If knife comes out clean, the custard is done.

Outrageous Chocolate Mousse

Garie Morgenstern Stein

The best chocolate mousse that you will ever taste.

2 bars German sweet chocolate
3 tablespoons confectioners' sugar
2½ tablespoons water

4 eggs, separated
¾ pint heavy or whipping cream whipped

- Melt chocolate in a pan with confectioners' sugar and water.
- Beat egg yolks for 3 minutes. Mix yolks and melted chocolate for 2 minutes.
- Beat eggs whites until stiff.
- Fold egg whites into chocolate mixture.
- Fold in cream. Refrigerate for a few hours. Serves 10-12.

Chocolate Mousse

Roma Joseph

Has become a tradition!

½ pound semisweet chocolate bits
1 teaspoon instant coffee
2 tablespoons water
¾ cup confectioners' sugar

6 egg yolks
4 tablespoons cognac or Kahlua
2 cups heavy cream

- Melt chocolate, coffee, and water in double boiler. Stir until smooth. Cool.
- Cream sugar and yolks until thick.
- Blend egg and chocolate mixtures. Add cognac and blend well.
- Whip cream until soft peaks form and fold into chocolate mixture.
- Put in glass bowl. Chill at least 4 hours. Freezes very well. Serves 12.

Chocolate Chip Cookie Pie with Walnuts

Karen Cohen

The pie is delicious and very rich. Can serve 8 to 12 people.

2 eggs
½ cup granulated sugar
½ cup flour (optional: use ¼ cup whole
    wheat flour and ¼ cup white flour)
½ cup firmly packed brown sugar
1½ sticks butter, softened

6 ounces chocolate chips
1 cup chopped walnuts
ice cream and/or whipeed cream, optional
pie crust (I use ready-made graham
    cracker brust)

- Preheat oven to 325°F.
- In a large bowl, beat eggs until foamy, approximately 2–3 minutes. For a cakier pie, beat eggs for 3 minutes, for a chewier, gooey pie, beat eggs for 2 minutes. I much prefer the richer, gooey pie and would recommend a 2 minute moderate beating.
- Blend in granulated sugar, flour, and brown sugar until well mixed.
- Fold in softened butter. I melt the butter on very low heat and let it cool down, and then add it to the batter.
- Finally, add the chocolate chips and the walnuts and mix well. Pour into the pie crust.
- Bake for 55–60 minutes.
- Serve warm with ice cream and/or whipped cream. Serves 8–12 people.

Chocolate-Toffee Pie

Lolita Baker

Excellent and simply heavenly

Crust:
½ package pie crust mix
1 tablespoon water
1 teaspoon vanilla
¼ cup brown sugar
¾ cup chopped walnuts
1 bitter chocolate square, grated

Filling:
½ cup butter
¾ cup granulated sugar
1 1-ounce bitter chocolate square, melted
2 teaspoons instant coffee
2 eggs

Topping:
2 cups heavy cream
2 tablespoons instant coffee
½ cup confectioners' sugar

Crust:
- Mix crust ingredients and press into a 9- or 10-inch pie plate. Bake 15 minutes at 375°F. Cool.

Filling:
- Beat butter until creamy. Add sugar, instant coffee, and melted chocolate. Beat until fluffy.
- Add 1 egg, beat for 5 minutes. Add other egg and beat for another 5 minutes.
- Pour into cooled pie shell. Refrigerate overnight.

Topping:
- Whip cream, sugar, and coffee until stiff. Spread over pie. Refrigerate another 2 hours. Serves 8.

⌂ Kiss Torte

Mrs. Samuel O. Chandler

6 egg whites	1 teaspoon vinegar
2 cups sugar	whipped cream
1 teaspoon vanilla	berries

- Beat egg whites until stiff peaks form. Then slowly beat in 6 tablespoons sugar, beating thoroughly.
- Add vanilla, vinegar, and fold in remainder of sugar.
- Pour ²/₃ of the mixture into a greased springform pan.
- Make small kisses dropped from a teaspoon with the remainder of the mixture and form a circle on a greased tin, the same size and shape as the spring form.
- Bake both springform and tray of kisses 1 hour or longer in slow 275°F oven.
- Fill with whipped cream and sliced fresh berries, slightly sweetened and decorate top with circle of baked kisses.

⌂ Linzer Torte

Mrs. Joseph Muller

This cake may be baked several days before serving.

²/₃ cup sugar	grated rind of 1 lemon
1¹/₃ cups flour	1 tablespoon lemon juice
1¹/₄ cups walnut meats, ground very fine	1 teaspoon cinnamon
²/₃ cup butter	¹/₂ teaspoon cloves
2 large egg yolks	¹/₃ cup apricot or raspberry preserves

- Knead together all ingredients except preserves. Pat ²/₃ of mixture in ungreased springform or a 9 x 9-inch square pan.
- Spread with apricot or raspberry preserves. Do not substitute jelly.
- With remaining dough, make bars the size of a pencil and place on top, making a lattice effect.
- Brush bars with an additional egg yolk if you desire.
- Bake for about 45 minutes in a 350°F oven until brown. Remove from pan when completely cool.

Torte with Chocolate Buttercream

M. Zuckerman

Cake:
6 eggs, separated
1 cup granulated sugar
1 cup ground nuts
2 tablespoons graham cracker crumbs
1 teaspoon vanilla

Frosting:
1 cup sweet butter
1 cup confectioners' sugar
4 ounces chocolate, melted and cooled
marmalade
2 teaspoons sherry

- Beat egg yolks, gradually adding granulated sugar.
- Add ground nuts and cracker crumbs, then vanilla. Fold in stiffly beaten egg whites.
- Bake in 2 greased and floured 9-inch pans in 350°F oven for about 30 minutes. Cool.
- To prepare frosting, cream butter and sugar, and whip until fluffy.
- Add chocolate and mix well.
- Spread 1 layer with marmalade. Sprinkle with sherry. Place other layer on top and cover top and sides of cake with butter icing.

Frozen White Chocolate Mousse

Jenique Radin

9 ounces white chocolate, chopped
6 egg yolks, at room temperature
1 tablespoon granulated sugar
1 tablespoon water

$1/4$ cup white creme de cacao
3 cups whipping cream
1 pint raspberries
2 tablespoons confectioners' sugar

- Melt chocolate in top of double boiler over hot, not simmering, water, stirring until smooth. Remove from heat.
- Whisk yolks, sugar, and water in large metal bowl set over saucepan of simmering water until pale yellow and slowly dissolving ribbon forms when whisk is lifted, about 5 minutes.
- Remove from water. Whisk in chocolate and creme de cacao.
- Whip cream and gently fold into mixture. Cover and freeze overnight. Can be prepared up to 4 days ahead.

Sauce:
- Purée raspberries and 1 tablespoon confectioners' in processor until smooth. Add more sugar to taste.
- Sieve to eliminate seeds. Store to use as topping.

Assembly:
- Serve in deep wine glasses with sauce on bottom and top or serve in chocolate cups with sauce on top. You can place the mousse in the chocolate cups and freeze all ready to be served, add sauce just before serving. Allow cups or frozen container to slightly thaw in refrigerator before serving. Serves 24.

Sabra Mousse

Ruth Margolis

Enjoy! Enjoy!

2 packages ladyfingers, separated into
single pieces
6 ounces semisweet chocolate bits
8 ounces cream cheese. softened

1 cup brown sugar
3 eggs separated, at room temperature
1 1/2–3 teaspoons Sabra (orange liqueur)
2 cups heavy cream

- Place mixing bowl and whipping tool in freezer. Butter the interior of a 9-inch springform pan.
- Arrange about 22 pieces of ladyfingers vertically around the edge and most of the balance on the bottom of the pan. Cover and set aside.
- Melt chocolate over hot water, or on medium heat in a microwave, taking care not to burn. Stir until melted. Cool.
- Combine the cream cheese and 1/2 cup of brown sugar and beat until creamy. Add egg yolks and beat again.
- Stir in the melted chocolate and liquer and mix again.
- Beat egg whites and gradually beat in 1/2 cup of brown sugar. Beat until stiff, satiny peaks form.
- Whip cream in the chilled bowl until peaks form.
- Fold egg whites into the chocolate mixture. Fold in the whipped cream until it is blended well.
- Pour into the lady finger lined pan. Comb surface to finish. Freeze overnight.
- Place in refrigerator 1 hour before serving. Serves 20–30.

Hot Fudge Sauce

Sue Seder

1/4 pound butter
5 squares unsweetened baking chocolate
1 can evaporated milk

3 cups confectioners' sugar
1 teaspoon vanilla

- Melt butter and chocolate in a saucepan.
- Slowly add evaporated milk and then confectioners' sugar. Cook slowly and wait until mixture comes to a boil.
- Remove from heat. Add vanilla.
- Refrigerate. Reheat before using.

*Pastries, Bars,
and Cookies*

Nana Schultz's Strudel

Gina Schultz

This recipe has been handed down from my husband's grandmother.

Filling I:
12–16-ounce package pitted prunes
1 cup seedless raisins
1/2 teaspoon cinnamon

Filling II:
3–4 apples, peeled, cored, and sliced
1/2 cup chopped walnuts, optional
1/3 cup sugar
cinnamon, to taste

Dough:
5 tablespoons vegetable shortening
   (crisco)
2 teaspoons baking powder
2 cups flour
1 teaspoon salt
1 egg, slightly beaten
1/2 cup sugar
1/2 cup strong tea, cooled

1 1/2 cups crushed corn flakes
1 16-ounce jar orange marmalade
cinnamon and sugar

- Stew together prunes, raisins, and cinnamon. Cool.
- Mix apples, chopped walnuts, 1/3 cup sugar, and cinnamon to taste. Set aside.
- Blend ingredients for dough. Refrigerate until well chilled.
- Divide dough into quarters. Roll out 1 quarter at a time, keeping remaining dough refrigerated. Roll out on a well floured board to fit a 9 x 13-inch pan. If dough is too difficult to roll, it can be pressed into pan.
- Place in greased pan and sprinkle with crushed corn flakes. Place prune and raisin filling on top. Roll out another quarter. Sprinkle with corn flakes. Top with apple walnut mixture.
- Roll out third quarter. Spread top with orange marmalade. Roll out remaining dough and, sprinkle with a mixture of cinnamon and sugar.
- Bake in a 350°F oven for 1 1/2 hours. Cut into 1-inch sqaures with sharp knife. Makes 20 pieces.

Phyllis's Easy Strudel

Phyllis Dorfman

Everyone adores it.

1/2 pound butter, at room temperature
2 cups flour
1 cup vanilla ice cream

Filling:
1 10-ounce jar apricot jam
1 cup shredded coconut

1 cup white raisins
1 cup chopped walnuts, optional

Topping:
milk
cinnamon
sugar

- Knead first 3 ingredients together until ball is formed. Refrigerate overnight.
- Bring to room temperature and divide into 4 parts.
- Roll each part on floured board into a rectangle. Spread with above filling. Roll like jelly roll. Cover each roll with milk, cinnamon, and sugar.
- Bake 20–30 minutes at 350°F on a slightly buttered cookie sheet. Cool. Cut on a diagonal. Freezes well. Makes about 40 pieces.

Strudel

Ethel Slovin

Delicious and easy to make.

2 cups flour
1/2 pound margarine
1/2 cup club soda
confectioners' sugar
apricot jam

chopped walnuts, optional
raisins, rinsed in hot water
coconut
cinnamon and sugar

- Knead flour and margarine. Add soda. Make 3 balls of dough and wrap in waxed paper. Refrigerate overnight.
- Take out 1 hour before rolling out. Roll out on confectioners' sugar.
- Spread with apricot jam, chopped nuts, raisins, and coconut. Top with cinnamon and sugar. Cut top where you plan to slice.
- Bake in a 350°F oven 45–60 minutes on Pam-sprayed cookie sheet. Makes about 48 slices.

Cookie Dough Strudel

Tillie Katz

Dough:
1/2 cup shortening
1/2 cup sugar
3 eggs, beaten
3 cups flour
2 teaspoons baking powder
1/2 teaspoon salt

Filling:
1 15-ounce box raisins, rinsed in hot water
1 whole orange, cut-up
2 teaspoons sugar and cinnamon

Dough:
- Rub together shortening and sugar. Add eggs 1 at a time.
- Sift together flour, baking powder, and salt. Add dry ingredients to egg mixture and form dough. Put in freezer for 10 minutes.
- Roll out 3 parts. Grind orange and raisins together. Mix with sugar and cinnamon and spread 1/3 of mixture on each part. Roll up.
- Bake on greased cookie sheet in 325°F oven for 30 minutes or as necessary. Slices best when frozen.

"Rogelach"

Ruth Jacobs

Scrumptious!!!

Sour Cream Pastry:
2 cups all-purpose flour
1/4 teaspoon salt
1 cup (2 sticks) unsalted butter, cut into
  tablespoons
3/4 cup sour cream
1 large egg yolk

Chocolate-Walnut Filling:
2 ounces semisweet chocolate, coarsely
  chopped, or 1/3 cup semisweet
  chocolate chips
1/2 ounce unsweetened baking chocolate,
  coarsley chopped
1/3 cup walnut meats
3 tablespoons sugar
1/2 teaspoon cinnamon

Topping:
2 tablespoons unsalted butter, melted
3 tablespoons sugar
1/2 teaspoon cinnamon

Sour Cream Pastry:
- In a food processor fitted with the metal chopping blade, combine flour and salt. Process 5 seconds, until blended.
- Evenly distribute the butter cubes and sour cream over flour mixture. Add egg yolk. Process 10–20 seconds, just until the dough starts to hold together and comes away from the sides of the workbowl.
- Wrap the dough in plastic wrap and refrigerate overnight or at least 2 hours, until firm.

Filling:
- In a food processor, process the chocolates, walnuts, sugar, and cinnamon until finely chopped. Transfer mixture to a small bowl.

Assembly:
- Position 2 racks in the top and bottom thirds of the oven and preheat to 375°F.
- Divide the dough into quarters. Leave 3/4 in the refrigerator, place the fourth on a lightly floured work surface, and roll into a 9-inch circle. Spread 3 tablespoons of the filling onto the dough and press it down gently.
- With a sharp knife, cut the circle into 12 wedges. Beginning with the outside edge, roll each wedge tightly.
- Place the "rogelach," point side down, on an ungreased baking sheet leaving 1/2-inch between the cookies.
- One fourth at a time, prepare the remaining "rogelach," keeping the already assembled cookies in the refrigerator while you work.

Topping:
- Brush the "rogelach" with the melted butter. Sprinkle sugar and cinnamon over the top.
- Bake 30 minutes until golden brown. Transfer them to a wire rack to cool completely. Store cookies in airtight container for up to 1 week. **Enjoy!!**

Melissa's Biscotti

Melissa Benjamin

2³/₄ cups sifted flour
1¹/₂ cups sugar
¹/₂ cup unsalted butter
2¹/₂ teaspoons baking powder
1 teaspoon salt

5 ounces white chocolate
1²/₃ cups almonds, toasted
2 eggs
¹/₄ cup brandy or rum
2 teaspoons almond extract

- Combine flour, sugar, butter, baking powder, and salt in food processor. Process until it forms a fine texture.
- Add white chocolate and process until finely chopped. Add almonds and coarsley chop.
- In another bowl, beat eggs, brandy, and extract. Add flour mixture and stir until moist dough forms.
- Grease cookie sheet. Form dough on sheets into 3 12-inch long strips. Shape each dough strip into 2-inch wide log. Refrigerate until dough is firm, about 30 minutes.
- Preheat oven to 350°F. Bake logs until golden, about 30 minutes. Cool.
- Reduce oven to 300°F. Cut logs into ³/₄-inch slices. Place cut side down. Bake 10 minutes on each side. Cool.

Mandel Brot

Natalie N. Seder

This is the best recipe I have had for mandel brot.

1 stick butter
³/₄ cup sugar
2 eggs
1 teaspoon vanilla
2¹/₂ cups flour

¹/₄ teaspoon salt
1 teaspoon baking powder
1 cup chopped almonds, lightly toasted
cinnamon and sugar

- Cream butter and sugar. Add eggs, one at a time. Beat well. Add vanilla.
- Sift flour, salt, and baking powder. Add to mixture, Add almonds.
- Make 3 small loaves. Bake on jelly roll pan at 350° for 30 minutes.
- While **hot**, cut diagonally in slices about ¹/₂-inch thick. Sprinke with cinnamon and sugar.
- Turn each piece, sprinkle with cinnamon and sugar, and bake for an additional 10 minutes. *Happy munching!* Makes 3 small loaves.

Mandel Bread

Mollie Steinberg

4 eggs
1 cup sugar
1 cup shortening (oil)
1 teaspoon vanilla
2¹/₂ cups sifted flour

1 teaspoon baking powder
1 cup walnut meats
10 marachino cherries, drained
    and cut-up

- Beat eggs. Add sugar, oil, and vanilla. Beat well.
- Fold in sifted flour and baking powder. Add nuts and cherries.
- Place dough on cookie sheets. Cut in 10 strips on 2 cookie sheets.
- Bake 350°F oven for 15 minutes. Cut into pieces after it is baked. Shut off oven and put pieces back in to crisp for 10 minutes.

Chocolate Chip Mandel Bread

Bette Jagodnik

3 cups all-purpose flour
2 teaspoons baking powder
¹/₂ teaspoon salt
3 eggs
1 cup plus 1 tablespoon vegetable oil
1 scant cup sugar

1 cup chopped pecans
4 ounces chocolate chips
5 tablespoons sugar
1 teaspoon cinnamon

- Preheat oven to 375°F. Grease or spray cookie sheet.
- Mix all dry ingredients in small bowl.
- Beat eggs, oil, and sugar until well blended. Gradually add 2 cups of flour mixture, beating constantly.
- Fold in nuts and chocolate chips. Add remaining flour mixture and mix well.
- Form dough in 4 strips on wide side of cookie sheet. Combine sugar and cinnamon and sprinkle over strips.
- Bake for 20 minutes. Cut, at an angle, into ¹/₂-inch slices. Separate. Return to oven for toasting, watching carefully, for 10–15 minutes.

🗂 Bird's Nest

Mrs. David Israel

1/2 cup butter
1/2 cup brown sugar
1 egg, separated
1 cup flour

pinch of salt
1/2 teaspoon vanilla
1 cup chopped nuts or coconut, optional

- Cream butter and sugar. Add yolk of egg and beat well. Add flour, pinch of salt, and vanilla. Mix well.
- Form dough into small balls (smaller than walnut). Dip in slightly beaten egg white and then roll in nuts or coconut if desired. Press center with tip of fingers to make a nest.
- Bake about 8 minutes in 350°F oven. Remove from oven and press center in again. Return to oven for 10 minutes. When cool fill centers with jam.

Lacey Oatmeal Cookies

Esty Lieberman

Better than candy!

2 tablespoons plus 1 teaspoon flour
1 cup quick-cooking rolled oats
1/4 teaspoon baking powder
1/2 teaspoon pinch salt

1 egg, beaten
1/4 pound margarine or butter, melted
1 cup sugar
2 teaspoons vanilla

- Combine dry ingredients.
- Beat egg and add margarine, sugar, and vanilla. Add to dry mixture.
- Cover cookie sheet with aluminum foil. Drop 1/2 teaspoonful at a time 2–3 inches apart.
- Bake in a 350°F oven, 10–12 minutes or until edges are brown. Cool then peel off foil.

Grandma Starr's Twists

Reva Thomashow

½ cup raisins
⅓ cup warm water
2 large eggs
½ cup sugar
pinch salt
⅓ cup oil
1 teaspoon baking powder
3 cups all-purpose flour

Topping:
1 cup sugar
2 teaspoons cinnamon
oil, as needed

- Soak raisins in warm water for a few minutes, drain, and set aside.
- Mix eggs, sugar, and salt. Add oil and mix well. Add drained raisins and warm water.
- Mix in baking powder and flour. Form into a ball. Cut into 4 small balls.
- On floured board, roll each ball into oblong shape. Spread oil on top, then sprinkle generous amounts of cinnamon and sugar mixture. Cut into strips, not too long, then twist once or twice. Place on well oiled cookie sheet.
- Bake 375°F oven for 15–20 minutes till brown, or bake 15 minutes, turn over, and bake 5 minutes longer.

Peanut Butter Cookies

Nancy Benjamin

1 stick unsalted butter, at room
    temperature
½ cup light brown sugar
2 tablespoons granulated sugar
½ cup chunky peanut butter
1 egg
2 teaspoons vanilla

1 cup flour
½ teaspoon baking soda
pinch salt
6 ounces white chocolate, coarsely
    chopped
1 cup coarsely chopped macadamia nuts

- Preheat oven to 375°F.
- In a large bowl, use electric mixer to cream butter and both sugars until light and fluffy. Add peanut butter and mix well. Add egg and vanilla and mix until incorporated .
- Mix in flour, baking soda, and salt until well blended and then add white chocolate and nuts.
- Spoon heaping tablespoons on ungreased cookie sheets. Flatten slightly.
- Bake 12–15 minutes until tops are just set. Do not over bake.

☐ Poppy Seed Cookies

Mrs. Herman H. Saltz

3¹/₂ cups flour
3 teaspoons baking powder
¹/₂ teaspoon salt
1 cup butter or margarine

1 cup sugar
1 teaspoon vanilla
3 eggs, beaten
³/₄ cup poppy seeds

- Sift all dry ingredients together.
- Cream butter or margarine, and sugar, vanilla, and eggs.
- Add dry ingredients, about 1 cup at a time. Add poppy seeds.
- Drop from a teaspoon onto greased cookie sheet. Flatten cookies by stamping with a glass covered with a damp cloth.
- Bake in a moderate oven 350°F about 10–12 minutes.

Joyce Anne's Aspen Cookies

Harriet Chandler

A cinch to make and everyone loves them.

1 box honey-cinnamon graham crackers
1 10-ounce package sliced almonds, lightly toasted

2 sticks butter
¹/₂ cup sugar

- Place individual crackers on ungreased cookie sheet. Cover with nuts.
- Mix butter and sugar in a small saucepan. Boil 4 minutes until mixture starts to thicken. Spoon over grahams.
- Bake for about 7 minutes at 350°F. Check to make sure done. Remove from pan while still hot. Can be stored in tin or plastic bag. Makes about 3 dozen.

Esther's Crescents

Evelyn Plotkin

They make a big hit at our Onegs.

1 pound butter or margarine
1 cup granulated sugar
4 teaspoons vanilla
4 cups sifted flour

2 cups oatmeal, not instant
12 ounces chocolate chips
confectioners' sugar

- Cream butter and granulated sugar. Add vanilla. Add flour, oatmeal, and chocolate chips, and mix by hand. Chill dough for easier handling.
- Roll a teaspoon of dough in hands and shape like crescents or pretzels.
- Bake in 325°F oven for 15–20 minutes (not too brown) on an ungreased baking sheet. Sprinkle confectioners' sugar on crescents while still warm. They freeze well. Makes over 100 pieces.

Walnut Clusters

Suzanne Feldman

Takes a short time to prepare — easy to handle.

$1/4$ cup butter
$1/2$ cup sugar
1 egg
$1/2$ teaspoon vanilla
$1 1/2$ squares baking chocolate, melted

$1/2$ cup flour
$1/4$ teaspoon baking powder
$1/2$ teaspoon salt
2 cups walnuts, cut or broken into medium-sized pieces

- Preheat oven to 350°F.
- Cream butter and sugar. Add egg and vanilla, then melted chocolate.
- Sift dry ingredients. Add to creamed mixture. Fold in walnuts.
- Drop by teaspoonfuls onto greased baking sheet. Bake for 10 minutes. Makes approximately 48.

⌂ Almond Crescents

Mrs. Elias S. Grace

1 cup vegetable shortening, softened (half
   butter for flavor)
1/3 cup sugar
2/3 cup ground blanched almonds

1 2/3 cups sifted all-purpose flour
1/4 teaspoon salt
1 cup confectioners' sugar
1 teaspoon cinnamon, optional

- Mix together shortening, granulated sugar, and almonds.
- Sift together and work in flour and salt. Chill dough.
- Roll into pencil-thick rolls and cut into 2 1/2-inch lengths. Place on ungreased baking sheet in the form of crescents.
- Bake at 325°F until set but not brown, about 14–16 minutes. While still warm roll in 1 cup confectioners' sugar which can be mixed with 1 teaspoon cinnamon or left plain. Makes about 5 dozen cookies.

Positively-the-Absolute-Best Chocolate Chip Cookies

Wendy Honig Krintzman

8 ounces (2 sticks) sweet butter
1 teaspoon salt
1 teaspoon vanilla extract
3/4 cup granulated sugar
3/4 cup light brown sugar, firmly packed
2 large or extra-large eggs
2 1/4 cups unsifted all-purpose flour

1 teaspoon baking soda
1 teaspoon hot water
8 ounces (2 generous cups) walnuts, cut
   or broken into medium-sized pieces
12 ounces (2 cups) semisweet chocolate
   chip morsels (or chunks)

- Adjust 2 racks to divide the oven into thirds and preheat oven to 375°F. Cut aluminum foil to fit cookie sheet.
- In the large bowl of an electric mixer, cream the butter. Add the salt, vanilla, and both sugars, and beat well. Add the eggs and beat well.
- On low speed, add about half of the flour, scraping the bowl with a rubber spatula. Beat only until incorporated.
- In a small cup, stir the baking soda into the hot water to dissolve it. Then mix it into the dough. Add the remaining flour and beat only to mix. Stir in the walnuts and the morsels.
- Spread out a large sheet of waxed paper . Use a rounded teaspoonful of the dough for each cookie and place the mounds on the waxed paper. Wet your hands with cold water and shake off excess water. Pick up a mound of dough and roll it between your wet hands to form a smooth round shape. Press it between your hands to flatten it evenly into a round shape about 1/2-inch thick and place it on the foil lined cookie sheets, 2 inches apart.
- Bake 2 cookie sheets at a time, reversing the sheets top to bottom and front to back as necessary during baking to ensure even browning. Bake for 12 minutes or a little longer until the cookies are browned all over. If you bake only one sheet at a time, bake it on the upper rack. They must be crisp — do not underbake. Let the cookies cool for a few seconds on the foil until they are firm enough to be moved. Then with a wide spatula, transfer them to racks to cool. Store airtight. Can be frozen. *Enjoy*. Makes about 55 3-inch cookies.

Sisters' Chocolate Chip Cookies

Judy Freedman Fask

1 cup butter
1 cup brown sugar
1 cup granulated sugar
2 eggs
1 teaspoon vanilla
1/2 teaspoon almond extract

2 cups flour
2 1/2 cups oatmeal
1/2 teaspoon salt
1 teaspoon baking powder
1 teaspoon baking soda
12 ounces chocolate chips

- Cream butter, and sugars. Add eggs, vanilla, and almond extract.
- Mix together flour, oatmeal, salt, baking powder, and baking soda. Add to creamed mixture. Add chocolate chips.
- Roll into balls and put on a cookie sheet. Bake for 10 minutes in a 375°F oven.

Mocha Truffle Cookies

Barbara Robbins

1/2 cup margarine
1 1/2 cups semisweet chocolate morsels
1 tablespoon instant coffee (Decaf or regular)
3/4 cup granulated sugar
3/4 cup packed brown sugar

2 eggs
2 teaspoons vanilla
2 cups all-purpose flour
1/3 cup unsweetened cocoa powder
1/2 teaspoon baking powder
1/4 teaspoon salt

- In large saucepan, melt margarine and 1/2 cup chocolate morsels over low heat. Remove from heat. Stir in coffee and cool for 5 minutes. Stir in both sugars, eggs, and vanilla.
- In a medium-sized mixing bowl, combine flour, cocoa, baking powder, and salt. Stir this into coffee mixture. Stir in 1 cup chocolate morsels.
- Drop dough by rounded tablespoonfuls onto lightly greased cookie sheets. Bake at 350°F for 10 minutes. Let cool 1 minute before removing from cookie sheets. Makes about 30 cookies.

Best Chocolate Cookies

Nancy Benjamin

Great as large cookies.

2 cups semisweet chocolate bits
　　(12 ounces)
2 ounces unsweetened chocolate
3 ounces unsalted butter
2 eggs
3/4 cup granulated sugar

1 teaspoon instant coffee
2 teaspoons vanilla
1/4 cup flour
1/4 teaspoon baking powder
1/2 teaspoon salt
1 1/2 cups walnuts, in large pieces

- Melt 1 cup chocolate bits, unsweetened chocolate, and butter over low heat. Remove and let cool slightly.
- Beat eggs, sugar, and coffee at high speed. Add the melted chocolate and vanilla.
- Add flour, baking powder, and salt and mix to blend. Add remaining chocolate bits and nuts. Spoon heaping tablespoonfuls on cookie sheet.
- Bake in 350°F oven for 12–16 minutes until tops are slightly firm to the touch. Reverse sheets, top to bottom and front to back, once during baking.

Grammy's Surprise

Nancy Hodes

1 cup butter
3/4 cup sugar
1 egg
2 teaspoons vanilla

2 1/2 cups flour
1/2 teaspoon salt
5 small Hershey's candy bars
　　(12 squares each)

- Cream butter and sugar. Add egg and vanilla and beat well.
- Add the dry ingredients and mix well.
- Press dough through a cookie press (using saw tooth plate) into strips on an ungreased cookie sheet.
- Break the candy bars into the scored squares, place squares 1/4-inch apart on the dough. Press a strip to cover. Make a slight indentation between pieces of candy.
- Bake at 375°F for 12–15 minutes. Cut while warm at indentations.

Chocolate-Tipped Sandwich Cookies

Mrs. Albert Hoffman

Cookie:
1/2 cup sugar
1/2 cup butter or margarine
1 egg
1 teaspoon vanilla
1 1/2 cups sifted flour

Melted Chocolate:
1/2 cup semisweet chocolate morsels
1 1/2 tablespoons water

Filling:
raspberry jelly, or your choice

- Gradually add sugar to butter or margarine, creaming well. Add egg and vanilla. Beat well.
- Blend in flour gradually, mixing thoroughly.
- Press through cookie press, using mold with a thin, narrow slit. Press dough in strips across greased baking sheets.
- Bake in 400°F oven for 6–8 minutes. Immediately cut into 2-inch pieces and remove from sheet, matching each 2 cookies with bottom sides together. Cool.

Melted Chocolate:
- Combine semisweet chocolate morsels and water. Melt over low heat — microwave is preferable. Blend well.
- When cooled, spread jelly between each 2 matched cookies. Dip ends of sandwich cookies in melted chocolate, then in chocolate shot or chopped nuts. Makes approximately 30–35 cookies.

Low-Fat Cookies with Applesauce

Diane C. Stone

Excellent.

1 cup all-purpose flour
1 teaspoon baking powder
1/2 teaspoon baking soda
1/2 teaspoon salt
2 tablespoons vegetable shortening
1/4 cup cinnamon applesauce

1/2 cup granulated sugar
1/2 cup light brown sugar
1 whole egg, or 1/3 cup egg substitute
1 teaspoon vanilla extract
1 1/3 cups rolled oats
1/2 cup raisins, optional

- Preheat oven to 375°F. Lightly spray cooking sheet with Pam.
- If using plain applesauce add 1/2 teaspoon cinnamon to flour.
- In a large bowl, mix flour, baking powder, baking soda, and salt.
- In a separate bowl, whisk together shortening, applesauce, granulated sugar, brown, sugar, egg, and vanilla until shortening breaks into pea-sized pieces. Add flour mixture to applesauce mixture. Mix well.
- Fold in oats and raisins. Drop by rounded teaspoonfuls onto cookie sheet, 2 inches apart.
- Bake for 10–12 minutes. Remove cookies and place on cooling rack. Yields 36 cookies.

Ginger Snaps

Mrs. Elias S. Grace

4 1/2 cups flour
1 tablespoon baking soda
1 tablespoon ginger
2/3 cup shortening
1/2 cup sugar

1 egg, beaten
1 cup molasses
1 tablespoon vinegar
2 tablespoons cold water

- Sift together flour, soda, and ginger.
- Cream shortening with sugar. Add egg, molasses, vinegar, and water. Mix well.
- Add sifted dry ingredients. Mix by hand to incorporate thoroughly.
- Roll out and cut into desired shapes.
- Bake 10–12 minutes in moderate oven 350–375°F.

Aunt Belle's Apple Squares

Lois Edinberg

2 medium-sized apples
1 cup sugar
1 1/2 cups flour
1 teaspoon baking soda
1/4 teaspoon cinnamon
1/4 teaspoon nutmeg
1/4 teaspoon allspice

1/4 teaspoon ginger
dash salt
1/2 cup nuts
1/2 cup raisins, optional
1/4 cup butter, melted
1 egg, beaten
1 teaspoon vanilla

- Grease a 9 x 9-inch pan.
- Peel and dice apples and place in pan. Add sugar to apples.
- Sift flour, baking soda, spices, and salt. Sprinkle over apples and mix to combine. Add nuts and raisins.
- Combine butter, egg, and vanilla. Pour over mixture and combine.
- Bake at 350°F for 35–40 minutes. Cut into squares. Serves 8–10.

Date Nut Squares

Nancy Seder

1/4 pound butter, melted
1 cup sugar
2 eggs, well beaten
3/4 cup all-purpose flour

1/4 teaspoon baking powder
1/4 teaspoon salt
1 cup chopped walnuts, optional
1 cup chopped dates

- Mix melted butter with sugar and eggs.
- Sift flour, baking powder, and salt and add to butter mixture. Add nuts and dates.
- Turn into a greased 8 x 8-inch pan. Bake in a 375°F oven for 20–25 minutes or until light brown. (I like to undercook a bit.)

Apricot Squares

Faye Levine

My mom's special desert!

1/2 pound dried apricots
3/4 cup granulated sugar
1/4 pound butter

1 1/2 cups rolled oats
1 cup brown sugar
1 1/4 cups flour

- Soak apricots for 1/2 hour in enough water to cover. Retain 3/4 cup water with the apricots and add granulated sugar. Cook in saucepan until thick and mushy.
- Melt 1/4 pound butter.
- Mix rolled oats, brown sugar, and flour together. Add melted butter to dry mixture.
- Butter a 9 x 11-inch pyrex dish. Spread half of the flour mixture on the bottom and pat down well. Spread apricot mixture over crust. Cover with remaining flour mixture. Pat down well.
- Bake about 30–35 minutes in a 350°F oven. Cut into squares.

Apricot Jam Squares

Suzanne Feldman

1 cup butter or margarine, at room
    temperature
1 cup sugar
1 egg yolk

2 cups flour
3/4 cup finely chopped walnuts, optional
1 10-ounce jar apricot jam

- Preheat oven to 350°F.
- Cream butter with sugar in large bowl. Add egg yolk and mix well. Stir in flour. Add nuts and blend well. Dough will be soft.
- Divide dough in half. Spread half loosely into bottom of 9 x 13-inch baking pan. Cover with jam.
- Drop remaining dough by spoonfuls over jam, spreading carefully to edges with knife.
- Bake until top is golden, 40–45 minutes. Cool slightly before cutting into squares.

Gertie's Brownies

Nancy Hodes

This is my mother's recipe, hence their name. Certainly one of the best recipes ever.

1/2 pound butter
4 1-ounce squares unsweetened
    chocolate, melted
2 cups sugar
4 eggs

2 teaspoons vanilla
1 cup flour
1 cup walnuts, cut or broken into medium-sized pieces

- Melt the butter and chocolate either in the microwave or on the stove using a container large enough to hold the whole recipe.
- Add the rest of the ingredients in the order they are listed, mixing well after each addition.
- Turn into a greased 9 x 13-inch tin pan.
- Bake for 30 minutes at 350°F.

Chocolate Cheesecake Brownies

Lisa Honig

Brownie Batter:

6 ounces semisweet chocolate, chopped
6 tablespoons butter
1 tablespoon instant coffee powder
4 large eggs
1 1/2 cups sugar
1 cup flour
1/4 cup unsweetened cocoa powder
1 teaspoon vanilla extract
1 tablespoon Kahula coffee liqueur

Cream Cheese Mixture:

1 8-ounce package cream cheese, at room temperature
1/4 cup butter, at room temperature
1/2 cup sugar
2 large eggs
2 tablespoons flour
1 tablespoon Kahula coffee liqueur
1/4 cup semisweet mini chocolate chips

Brownie Batter:

- Preheat oven to 350°F. Butter a 13 x 9-inch baking pan.
- Combine chocolate, butter, and coffee powder in saucepan. Stir over low heat until melted and smooth. Cool.
- In a large bowl, beat eggs until frothy. Gradually add sugar and beat until mixture is pale yellow and slightly thickened. Stir in flour and cocoa. Add vanilla, liqueur and melted chocolate. Stir until blended.

Cream Cheese Mixture:

- With electric mixer, in a large bowl, beat cream cheese and butter until smooth. Add sugar and beat until fluffy. Beat in eggs, flour and coffee liqueur. Set aside 1/2 cup brownie batter for topping.
- Pour remaining batter into prepared pan. Carefully spoon cream cheese mixture over batter, covering completely.
- Sprinkle chocolate chips evenly over cream cheese layer. Drop reserved batter by teaspoon over cream cheese layer. Using a sharp knife, swirl batter into cream cheese mixture to create marble pattern.
- Bake brownies until toothpick inserted into center comes out with some crumbs, about 30 minutes. Cool and cut into squares.

My Best Brownies

Barbara Rothstein

The fear of fat is at a minimum — so indulge!!

1/2 cup canola oil
1 cup sugar
1 teaspoon vanilla
2 eggs
1/2 cup all-purpose flour
1/3 cup baking cocoa
1/4 teaspoon baking powder
1 pinch salt
1/2 cup chopped walnuts, optional

- Blend oil, sugar, and vanilla. Add eggs. Beat well with spoon.
- Combine flour, cocoa, baking powder, and salt. Gradually add to egg mixture until well blended. Stir in nuts.
- Spread in greased and lightly floured 9-inch square pan.
- Bake at 350° for 20–25 minutes or until brownies begin to pull away from edges of pan. Cool in pan. Cut into squares.
  Makes 16 brownies.

Chocolate Mint Brownies

Janet Gordon

2 squares unsweetened baking chocolate
1/2 cup margarine
1 cup sugar
1 teaspoon vanilla
2 eggs
1/2 cup flour

Frosting:
1 cup sifted confectioners' sugar
2 tablespoons margarine, softened
1 tablespoon milk
1/2 teaspoon peppermint extract
2 drops green food color

Glaze:
2 tablespoons margarine
2 ounces chocolate, melted

- Melt chocolate and margarine. Add sugar, vanilla, and eggs. Blend well. Add flour and blend.
- Bake 25 minutes in a 350°F oven in greased 8 x 8-inch pan. Cool completely before frosting.
- Mix frosting ingredients together spread on brownies. Refrigerate

Chocolate Glaze:
- Melt margarine and chocolate.
- When frosting is cooled, spoon glaze on brownies. Refrigerate again until set, then cut into squares.

Raspberry Chocolate Bars

Eleanor Burke

2 1/2 cups flour
1 cup sugar
3/4 cup finely chopped pecans
1 cup butter or margarine

1 egg
1 12-ounce jar seedless red raspberry jam
1 2/3 cups chocolate chips

- Stir together first 5 ingredients until crumbly. Set aside 1 1/2 cups of crumb mixture. Press remaining crumb mixture on bottom of 13 x 9-inch greased pan.
- Spread jam on the top. Sprinkle with chocolate chips then the reserved crumb mixture.
- Bake in 350°F oven for 40–45 minutes or until lightly browned. Cool. Cut into bars. Makes about 3 dozen bars.

Walnut Squares

Barbara W. Burwick

Batter:
1 cup sugar
$1/2$ pound butter, melted
1 teaspoon cinnamon
2 cups flour
1 teaspoon vanilla
1 egg yolk

Topping:
1 egg white, beaten
cinnamon
sugar
chopped walnuts

- Mix batter ingredients together to form dough. Press with heel of hand into a jelly roll pan.
- Brush with egg white and top with cinnamon, and sugar, and chopped walnuts.
- Bake in 350°F oven for 30 minutes. Cut in squares while hot. Cool in pan.

Magic Cookie Bars

Nell Goldberg

Family favorite

$1/2$ cup margarine or butter
$1^1/2$ cups graham cracker crumbs
1 14-ounce can sweetened condensed milk

1 cup (6 ounces) semisweet chocolate chips
1 $3^1/2$-ounce can flaked coconut

- Preheat oven to 350°F.
- In 13 x 9-inch baking pan, melt margarine or butter. Sprinkle crumbs over margarine. Pour sweetened condensed milk evenly over crumbs. Top with remaining ingredients. Press down firmly.
- Bake 25–30 minutes or until lightly browned. Cool-chill if desired. Cut into bars. Store loosely covered at room temperature. Makes 20–24 bars.

Oh Henry Bars

Mim Lazerowich

Yummy.

²/₃ cup butter or margarine
1 cup brown sugar, firmly packed
1 tablespoon vanilla
¹/₂ cup light corn syrup

4 cups quick-cooking rolled oats
6 ounces (1 cup) chocolate chip morsels
²/₃ cup chunky peanut butter

- Cream butter and sugar. Add vanilla, corn syrup, and oats. Pat dough into lightly greased 9 x 13-inch pan.
- Bake at 350°F for 15–16 minutes. Do not overbake.
- While dough is baking. melt chocolate chips and peanut butter together over low heat. Cool dough slightly then spread chocolate mixture on top. Cool further, then cut into bars. Makes about 40.

Caramel Nut Squares

Rose Gould

Crust:
¹/₄ pound butter, softened
1 cup flour
1 egg

Filling:
2 eggs
1¹/₂ cups brown sugar
2 tablespoons flour
¹/₂ teaspoon baking powder

Topping:
1 cup chopped walnuts
1 package shredded coconut
1 teaspoon vanilla
³/₄ cup confectioners' sugar
juice of 1 lemon

Crust:
- Blend ingredients. Pat on bottom of greased 9 x 13-inch pan. Bake at 425°F for 15 minutes.

Filling:
- Mix together until blended. Pour on baked crust.

Topping:
- Combine walnuts, coconut, and vanilla. Sprinkle on top.
- Bake at 350°F for 30 minutes. After removing from oven, pour confectioners' sugar mixed with lemon juice over the filling.

Turtle Squares

Nancy Benjamin

Crust:
2 1/4 cups flour
1 cup butter
2/3 cup granulated sugar
3 cups whole pecans

Filling:
3/4 cup butter
1/4 cup honey
1 cup brown sugar
3 tablespoons heavy cream
2 teaspoons vanilla
pinch salt

Topping:
1–2 cups dark chocolate or white
  chocolate bits

Crust:
- Mix flour, butter, and sugar until blended in food processor. Pat into a 10 x 15-inch pan.
- Bake in 350°F oven for 10–15 minutes. Remove from oven and spread whole pecans evenly over crust.

Filling:
- Combine in saucepan, butter, honey, and brown sugar. Stir over medium heat until melted. Boil for 5–7 minutes not stirring. Removed from heat.
- Add heavy cream, vanilla, and salt. Pour evenly over pecans.
- Bake 20 minutes in 350°F oven. Remove from oven.
- Sprinkle chocolate over evenly. Let sit until softened. Then swirl with a knife for frosted or marbled effect.

Hermits

Ann Kulin

Can be used for parties — children enjoy these.

6 tablespoons butter or margarine
3/4 cup sugar
1 egg, leaving a little for topping
1 1/2 cups flour
1/2 teaspoon baking soda
1/2 teaspoon cinnamon
1/2 teaspoon nutmeg
1/2 cup raisins
1/4 cup walnuts
2 tablespoons molasses
1 tablespoon sherry

- Cream butter and sugar together. Add the remaining ingredients and mix together. Spread on a greased cookie sheet. Brush with remaining part of egg.
- Bake for 20 minutes at 350°F. Cut in squares when cool. Makes 2 dozen hermits.

▢ Tayglalch

Mrs. Alex Hiatt

6 eggs, plus 3 egg yolks
2 teaspoons ginger
1 tablespoon sugar
1 pinch salt
1 tablespoon oil
1 teaspoon orange rind

1 teaspoon vanilla
3 cups flour, approximately
2 pounds honey
4 cups sugar
1/2 cup water
1/2 cup nut meats

- Beat eggs well and add 1 teaspoon ginger, 1 tablespoon sugar, salt, oil, rind, and vanilla. Add enough flour to make a soft dough. Knead well and let stand for 1 hour.
- In a large pot, put honey, 4 cups sugar, and water. Simmer slowly until it comes to a boil.
- Pinch off pieces of dough and roll in strip about 1-inch thick and cut to 3/4-inch pieces. Put pieces on a floured board so they will not stick together.
- When all the dough has been cut into pieces, put into the boiling honey. Cover pot and boil gently for 35 minutes. Take cover off and stir gently with a wooden spoon.
- Add 1 teaspoon ginger and nut meats, cover, and boil about 20 minutes until brown. Turn off heat and pour 3/4 cup boiling water over. Cover and let stand until it bubbles down. Stir. Left over honey from the pot can be used for Honey Cake.

Taglech

Nancy Hodes

Honey Mixture:
3 pounds honey
6 cups sugar
2 cups orange juice
2 teaspoons ginger

Dough:
1 cup vegetable shortening
2 1/2 heaping tablespoons sugar
9 eggs
1 teaspoon nutmeg or ginger
1/2 teaspoon allspice
2 tablespoons baking powder
4 plus cups flour
raisins
coconut

- Put honey, sugar, orange juice and ginger into pan. Set aside.
- To prepare the dough, cream shortening and sugar. Add eggs and spices. Add baking powder. Add flour a little at a time.
- Turn onto floured board and add more flour and knead as if it were bread. Dough should be elastic but not sticky.
- Divide into 8 parts. Work with only 1 part at a time. Roll out, not too thin, into a rectangle, sprinkle with raisins, roll up like a jelly roll, and slice. For plain ones, cut rectangle into strips and tie into knots.
- Bring honey mixture to a boil, gently drop cookies in, cook for 20 minutes covered, move to preheated 350°F oven, uncover and cook for 1 hour.
- Pour 1/2 cup boiling water over to soften the honey. When cool, roll some in coconut.

Taglech from the Hands of
Sadie Schwartzberg

Ethel Chaifetz

A real treat from bygone days! My mother's recipe.

3 cups flour
2 tablespoons sugar
2 teaspoons ginger
7 large egg
3 tablespoons oil
3 tablespoons whiskey

Syrup:
1 cup water
2 cups sugar
2 pounds honey
2 cups orange juice

- Mix flour, sugar, ginger, eggs, oil, and whiskey together to form a soft ball. If too sticky, add more flour. Roll into long ropes and make loose bow knots and cut. Let stand on a floured towel until syrup is ready.
- Bring water and 2 cups sugar to a boil. Add honey and let come to a roaring boil. Lower to simmer.
- Add bow knots and cook until they brown. When browned to satisfaction, pour on 2 cups heated orange juice! This sets the taglech. Remove pot from heat and let stand until cooled.
- Can be rolled in grated walnuts or flaked coconut. Mother reused honey syrup for baking honey cake.

Hamantashen

Ethel Chaifetz

1 package quick-rise yeast
$1/2$ teaspoon sugar plus 1 tablespoon
$1/4$ cup warm water
$1^1/2$-2 cups flour

2 tablespoons orange juice
1 large egg
1 tablespoon margarine, melted
1 egg white, beaten

- In a large mixing bowl mix yeast, $1/2$ teaspoon sugar, and warm water until blended. Let stand about 3 minutes, or until quite foamy.
- Add remaining sugar, flour, juice, egg, and melted margarine. Mix on low speed until all ingredients are blended to a soft ball of dough and leaves the sides of the bowl.
- Lightly spray mixing bowl with vegetable spray and place dough in bowl to rise. Cover with plastic wrap and let rise in a warm place until double in bulk.
- When dough has risen, punch down. On a lightly floured board, roll out dough to $1/8$-inch thickness. Cut into 3-inch rounds, rerolling scraps.
- Using any prepared poppy seed filling or fruit filling, place rounded teaspoonfuls in center of each round and pinch into a triangle shape. Place 2 inches apart on a greased cookie sheet. Cover and let rise again about 15–20 minutes.
- Brush with beaten egg white. Bake in a 350°F oven for 15–20 minutes until brown. Makes about 16 pieces.

Lillian "Billie" Glass' Hamantashen

Kathy Glass

Fabulous cookie dough which could be used for many other fillings. In memory of her mother-in-law.

Filling:
12 ounces pitted prunes
6 ounces dried apricot halves
6 ounces seedless raisins
4 ounces walnut meats
$^1/_2$ jar orange marmalade or apricot jam
juice of 1 lemon
$^1/_4$ cup honey

Cookie Dough:
$^1/_2$ cup vegetable shortening
1 cup sugar
2 eggs
2 tablespoons sour cream
1 teaspoon vanilla
$2^1/_2$ cups flour
$^1/_4$ teaspoon baking soda
$^1/_2$ teaspoon salt

Filling:
• Grind dried fruit and nuts. Mix all filling ingredients together.

Cookie Dough Preparation:
• Cream shortening and sugar. Add eggs one at a time. Add sour cream and vanilla. Beat till smooth.
• Add dry ingredients $^1/_3$ at a time. Beat until smooth.
• Divide dough in $^1/_2$ and wrap dough in waxed paper. Refrigerate overnight.
• Roll out dough $^1/_4$-inch thick and cut into $2^1/_2$-inch circles. Fill and fold up 3 sides to make 3 corner hat shape.
• Bake about 20 minutes at 350°F degrees on greased and floured cookie sheet.

"Homentaschen"

Simone Weinert

Dough:
$^1/_4$ pound butter or margarine
3 ounces cream cheese (regular only)
1 cup flour
1 teaspoon vanilla

Filling:
1 12-ounce box pitted prunes
$^1/_2$ cup sugar
juice of $^1/_2$ lemon
$^1/_2$ cup orange juice
$^1/_2$ cup chopped walnuts

• Make dough by processing all dough ingredients in food processer. Refrigerate at least 3 hours.

Filling:
• Grind prunes in food processor and put in double boiler. Add sugar, juices, and enough water to cook. Cook until liquid evaporates, about 30 minutes. Add nuts.
• Roll dough $^1/_2$-inch thick with rolling pin on cloth. Cut with 3-inch glass. Spoon heaping tablespoonfuls of filling in centers. Fold sides in to form triangle. Place on ungreased cookie sheet.
• Bake at 375°F for 15–20 minutes, until light brown.

Passover

"Haroset"

Nancy Greenberg

A Sephardic variation which is very flavorful and a nice addition to the traditional apples/walnut version.

1/4 pound dried apricots
1/4 pound prunes
1/4 pound dates
3 apples, peeled and quartered
1 orange, unpeeled and quartered
1/2 pound walnuts

1/2 cup Concord grape wine
1/2 teaspoon cinnamon
1/8 teaspoon nutmeg
1 tablespoon lime or lemon juice

- Chop all fruits and walnuts in batches in food processor. Add wine, spices, and lime/lemon juice.

"Charosis"

Mahvash Haimi

Very delicious Persian recipe.

1/2 cup almonds
1/2 cup pistachio nuts
1/2 cup hazelnuts
1/2 cup pecans
1/2 cup cashews
1 cup black raisins

1 cup pitted dates
pomegranate juice, as much as needed
orange, pineapple or kiwi juice, or any
    other fruit juice you like, optional
1 cup red sweet wine

- First grind all the nuts together. Grind raisins and pitted dates.
- Add pomegranate juice, which is the most important part of this recipe. You may want to add some other kind of juice to the ingredients. Add wine.
- Remember! It has to be thick.

□ "Charoseth"

6 tart apples, peeled and grated
2 cups ground or chopped blanched
    almonds
1/2 cup walnut meats, ground or chopped
3 tablespoons sugar or honey
1 teaspoon cinnamon

1 teaspoon ground ginger
grated rind of 1 lemon or orange
3 tablespoons lemon or orange juice
Passover wine, to make mixture of right
    consistency

- Combine thoroughly to make a tasty mixture, thick enough to keep its shape when served on pieces of matzoh at the Seder.

Roasted Crispy Knaidels

Gloria Thomashow

1 teaspoon salt
2 cups matzoh meal
3 eggs

1/2 cup peanut oil
1 cup warm water

- Preheat oven to 400°F.
- Mix salt and matzoh meal together. Set aside.
- Beat eggs by hand. Add peanut oil and water. Mix well.
- Slowly add matzoh meal to egg mixture. Wet hands with cold water and form into egg shaped knaidels. Put in well greased oblong pan.
- Turn each knaidel until they get nice and brown and crisp, about 30–45 minutes.

🗂 Matzo Brie or Fried Matzo

2 eggs
1/2 cup milk or water
1/4 teaspoon salt
dash of cinnamon
2 matzohs

3 tablespoons shortening
sugar and cininamon, for topping,
    optional
applesauce, for topping, optional
honey, for topping, optional

- Beat eggs, add liquid, salt, and cinnamon, and break matzoh into this mixture. Stir well and turn into melted shortening in a well-heated frying pan. Cover.
- Cook over moderate heat about 10 minutes or until browned on under side. Turn and brown, uncovered, for about 3 minutes. Serve hot, plain or with sprinkling of sugar and cinnamon, applesauce, or honey.

🗂 Popovers

Mrs. Julius Goldman

1 cup boiling water
1/8 pound shortening
pinch salt

1 scant teaspoon sugar
1 cup matzoh meal
4 eggs

- To boiling water, add shortening, salt, and sugar. When mixture is cool, stir in matzoh meal.
- Add eggs, one at a time, beating well after each egg is added. (This is same procedure as for cream puffs.)
- Drop into greased muffin tins and bake in 400°F oven till brown. Makes very nice cream puffs.

Blueberry Muffins

Marsha Bernstein

1 stick margarine
1 cup sugar
3 eggs
1/4 cup potato starch

1/2 cup cake meal
1 teaspoon vanilla
dash salt
1 cup frozen drained blueberries

- Cream together margarine and sugar. Add remaining ingredients except blueberries.
- Fold in blueberries. Spoon into muffin papers in cup cake holder.
- Bake at 350°F for 45 minutes to 1 hour. Makes 12–14.

Lena Price's Fruit Fritters

Diane Price

Can't have family seder without them!

1/3 cup shortening or margarine
1/2 cup cake meal
1/2 cup sugar
1 cup orange juice
1 cup chopped nuts

2 cups dried prunes and apricots, cooked,
coarsely chopped
1 cup diced, fresh banana
1/2 cup matzo meal
1 egg
2 tablespoons water

- Melt shortening and add cake meal and sugar until well blended. Remove from heat and gradually stir in orange juice.
- Bring to a boil, stirring, and boil 1 minute. Remove from heat and stir in nuts, prunes, apricots, and banana. Chill thoroughly.
- Shape into patties and roll in matzo meal. Combine egg and water. Dip patties into egg mixture and then roll in matzo meal again .
- Fry until brown. Freeze. Reheat at 250°F for 20 minutes. Makes a dozen or more.

Apple Farfel Kugel

Terri Witkin

Very delicious!

3 apples, peeled and coarsely chopped
2 teaspoons cinnamon
6 eggs, beaten
1/4 teaspoon salt
rind of 1 lemon, grated

3/4 cup brown sugar
4 tablespoons oil
1/4 teaspoon nutmeg
3 cups farfel, soaked and drained

- Mix all ingredients.
- Grease a 9 x 13-inch pan. Bake 45 minutes to one hour in 350°F oven. Serves 12–14.

Farfel Mold

Trudy Cohen

2 cups matzoh farfel
2 eggs, beaten
1/2 cup sugar
1/2 teaspoon salt

1/2 teaspoon cinnamon
3 tablespoons butter, melted
2 cups grated and peeled apples
3/4 cup white raisins

- Cover farfel with hot water. Drain.
- Add beaten eggs, sugar, salt, cinnamon, butter, apples, and raisins.
- Bake in muffin tins greased with butter for 30 minutes at 350°F.

Matzoh Farfel Kugel

Judy Shriber

Better than regular kugel!!

3 cups farfel
3 cups boiling water
1 stick margarine, melted
6 eggs
3/4 cup sugar
1/2 pound cream cheese

1 teaspoon salt
4 heaping tablespoons cottage cheese
4 heaping tablespoons sour cream
2 cups milk
cinnamon

- Mix farfel with 3 cups boiling water. Let stand until absorbed.
- Add all ingredients except cinnamon, to farfel. Pour into a greased 9 x 13-inch pan.
- Bake at 400°F for 1/2 hour. Lower temperature to 350°F. Sprinkle cinnamon all over top of kugel and continue to bake another 20 minutes. Serves 6–8.

Farfel Pudding

Dorothy Kaplan

So good you'll make it year round.

1 1/2 cups matzoh Farfel
1/2 cup hot water
1 cup milk, heated
6 tablespoons butter, melted
3 eggs, beaten with 6 tablespoons sugar
4 tablespoons cottage cheese
3 ounces cream cheese
pinch salt

Topping:
sugar and cinnamon

- Preheat oven to 400°F. Butter a deep pie plate.
- Soak farfel in liquids for 15 minutes. Add next 5 ingredients.
- Pour into pie plate and bake 1/2 hour or until brown. Top with sugar and cinnamon. Serves 6.

Joyce's Farfel "Koogle"

Joyce C. Covitz

Delicious. Freezes well.

1 cup cold water
3 cups matzoh farfel
3 eggs (eggbeaters, if desired)
1 cup milk
1/8 teaspooon salt

2 tablespoons sugar
1 teaspoon vanilla
1 pound cottage cheese
cinnamon and sugar

- Grease pan with melted butter or margarine. Soak farfel in cold water. Let stand 15 minutes.
- Beat eggs in a bowl. Add milk, salt, sugar, and vanilla. Beat well. Add farfel to mixture. Add cottage cheese.
- Pour mixture into pan. Sprinkle cinnamon and sugar on top.
- Bake at 375°F for 40 minutes. Lower heat to 350°F and continue baking until brown. Serves 6.

Gloria's Peach Farfel Kugel

Ethel Chaifetz

7 large eggs, beaten
3/4 pound margarine, melted
1 1/2 cups peach liquid (add water if necessary)
1 teaspoon vanilla

1 cup sugar mixed with 1 teaspoon cinnamon
1 pound matzo farfel
1 large can sliced peaches
1 medium can sliced peaches

- Preheat oven to 375°F.
- Combine and mix all ingredients except peaches. Pour into greased 9 x 13-inch pan. Top with sliced peaches and sprinkle with cinnamon and sugar.
- Bake for 1 hour or for 45 minutes and freeze. Pears or pineapple can be substituted.

Dairy Lasagna

Helen Sigel

A change for Passover

2 eggs
1 pound cottage cheese
1 clove garlic, minced or 1/2 teaspoon
    garlic powder
3–4 whole matzohs

milk, as needed
2 10 1/2-ounce cans tomato sauce
salt and pepper, to taste
1/2 pound shredded Muenster cheese

- In medium-sized bowl, beat eggs. Add cottage cheese and seasonings. Mix well.
- Wet matzohs with milk until moistened.
- Pour a little tomato sauce into 8 x 8-inch baking pan. Layer remaining ingredients alternating matzo, cottage cheese, tomato sauce and Muenster cheese. Repeat ending with muenster.
- Bake at 350°F for 45–50 minutes. Let rest 5–10 minutes before cutting. Serves 6.

Vegetable Kugelach

Rose Singer

1/4 cup chopped green bell peppers
1 cup chopped white onions
1/2 cup chopped celery
1 1/2 cups grated raw carrots
6 tablespoons butter or margarine
10-ounce package prewashed spinach,
    chopped

3 eggs, beaten
1 teaspoon salt
1/8 teaspoon pepper
3/4 cup matzoh meal
oil for sautéing
sour cream

- Sauté green pepper, onion, celery, and carrot in the butter or margarine about 10 minutes, stirring occasionally.
- Cook spinach and drain.
- Combine with vegetables.
- Add eggs, salt, pepper, and matzoh meal. Spoon into 12 well-greased large muffin tins or 8 x 11-inch pyrex dish.
- Bake in a moderate oven, 350°F for 45 minutes or until firm. Allow to cool for 10 minutes before removing from pan. Serve plain, or with sour cream for a dairy meal.

Sephardic Vegetable Kugel

Ethel Chaifetz

4 tablespoon cooking oil
1 large onion, peeled and thinly sliced
1 large bell pepper, cut into 1/2-inch
    chunks
1 medium-sized eggplant, peeled and cut
    into 1-inch chunks
2 ribs celery, sliced 1/2-inch thick

1 teaspoon crushed fresh garlic cloves
1/2 teaspoon salt
1/4 teaspoon pepper
1 large tomato, cut into wedges
2 cups coarsely chopped fresh spinach
2 eggs and 4 egg whites, slightly beaten
1/3 cup matzoh meal

- Preheat oven to 350°F. Grease 9 x 9 x 2 -inch baking dish.
- In a large skillet, heat oil. Add onion, pepper, eggplant, and celery. Sauté 8–10 minutes until slightly softened.
- Remove from heat and add garlic, seasonings, tomato, and spinach. Cool 10 minutes in pan.
- Quickly stir in eggs and matzoh meal. Turn into prepared baking dish.
- Bake for 40–45 minutes until center is firm, or until knife inserted in center comes out clean. Serves 6.

Potato-Carrot Kugel

Natalie Rosenkrantz

5 medium-sized potatoes, grated
2 large carrots, grated
2 onions, minced
1 cup matzoh meal
3 eggs

1/4 cup oil
salt and pepper, to taste
dill and chives, to taste
cheese, optional

- Combine all ingredients and mix well.
- Pour into baking dish and bake at 350°F for 40–60 minutes until firm. Can top with cheese or add cheese before baking. Serves 8.

Spinach Kugel

Harriet G. Tullman

Serve as an entree or cut up small for appetizers.

1/4 cup chopped green pepper
1/4 cup chopped onions
1/2 cup chopped celery
1/2 cup grated carrots
6 tablespoons margarine

10 ounces frozen chopped spinach,
   defrosted and squeezed
3 eggs, beaten
1/2 teaspoon salt
1/2 teaspoon pepper
1/4 cup matzoh meal

- Sauté the vegetables in margarine. Add defrosted spinach. Add eggs. Add salt, pepper, and matzoh meal, and mix well.
- Grease an 8 x 8-inch baking dish. Bake at 350°F for 45 minutes. Use a 9 x 13-inch pan for a double recipe. Freezes well.

Eggplant Cheese Bake

Jenique Radin

1 red onion, sliced
3 tablespoons peanut oil, Passover oil
1 1/2 pounds eggplant
1 cup chopped white mushrooms
1 15-ounce can tomato sauce
1/2 teaspoon pepper

1 1/2 teaspoons garlic, minced
1 teaspoon oregano
1 teaspoon salt
8–12 ounces shredded Cheddar cheese
2 cups matzo farfel

- Sauté onion in oil. Peel and cut eggplant into cubes. Combine onion, eggplant, mushrooms, tomato sauce, and spices. Cover and cook 10–15 minutes until eggplant is tender.
- Grease a 2-quart baking dish. Arrange alternating layers of the eggplant mixture, Cheddar cheese, and matzo farfel. Repeat ending with eggplant mixture.
- Bake at 350°F uncovered for 20 minutes. Sprinkle some additional cheese on top during the last 5 minutes of baking time. For a lasagna effect, bake in shallow 13 x 9-inch pan.

Turkish Mina

Nancy Hodes

This is a favorite of my family!

1 cup heated oil
4 matzohs
2 pounds cooked spinach

1 cup Feta cheese
4 eggs, beaten
garlic, salt, and pepper, to taste

- Put ½ cup of oil into a casserole. Dip the matzoh into water quickly so they do not get soggy. Line the bottom of the casserole with 2 of the matzohs.
- Mix spinach and cheese and seasonings, and put this mixture on top of the matzohs. Cover with 2 remaining matzohs. Cover with eggs.
- Bake at 400°F for 10 minutes.
- Pour remaining hot oil over the eggs. Bake for 30 minutes longer. Pour off excess oil. Best when served hot. Any combination of cooked meats and vegetables can be used as the filling.

Sweet and Sour Meatballs

M. Zuckerman

2 pounds ground beef
²/₃ cup matzoh meal
½ cup water
2 eggs, slightly beaten
½ cup minced onions
1 teaspoon salt
¼ teaspoon pepper

Sweet–Sour Sauce:
1 large onion, diced
½ cup lemon juice
1 cup sugar
11-ounce can tomato-mushroom sauce
½ cup water

- Combine beef, matzoh meal, water, eggs, minced onions, salt and pepper, Shape into meatballs.
- Combine sauce ingredients and bring to a boil. Add meat balls. Reduce heat and simmer about one hour. Serves 6.

Rosie's Sponge Cake

Nancy Hodes

This recipe comes from Rose Grossman who owned Sheppies Fruit Store on Water Street. I have been making this cake for more than 30 years, at least 2 cakes and some years as many as 6. It has never failed me or anyone that I gave the recipe to. All you need to do is follow the directions exactly.

9 extra large eggs, separated
1 1/2 cups sugar
4 tablespoons lemon juice

1/2 cup cake meal
1/2 cup potato starch, sifted twice

- Beat the yolks for 5 minutes. Add the sugar and lemon juice slowly. Add the cake meal and potato starch slowly and beat until well mixed.
- Using clean dry beaters, beat the egg whites until stiff. If a butter knife will stand upright in the egg whites, they are stiff. Fold yolk mixture into the whites. Turn into an angel food pan with a removable bottom.
- Bake at 325°F for 1 hour. Turn upside down to cool. Do not remove from the pan until it is **cold**.

Potato Starch Sponge Cake

Anna L. Baker

Great for Passover.

8 eggs, separated
2 tablespoons lemon juice
1 1/2 cups sugar, sifted

1 1/2 teaspoons grated lemon rind
1 cup potato starch, sifted
dash salt, if desired

- Using electric mixer, beat egg yolks for 2 minutes at high speed. Add lemon juice, sugar, and lemon rind, and mix 2 minutes at medium speed. Gradually add the sifted potato starch and continue mixing at medium speed for an additional 2 minutes.
- Beat egg whites until stiff. Gently, but thoroughly, fold in egg yolks, lemon juice, and rind mixture.
- Place in an ungreased 2-piece 10-inch tubepan and bake at 350°F for 60–70 minutes, or until cake springs back when firmly touched with fingers. Invert pan and cool thoroughly before removing cake from pan. Serves 12.

Sponge Cake

Mrs. E. David Pemstein

7 eggs, separated
2 additional eggs
1³/₄ cups sugar

rind of whole lemon
juice of whole lemon
1 scant cup of potato starch

- Beat egg yolks and 2 whole eggs until light. Add sugar gradually and rind and juice of lemon. Beat thoroughly, add potato starch and beat again.
- Beat egg whites until stiff, but not dry. Fold into yolk mixture very carefully.
- Bake in ungreased tube pan in 350°F oven, 40–50 minutes. Invert to cool.

Banana Sponge Cake

Mrs. Louis Friedberg

7 eggs, separated
1 cup sugar
1 cup mashed bananas
³/₄ cup matzo cake meal

¹/₄ cup potato starch
¹/₂ teaspoon salt
1 cup chopped walnuts
1 tablespoon potato starch

- Beat egg yolks until light in color. Add sugar and continue beating until thick and lemon colored. Add mashed bananas and beat thoroughly. Add dry ingredients which have been sifted together. Blend well.
- Fold in stiffly beaten egg whites. Coat nuts with potato starch and fold into batter.
- Bake in ungreased springform pan in 325°F oven, 1 hour.

Wine and Nut Cake

Sara E. Miller

9 eggs, separated
1¼ cups sugar (reserve 2 tablespoons for egg whites)
¼ cup wine
¼ cup orange juice
¾ cup cake meal
¼ cup potato starch
½ cup walnuts, finely chopped

- Beat egg yolks and sugar until thick. Add wine and juice. Fold in meal and starch and walnuts.
- Beat egg whites with 2 tablespoons sugar until peaks form. Fold into yolk mixture.
- Bake in 350°F oven for 55 minutes in angel cake pan. Place pan on a bottle and cool completely.

Mom's Nut Cake

Mari Seder

A moist cake. Good for breakfast, too.

6 eggs
1 cup sugar
½ cup cake meal
2 tablespoons potato starch
½ teaspoon salt
2 teaspoons orange juice
2 tablespoons orange rind
½ cup chopped nuts

- Beat eggs well. Add all ingredients except nuts. Mix well. Fold in nuts.
- Bake in 325°F for 50–60 minutes in an angel food cake pan. (Test in 30–40 minutes.) Invert for 1 hour.

Chiffon Cake

Ethel Chaifetz

10 eggs, separated
1 1/4 cups sugar
1/4 cup oil
1/4 cup orange juice

juice of 1/2 lemon
rind of 1 lemon
8 tablespoons potato starch, sifted

- Beat egg whites until stiff. Add half the sugar.
- Beat yolks with remaining sugar, oil, juices, and rind. Fold in egg whites and blend with potato starch, 1 tablespoon at a time. Pour batter into a 10-inch tube pan.
- Bake at 350°F for 50–60 minutes. Invert pan and let cool.

Raisin or Date Torte

Mrs. Jacob D. Freelander

4 eggs, separated
1/2 cup sugar
4 tablespoons matzoh meal
1/2 cup raisins or chopped dates

1/2 cup nuts, chopped
1 teaspoon vanilla
raspberry jam and whipped cream,
   optional

- Beat egg whites until stiff. Beat yolks a long time until lemon colored and thick. Add sugar gradually.
- Fold in matzoh meal, raisins or dates, nuts, and vanilla carefully. Fold in egg whites.
- Bake 40–50 minutes in a 325°F oven in a springform pan. Top with raspberry jam, chopped nuts, and whipped cream, if desired.

Meringue Torte

Mari Seder

Bakes overnight.

1½ cups egg whites (9–11 eggs)
¼ teaspoon cream of tartar
3 cups plus 1 tablespoon sugar
1 teaspoon vanilla extract

½ teaspoon almond extract
1 cup heavy cream
3 10-ounce packages frozen raspberries

- Preheat oven to 425°F. Brush inside of angel food cake pan with butter or shortening.
- Put egg whites in bowl of electric mixer and beat on medium speed until frothy. Add cream of tartar and continue to beat. Slowly add 2½ cups of sugar on high speed. Add vanilla and almond extracts. Continue beating until mixture is stiff and shiny.
- Put meringue in cakepan and smooth over the top. Place in oven and turn off immediately. Keep in oven overnight and do not take out of oven (keep door closed until close to serving time.)
- Slice around the top with a knife to cut away the crust. It will be crumbly, but save the crumbs. Slide knife between bottom of cake and pan bottom. Loosen cake around cylinder. Unmold onto a plate.
- Whip cream and sweeten it with one tablespoon of sugar. Frost cake with whipped cream. Sprinkle crumbs on sides and top of cake. Defrost raspberries and add remaining sugar to make sauce for cake slices. Garnish with raspberries or strawberries. Serves 10–12.

Upside Down Cake

Selma Cherkas Snider

It is delicious and so simple to prepare.

15 stewed prune halves
15 stewed apricot halves
½ cup honey
6 slices pineapple
4 egg yolks

¾ cup sugar
4 egg whites, beaten until stiff
½ cup cake meal
1 tablespoon lemon juice
grated rind of 1 lemons

- Cover prunes and apricots with water and simmer 10 minutes.
- Use a 9-inch square pan. Spread ¼ cup honey on bottom. Add fruit which should be arranged in the pan.
- Beat yolks with sugar. Fold in whites and add cake meal, lemon juice, and lemon rind. Pour the batter over the fruit.
- Bake in a moderate oven, until done about 50 minutes. Let cool in pan about 5 minutes, then loosen sides of cake with knife or spatula. Serve warm or cold.

Fudge Roll

Miriam Levy

Excellent.

6 eggs, separated
¹/₂ teaspoon salt
1 cup sugar
6 teaspoons potato starch
7 teaspoons cocoa

Filling:
6 ounces bittersweet chocolate
2 eggs
¹/₂ cup shortening

- Beat egg whites with salt, gradually adding ¹/₂ cup sugar. Beat stiff.
- In second bowl, beat yolks with remaining sugar until thick. Stir in potato starch and cocoa. Fold in whites.
- Pour in greased 10 x15-inch jelly roll pan, lined with waxed paper. Bake at 400°F, 15–20 minutes.
- Turn on to linen towel, sprinkled with mixture of cocoa and potato starch. Roll on long side. Roll up and cool while preparing the filling.
- Melt chocolate over hot water. Beat eggs with shortening. Add melted chocolate. Beat well. Unroll cake, spread filling, and reroll.

Chocolate Torte

Lois Lopatin

1³/₄ cups semisweet chocolate squares
³/₄ cup sweet butter, or no-salt margarine, at room temperature
1¹/₃ cups sugar

11 eggs, separated
1 ounces semisweet chocolate for curls, to put on top of torte

- Preheat oven to 325°F.
- Melt the chocolate. (I put the squares in the mixing bowl and put the bowl in the microwave to melt the chocolate — it saves cleaning pots!)
- Add cooled chocolate to butter and sugar in mixing bowl and beat together at low speed. Gradually add egg yolks. Beat entire mixture for 25 minutes.
- Beat egg whites until stiff. May need to do ¹/₂ at a time if using a small mixing bowl. Fold into chocolate mixture.
- Put ²/₃ of batter into 10-inch springform pan. Put remainder of mixture in refrigerator and cover with waxed paper.
- Bake for 30 minutes or until tester comes out clean. Let cake stand until it reaches room temperature. Cake will sink in the middle.
- Spread remaining ¹/₃ (batter kept in the refrigerator until now) over the baked torte. Decorate with chocolate curls made from the extra 1 ounce of chocolate. Cover and store in refrigerator until ready to serve. Best if made a couple of days in advance!

Cheese Cake

Rebecca Meyer

4 8-ounce containers whipped cream
    cheese
16 ounces sour cream (Lite can be used)
$1/4$ pound sweet butter (one stick)
2 tablespoons potato starch

$1 1/4$ cups sugar
$1 1/4$ teaspoons vanilla
1 teaspoon lemon juice
5 eggs
cinnamon

- Let cream cheese, sour cream, and butter stand at room temperature for approximately 1 hour, then blend together. Add cornstarch, sugar, vanilla, and lemon juice. Beat on whip speed until well blended.
- Add eggs one at a time, continuing to beat until mixture is very smooth.
- Pour mixture into greased $9 1/2$-inch springform pan. Sprinkle cinnamon on top of batter. Place pan in large roasting pan half filled with warm water. Bake at 375°F for 1 hour or until top is golden brown. Turn off oven and let cake cool with oven door open for 1 hour.

Parve Chocolate Mousse

Ethel Chaifetz

6 ounces semisweet chocolate chips
$1/4$ cup boiling water
1 tablespoon instant coffee

6 egg, separated
$1/2$ cup granulated sugar
$2 1/2$ teaspoons vanilla

- Melt chocolate in water mixed with coffee. Set aside to cool.
- Beat yolks with sugar until smooth. Add chocolate mixture and vanilla.
- Beat egg whites stiff, but not dry. Take $1/3$ of whites and stir into chocolate mixture. Fold remainder of whites into mixture. Put in bowl, cover with plastic wrap and freeze.

Jam Cookies

Ruth Seder

½ pound butter	1½ cups cake meal
1 cup sugar	2 tablespoons potato starch
1 egg	jam

- Cream butter and sugar. Add egg and beat well. Add cake meal and potato starch. Divide into 4 rolls. Wrap each individually in waxed paper and freeze.
- Defrost until it can be sliced thinly. Put on a cookie sheet with a dab of jam on each.
- Bake 350°F for 10–12 minutes.

Butter Cookies

Thelma Lockwood

Quick, easy, melt in your mouth.

¼ pound butter or margarine	½ cup cake meal
⅓ cup sugar	½ cup potato starch
1 egg	½ cup nuts, chopped

- Cream butter with sugar. Add egg and mix well.
- Add cake meal, potato starch, and chopped nuts to creamed mixture. Chill ½ hour.
- Roll into small balls. Bake at 350°F for 15 minutes on a lightly greased cookie sheet. Makes 1½ dozen.

Toll House Cookies

Helen Sigel

Good and easy.

1 cup matzoh meal
1/2 cup sugar
1 cup matzo farfel
1/2 cup chopped walnuts

1/2 cup semisweet chocolate chips
2 eggs
1/3 cup oil

- In mixing bowl, combine matzo meal, sugar, farfel, nuts, and chocolate chips.
- In a small bowl, beat eggs with oil.
- Pour liquid mixture over dry mixture and mix until thoroughly blended.
- Drop by teaspoonful onto a greased baking sheet. Bake in preheated 350°F oven for 20–30 minutes until golden. Makes approximately 24 cookies.

Mandel Bread

Lillian Bass

3 eggs
1 1/2 cups cake meal
1/2 teaspoon salt
1 cup sugar

1 cup oil
1 cup nuts, chopped
1 12-ounce package chocolate chips
cinnamon and sugar

- Preheat oven to 350°F. Grease a cookie sheet.
- Beat eggs until thick and lemon colored. Add remaining ingredients. Let stand 1 hour.
- Form 2 rolls on cookie sheet. Sprinkle with cinnamon and sugar.
- Bake 35 minutes. Cut into slices while still hot. Put slices back in oven for 5 minutes to toast.

Chocolate "Mandle Brodt"

Eva Sherman

Delicious

2 cups sugar
$\frac{1}{2}$ pound butter or margarine
6 eggs
$2\frac{3}{4}$ cups cake meal
$\frac{1}{2}$ teaspoon salt

$\frac{3}{4}$ cup potato starch
2 3-ounce bars bittersweet chocolate
1 cup chopped walnuts
1 teaspoon cinnamon
2 teaspoons sugar

- Cream sugar and butter. Add eggs 1 at a time, beating after each.
- Sift cake meal, salt and potato starch. Fold into egg mixture.
- Add chocolate, which has been cut into small pieces, and chopped nuts. Mix well.
- Form into 2-inch wide (5 strips) loaves. Sprinkle with combined sugar and cinnamon. Place on greased cookie sheet.
- Bake in 350°F oven about 45 minutes. Slice when warm. Place back in oven to brown on all sides, about 5 minutes.

Nina Stoll's Chocolate Chip Mandel Bread

Mari Storm

Pesach dessert.

3 eggs
$\frac{3}{4}$ cup sugar
$\frac{1}{2}$ cup oil

$1\frac{1}{2}$ cups cake meal
1 tablespoon potato starch
1 6-ounce package chocolate chips

- Beat eggs and sugar. Stir in oil. Fold in cake meal and potato starch. Add chocolate chips.
- Make 2 long loaves on lightly greased baking sheet.
- Bake at 350°F for 25–30 minutes. Cool and cut into pieces.

⌂ Date-Nut Squares

Mrs. Eli Sandman

6 eggs
1 cup sugar
1/2 pound dates, cut-up

1 cup chopped walnuts, optional
1 cup matzoh meal
juice of 1/2 lemon

- Beat eggs and sugar together thoroughly. Add remainder of ingredients and bake in greased pan in 350°F oven for about 30 minutes.

Hermits

Eileen Levenson

1 package Passover Honey Cake Mix
1 tablespoon instant coffee
1 large egg
2 tablespoons peanut oil
water

1/2 teaspoon ginger
1/2 teaspoon cinnamon
1 cup seedless raisins
1 cup chopped nuts

- Stir coffee into cake mix. Break egg into measuring cup and add peanut oil. Add enough water to make 1/2 cup. Add ginger and cinnamon.
- Mix as directed on package. Fold in raisins and nuts and chill 1 hour.
- Drop by teaspoonfuls on greased cookie sheet and bake for 10–15 minutes in 350°F oven. Allow to cool for 1 minute and remove from cookie sheet.

Rocky Road Brownies

Toby Richmond

So good I make them during the year also. Can be made pareve.

2 3-ounce bars bittersweet chocolate
1/2 cup margarine
2 eggs
1/8 teaspoon salt
2/3 cup sugar

1/2 cup cake meal
2/3 cup miniature marshmallows
2/3 cup coarsely chopped walnuts
2/3 cup semi-sweet chocolate chips

- Melt the bittersweet chocolate and margarine on a very low heat. Set aside to cool.
- In a medium-sized mixing bowl, beat the eggs and salt until thick and lemon colored. Gradually add the sugar.
- Beat in the cooled chocolate mixture. Gradually add the cake meal and beat until well blended. Spread the batter in a well greased 8-inch square pan.
- Bake at 325°F for 10 minutes or so. Top should still be soft. Remove from oven and sprinkle marshmallows, walnuts, and chocolate chips over the top. Return to oven for around 10 minutes more. Watch to make sure marshmallows don't burn. Cool in pan and cut when cooled.

Brownies

Sylvia Stein

Easy and fantastic. Can be used year round.

7 ounces bittersweet chocolate or
    2 3-ounce bars of Elite chocolate
1/2 pound margarine
4 large eggs

1 1/2 cups sugar
1 pinch salt
1 cup cake meal, sifted
1 cup nuts

- Melt chocolate and margarine and set aside.
- Beat eggs until foamy. Add sugar and salt and beat well. Add chocolate mixture, sifted cake meal, and nuts.
- Bake at 325°F in greased 9 x 13-inch pan for 25 minutes. If using Pyrex, drop oven temperature 25°F. Cut while warm but do not have to be removed immediately. Makes about 16 squares, depending on size you want.

Date and Chocolate Chip Bars

Gloria Thomashow

Use mixer. Freezes well. Very good.

1 8-ounce package dates, cut-up
1¹/₂ cups boiling water
1¹/₂ teaspoons baking soda
2 eggs
1 cup sugar
³/₄ cup oil
³/₄ teaspoon baking soda
¹/₂ teaspoon salt
1¹/₂ cups cake meal
¹/₈ cup potato starch

Topping:
6 ounces or 1 cup chocolate chips
¹/₄ cup sugar
1 cup nuts, finely chopped

- Combine the cut-up dates, boiling water, and baking soda in a small saucepan. Bring to a slow boil, remove from heat, and set aside to cool.
- In a medium-sized bowl, cream the eggs with sugar and oil until well blended. Add the cooled date mixture.
- Sift together baking soda, salt, cake meal, and potato starch into a small bowl. Combine the dry ingredients with the date mixture. Blend thoroughly.
- Grease and dust with cake meal a 9 x 13-inch pan. Pour batter into pan. Sprinkle chocolate chips over batter. Sprinkle sugar and nuts over chocolate chips.
- Bake in 350°F oven for 40–45 minutes. Cool and cut into squares.

Chocolate Chip Kisses

Mrs. Louis Zellen

2 egg whites
pinch of salt
¹/₈ teaspoon cream of tartar
³/₄ cup sugar

¹/₂ cup chocolate morsels
¹/₂ cup walnuts, cut-up
1 teaspoon vanilla

- Beat whites until foamy. Add salt and cream of tartar, and beat until peaks are formed. Add sugar gradually and beat in well. Fold in morsels, walnuts, and vanilla.
- Cover a cookie sheet with brown wrapping paper. Do not grease the pan or the paper. Drop batter by teaspoonfuls on the paper.
- Bake in 300°F oven for 25 minutes. While slightly warm, remove from paper with spatula. Cool on a wire rack.

Variation: 1 cup dates cut into small pieces may be substituted for the chocolate morsels.

Chocolate Macaroons I

Anne Kulin

Excellent for children and parties

1 cup sweetened condensed milk
2¹/₂ squares bakers chocolate, melted

9 ounces unsweetened coconut
¹/₂ teaspoon vanilla

- Mix ingredients together and drop on cookie sheet with teaspoon.
- Bake in 350°F oven for 10 minutes. Remove and let cool. Serves 24.

Chocolate Macaroons II

Mrs. David I. Israel

2 egg whites
¹/₄ teaspoon salt
¹/₂ cup sugar
1 6-ounce package chocolate bits,
    semisweet

1 package shredded coconut
    (3¹/₂–4 ounces)
1 teaspoon vanilla

- Beat egg whites gradually, adding salt and sugar until stiff.
- Meanwhile, melt chocolate bits in top of double boiler. Keep the cover on to speed melting. When the melted chocolate is cool, fold it into the whites. Then fold in coconut and vanilla.
- Lay brown wrapping paper on cookie sheets. Do not grease the pan or the paper. Drop batter by teaspoonfuls onto the paper.
- Bake in 325°F oven for 13 minutes. Cool slightly for a couple of minutes before removing from paper with a spatula. Cool on a wire rack.

▢ Macaroons

Mrs. Samuel Writer

pinch of salt
6 egg whites
1¹/₂ cups sugar
1 pound shredded coconut

5 tablespoons sifted cake meal
3 tablespoons sugar
nuts
candied cherries

- Add pinch of salt to egg whites and beat until stiff, gradually adding sugar. Add coconut, stir thoroughly, and let stand for 5 minutes.
- In the meantime, mix sifted cake flour, and sugar together. Drop teaspoonfuls of coconut mixture into flour mixture, coating well and place on greased cookie sheet. Decorate with a piece of walnut or ¹/₂ cherry in center, after making center indentation with thumb.
- Bake in 350°F oven for 20 minutes.

Matzo Farfel Taiglach

Ethel Chaifetz

My husband's favorite Passover treat!

2 eggs, beaten
3 cups matzo farfel
1 pound honey

1 cup sugar
1 cup coarsley chopped nuts
¹/₂ teaspoon ginger

- In a bowl, put beaten eggs over farfel and mix.
- Bring honey and sugar to a rolling boil in a heavy soup pot, add farfel mixture and nuts. Cover pot. Boil until golden brown, stirring frequently.
- Put on a wet board; spread to about ¹/₂-inch thickness. Cut when cool.

Matzoh Brittle

Sylvia Stein

Delicious — like peanut brittle — easy for Passover.

4 matzohs
1 cup margarine
1 pinch salt

¾ cup light brown sugar
1 cup chopped nuts (walnuts or pecans)

- Grease cookie sheet. Line with matzohs.
- Bring to boil, at least 3 minutes, margarine, and brown sugar. Pour over matzoh. Spread then sprinkle with chopped nuts.
- Bake 350°F for 10 minutes or until light brown. Cool on waxed paper and break into pieces. Serves 8.

Index

"Master Chef" Sponsors

Nancy and Harold Benjamin

Leatrice and Morris Chafetz

Zelda and Samuel Chafetz

Harriet and Burton Chandler

Norma and Saul Feingold

Ceril and Howard Fish

Edith and Conrad Fisher

Joan and Richard Freedman

Liz and Robert Frem

Edward, Jon, and Larry Glick

Ina Gordon

Dorothy and Harry Heitin

Toby and Arnold Horowitz

Marjorie and Charles Housen

Roma and Burrill Josephs

Shirley and Benson Kane

Jean and Abraham Krintzman

Frances and David Lubin

Dorothy and Howard Lurier

Ruth and Jacob Margolis

Devy and Peter Pollock

Ruth Ravelson

Blossom and Jules Saide

Phyllis Sherwin

Rosalie Wolf